# public speaking

# made easy

## second edition

# public
# speaking made easy

### second edition

## Judith A. Rolls
Cape Breton University

THOMSON

NELSON

Australia    Canada    Mexico    Singapore    Spain    United Kingdom    United States

**THOMSON**

™

**NELSON**

Public Speaking Made Easy
Second Edition
Judith A. Rolls

**Associate Vice-President, Editorial Director:**
Evelyn Veitch

**Executive Editor:**
Anne Williams

**Senior Marketing Manager:**
Wayne Morden

**Marketing Manager:**
Sandra Green

**Developmental Editor:**
Linda Sparks

**Permissions Coordinator:**
Karen Becker

**Production Editor:**
Tammy Scherer

**Copy Editor:**
Erin Moore

**Proofreader:**
Joe Zingrone

**Indexer:**
Edwin Durbin

**Production Coordinator:**
Ferial Suleman

**Design Director:**
Ken Phipps

**Interior Design:**
Fernanda Pisani

**Cover Design:**
Johanna Liburd

**Cover Image:**
Anthony Marsland/Getty Images

**Compositor:**
Integra

**Printer:**
Transcontinental

**Library and Archives Canada Cataloguing in Publication**

Rolls, Judith A. (Judith Ann)
Public speaking made easy / Judith A. Rolls. — 2nd ed.

Includes bibliographical references and index.
ISBN 0-17-640699-9

1. Public speaking—Textbooks. I. Title.

PN4121.R64 2006    808.5'1
C2006-900742-X

# Contents

# PART 2: PREPARING AND DELIVERING THE SPEECH

## Chapter 4   Researching the Speech   97

## Chapter 6   Credibility   167

## Chapter 7    Using Good Visual Aids Well    203

## PART 3: DIFFERENT TYPES OF SPEECHES

## Chapter 8    Demonstrative, Informative, and Persuasive Speeches   237

# Chapter 9   Social Speeches   275

# Preface

An interesting thing about writing textbooks is that authors are actually given an opportunity to re-vamp their work. They can improve the writing, add new material, or shape the topics to meet the needs of their readers. It is kind of like taking a solid, sturdy older house and remodelling it. That is what I have attempted to do with the second edition of *Public Speaking Made Easy*. The basic structure and topics have been retained, but the overall backdrop is a little different and there are several renovations.

For instance, the text still focuses on providing a blend of the theoretical and the practical so that students are armed with the basic information they need to develop and present good speeches. It continues to examine topics from the cognitive (knowledge), affective (feelings), and behavioural (skills) perspectives. It is still designed for a semester-long, introductory public speaking course for college and university students. Student narratives, expert advice segments, and author experiences are still evident throughout. And, it is still "made in Canada." However, there are many new improvements.

The first major difference is the overall appearance of the book. The text now contains colour, a streamline approach, and sleeker visuals. I hope that this will make it more visually appealing.

In terms of the material, some of the chapters have been reorganized to make them clearer. The writing is tighter and less wordy in places. Some topics have been expanded, others shortened. New information has been added throughout. You will find segments on listening, visualization, relaxation, the ambiguity of nonverbal communication, culture and nonverbal communication, and vocal qualities such as projection, pitch, and inflection. More material on audience analysis, the reliability of research found on the Internet, citing sources in speech outlines, survey development, Maslow's Hierarchy of Needs, transitions, goal selection, turning speech outlines into notes, using PowerPoint, impromptu speaking, telephone etiquette, affective/personality conflicts, and interviewee perspectives have also been added.

In addition, there are two new pedagogical tools. The *Spotlight on Speakers* series highlights excerpts from and information about a variety of speakers. The *Public Speaking in the 21st Century* series directs readers to relevant Web sites. For example, in Chapter 2, you will be invited to check out the interactive *Talk to Me* site that offers a therapeutic approach to reducing nervousness. There are also lots of new cartoons, activities, examples, and helpful boxes. There are new *Expert Advice* pieces in every chapter.

Further, given that the majority of readers are business students, more of their world is reflected in this edition. Overall, I hope you find that the renovations provide stimulation, interest, and helpful public speaking instructions.

Unlike our American counterparts, public speaking courses are typically embedded within disciplines other than Communication and this makes it difficult for professors to come together. Therefore, do not hesitate to contact me at judy_rolls@capebretonu.ca. I would love to learn about your courses and I would appreciate any comments you may have regarding the text. Perhaps we can all meet at a future conference.

## ACKNOWLEDGMENTS

Neither edition of this text would have been possible without the Thomson Nelson team. Every individual I worked with has been helpful, professional, courteous, and patient—Bob Kohlmeier, Erin Moore, Rebecca Rea, Tammy Scherer, Linda Sparks, Evelyn Veitch, Anne Williams, and Joe Zingrone. I am also indebted to Christina Rostek for encouraging me to consider Thomson Nelson. Further, I wouldn't be writing this today had it not been for Murray Moman's diligence in uncovering potential readers and promoting the first edition. I am truly indebted to the instructors who gave the first edition a try and to Thomson Nelson that gave the go ahead for the second.

I am also grateful to the reviewers who examined early versions of the first edition and I own a huge thank you to the reviewers who took the time to make both general and detailed recommendations specific to the second edition—Linda Large of Canadore College, Andrea Lovering of Georgian College, Ruth Murdock of Mount Royal College, and Judy Ann Roy of the University of New Brunswick. Their advice has shaped this work and incorporating their suggestions has resulted in a much stronger text. I am also indebted to those writers who gave permission to include their work in the text and to the many professionals and public speaking instructors who so graciously offered their words for the *Expert Advice* feature.

In addition, thanks to my many students. Their honesty and dedication make teaching a joy and their voices and ideas ring throughout the text. In particular, I wish to credit Jamie Bailey, Amanda Benoit, and Allan MacDonald whose speeches serve as examples in this text.

I also wish to thank the faculty in the Department of Communication at Cape Breton University for wholeheartedly endorsing and supporting this project—Tanya Brann-Barrett, Carol Corbin, Michael MacDonald, Marlene MacInnes, Celeste Sulliman, and Dawn White. Thank you too to our part-time faculty who are typically called in last minute to help us reach as many students as possible—Dale Caume, Mike Hunter, Demetri Kachafanas, Amy LeMoine, Barbara MacDonald, Erna MacLeod, Bryce MacNeil, Jennifer Pino, and Eileen Smith Piovesan. Their collective input is also evident throughout the book.

Finally, thank you to my family for their never-ending love and encouragement—John MacLean and Jo-Anne, David, and Caleigh Rolls. They are always there for me.

## ABOUT THE AUTHOR

Judith A. Rolls received a B.A. from St. Francis Xavier University, a B.Ed. from Dalhousie University, an M.A. from the University of Maine, and a Ph.D. in speech communication from Indiana University. She is a professor in the Department of Communication at Cape Breton University where she has taught for 25 years. Her research interests focus on pedagogy and communication competence, experiential learning, health communication, gender communication, and women and recovery. Dr. Rolls's scholarly work has been published in Canadian, American, and international journals. She is also active as a communication consultant, organizational trainer, and guest speaker.

# Chapter 1
## Introduction to Public Speaking

## CHAPTER GOALS

In this chapter, you will learn
- the benefits of developing public speaking skills
- a new way to think about public speaking
- the role of listening in public speaking
- that a fear of public speaking is normal
- the characteristics of dynamic speakers

# INTRODUCTION

I had the good fortune a number of years ago to hear Yolanda King, daughter of Dr. Martin Luther King, Jr., speak at a large rally. Her message (that work is still needed to eliminate racism) was powerfully delivered in an almost theatrical manner. She kept us riveted by altering the rate of her speech and the tone and inflection of her voice. She used large, emphatic gestures and spoke in a vivid, descriptive language style that re-created for us some of her childhood experiences growing up in the South. She was passionate, articulate, and intelligent. Her presentation was by far one of the best I have ever witnessed.

Yolanda King obviously possesses natural speaking abilities. However, it was more than talent that enabled her to connect so convincingly with her audience. She obviously worked hard to develop a speech that, through the use of statistics, stories, and sarcasm, would captivate our imagination. She also relied heavily on her voice and vocal techniques, as well as her body, to further embellish her message. This all worked together to create a very enchanting presentation. Finally, the balance and timing of her address suggested that she was well rehearsed.

Good speakers like Yolanda King make public speaking look easy. This is because they both know and practise the public speaking techniques that result in dynamic, engaging speeches. They know how to structure their message, how to use their voices, and how to move their bodies to further enhance their meaning. The goal of this text is to teach you those very strategies.

Basically, many people think public speaking is difficult because they do not know how to do it. However, once they learn the fundamental ins and outs, they find that the process is rather straightforward. An environmental engineering student found that out. He wrote, "I feel quite a bit more prepared now that I have overcome some hurdles, especially in the speech delivery department. My confidence is peaking and I feel ready to try my skills in the workforce now. Perhaps the most impressive statement I can make is that I don't get the nervous butterflies in the pit of my stomach now when I think of getting in front of strangers but rather look forward to it. I never thought I would say that!"

# WHY DEVELOP PUBLIC SPEAKING SKILLS?

There are many reasons why it is worthwhile to develop your communication skills. Some of these are discussed in this section.

## A Useful Educational Skill

One obvious reason to hone your public speaking skills is that they transfer to other courses that require presentations. Professors from various disciplines often remark that they can identify public speaking students by their superior communication abilities; those students are comfortable on their feet, and their presentations are professionally crafted and delivered. Students too recognize the value of attaining such skills. For instance, a frequent comment among fourth-year business students in public speaking classes is that they wish they had taken the course in their first or second year. They say they would have done much better in their case competitions.

 **EXPERT ADVICE**

Individuals who take time to hone their public speaking skills have more opportunities for success than those who do not. Unfortunately, though, many people believe that public speakers are born, not made. This is not true. I have seen many students come into my courses feeling apprehensive and thinking they could never be effective speakers. Yet by learning about and practising public speaking, they leave with newfound skills and confidence, and hope for a brighter future.

*Professor Michael MacDonald, Department of Communication*
*Cape Breton University, Sydney, Nova Scotia*

## Employability

Another practical reason to develop public speaking skills has to do with employability. Based on employer input, the Conference Board of Canada's Corporate Council on Education identified the skills required for a successful Canadian workforce. "The ability to communicate, think, and continue to learn throughout life" was one of the top noted areas (McLaughlin, 1995). One need only check out the employment classified ads to verify the truth of this statement. Phrases like "good written and oral skills," "good interpersonal communication," and "ability to communicate with the public," are common. More and more frequently, requirements such as "public speaking a must" or "public speaking required" are showing up.

There was a time when individuals in high-ranking positions were the only ones called on to make presentations. But, people in today's work environment can expect to present briefs and reports; to conduct orientation, training, and information sessions; to present and receive awards; to give ceremonial presentations; and to motivate workers. Other responsibilities may include making technical presentations, case presentations, or convention and conference presentations. Union or association representatives may use a public forum to provide data, convey negotiation strategies, or persuade members to accept or reject proposed contract agreements. Even people in occupations least associated with public speaking are requested to do so. For example, librarians conduct student orientation and information sessions, and computer technicians train personnel in the use of new programs and applications. Health care workers, museum curators, and zookeepers all engage in public speaking activities. There is just no escape!

 **EXPERT ADVICE**

In the business world, you need to be aware that you have one chance to impress. Your superior or next employer may be out there. Be prepared! If you have done your homework, you are the expert. Your confidence will shine through. And, remember to speak to, and not at the audience—they will take more away from it. Use your personality, be comfortable with the audience. If you show your nervousness, they will be distracted and you won't get the message across.

*Kerensa Wotton, Director of Catering and Convention Services*
*Sheraton Vancouver Wall Centre Hotel, Vancouver, B.C.*

## Success in the Business World

Adler and Elmhorst (1996) approximate that "business people give an average of twenty-six presentations a year" and being good at it can be advantageous for several reasons. For one, you receive more recognition than equally hard-working individuals who keep a lower profile. For example, IT professionals, in keeping with industry trends, do much of their work in groups. But Boyd Rodman, an e-business professor, notes that the individuals who present the results of such work are the ones who get noticed. As he says, "Your technical skills will get you a job, but public speaking and communication skills will get you a promotion" (Rodman, as cited in Gittlen, 2004, p. 61). Berns (2004) argues that speaking in public also allows you to demonstrate your knowledge which in turn can "enhance your image as an expert" (p. 28). He goes on to say that public speakers also get clients in the process.

Clearly, public speaking serves as a great marketing tool. Agreeing to speak at luncheons, conferences, professional meetings, service clubs, seminars, or area home shows all provide an avenue to meet and attract customers. In fact, public speaking is so important in the business world that some organizational consultants recommend that businesses develop a speaking program as part of the overall advertising plan (Friesen & Markman, 2004). And they are not alone in their thinking. Public speaking programs are definitely catching on. For example, Toastmasters International charters "corporate clubs" that are housed in companies, organizations, and government departments. The number of new charters increases every year. In the last year alone, new clubs have been established at Sophos Inc. in Vancouver, at the *Ottawa Citizen*, at Siemens Building Technologies in Calgary, at the Ontario Securities Commission in Toronto, at the RBC Royal Bank in Scarborough, at Canada Revenue Agency in Penticton, at Yolles Partnership Inc. and at Blake, Cassels & Graydon LLP in Toronto (Toastmasters International District Newsletters, 2004–2005).

Finally, in today's media age, where the use of video, Internet, cell phones, and so forth is the norm, the opportunities for public speaking have increased tremendously. One never knows when a last-minute performance call will be issued. The story in the accompanying "Public Speaking in the 21st Century" box illustrates how being prepared to think on your feet can enhance marketing opportunities.

 ## PUBLIC SPEAKING IN THE 21ST CENTURY

I was watching an early-bird television coverage of a trade show being held in Halifax, Nova Scotia. The zany announcer was doing mini-interviews with the few kiosk representatives already on the scene. He approached one booth and asked the agent to describe her product. Unfortunately for the company she represented, she became flustered and tongue-tied, and could hardly identify her merchandise, let alone embellish its features. In addition to appearing uninformed and incompetent, the interviewee missed a wonderful opportunity to promote her wares, free of charge, to the television audience.

*Pat, Former Communication Student*

## Play a Bigger Advocacy Role

Finally, possessing public speaking abilities enables individuals to be responsible citizens. Doing advocacy work, making presentations before public boards and hearings, taking stands in groups such as parent–teacher associations, running for public office, or serving as a keynote speaker for community, provincial, federal, and professional organizations all require adept communication skills. An added bonus is that learning to present thoughts and ideas in a rational manner helps people to become better critical thinkers and to be more aware of the many persuasive messages to which they are subjected.

Clearly, the ability to be an effective public speaker is a must in today's world. Julia Wood (1997, p. 314) sums it up well: "It is a basic communication skill that we all need if we wish to have a voice in what happens in our work, personal lives, and society."

# PUBLIC SPEAKING AND THE COMMUNICATION PROCESS

## Public Speaking Defined

Public speaking, also referred to as oratory, has traditionally been defined as one person speaking to an audience. For instance, delivering a valedictory speech or making a political speech would be considered public speaking. However, with the modern media, the division among mass communication, public speaking, and even interpersonal communication has become skewed. For instance, when Canada's former prime minister, Pierre Elliott Trudeau, died in 2000, his son, Justin Trudeau, presented the eulogy at his funeral (a form of public speaking). This much-lauded presentation was simultaneously brought to the nation via Internet, radio, and television coverage, which constituted a mass communication event. But one might also argue that Justin Trudeau's interpersonal communication skills (such as the use of humour, self-disclosure, and sensitivity) were evident in his presentation. The dimensions are melded.

Thus far, the term *public speaking* has been used to describe very different communication events—speaking formally before an audience, making presentations in the workplace or community, or performing in front of a camera while a live audience somewhere out there in TV land looks on. I even see the employment interview process as a form of public speaking. This is because the human communication skills required for success in each of these contexts are similar. That is, regardless of the

## PUBLIC SPEAKERS EARN BIG BUCKS

Imagine yourself 10 years from today. You have accomplished your dreams, and now you have been invited to speak to audiences across Canada. Give this serious consideration—it could be worth your while financially. For example, Cathy Jones (from *This Hour Has 22 Minutes*), Susan Aglukark, Dini Petty, Margaret Trudeau, and Mike Duffy are each paid between $5000 and $10 000 to make a presentation. So too are Mike Bossy (NHL Hall of Famer), Colin Mochrie (*Whose Line Is It Anyway?*), and Shaun Majumder (*This Hour Has 22 Minutes*). But it gets even better: Donovan Bailey, Dr. Roberta Bondar, Rubin "Hurricane" Carter, Margot Kidder, and Dave Broadfoot all charge over $10 000 to make an appearance. This should be a good incentive to hone your public speaking skills.

Check out the following Web sites for more information on both hiring and becoming a professional public speaker:

Professional Speakers Bureau Inc.: *http://www.prospeakers.com*
The Lavin Agency: *http://www.thelavinagency.com*
Speakers' Spotlight: *http://www.speakers.ca*

situation, good speakers are organized, they speak in a clear and concise voice, and they make eye contact with the listener or listeners.

Because of the broad definition of public speaking contained in this text, the material can not only be applied in conventional public speaking contexts, but also be adapted to a wide variety of venues. The goal is to enable speakers to prepare quickly and efficiently and then to deliver the types of presentations that will meet their personal, professional, and public communication needs.

## Communication Process Defined

The elements in the communication process consist of senders, receivers, messages, feedback, noise, and channels. **Senders** are the individuals who *behave* in some manner to relay a message, **receivers** get and *decode* the message, the **message** refers to the content of what is being relayed, and **feedback** relates to how the receiver responds to the sender. Senders and receivers have only three vehicles, or **channels**, through which to create and convey messages. Known as the 3 V's, these include visual communication

### EXPERT ADVICE

A number of years ago, I was invited to attend the launch of a new recreational initiative in Sudbury, Ontario. There were about 200 people in attendance, including the mayor and other civic leaders. The keynote speaker was an "expert" brought in, at considerable cost, from the United States. As we entered the auditorium, copies of his address were made available. While he was speaking, some of us followed the text to see if there were any differences between what was written and what he said. There weren't.

Shortly after the speech started, I noticed a strange, buzzing sound—loud enough to be a little annoying, but not to really interfere with the speech. After some 20 to 25 minutes, which was about one-third to one-half of the way through (judging by the written text), Mr. Authority suddenly stopped, and so too did the buzzing noise. This well-paid, keynote presenter simply stood there, not saying a word, while a couple of members of his entourage moved about in an agitated manner. His silence lasted about 15 minutes, as the audience grew more and more restless. Suddenly, as abruptly as he had stopped speaking, and with absolutely no explanation for the interruption, he started up again. And so did that buzzing noise.

After a few more minutes, I figured out what was going on. He had a tape-recorded version of his speech playing in another room, and it was being simultaneously rerouted to a receiver in his ear, and he just repeated the words verbatim to the audience. When the tape player stopped working, this "expert" was at a complete loss and did not have a single thing to say. That's when I left.

*Brian Seville, Retired Business Professor*
*Cape Breton University, Sydney, Nova Scotia*

(what the body does), vocal communication (how the voice is used in the transmission of the message), and verbal communication (how words are used to create the message). These three channels work in concert with one another.

Anything that interferes with the transmission and interpretation of a message is known as **noise**. Noise can come in many forms, some of which include physical distractions (an aching head), psychological distraction (worrying about something), environmental factors (too much perfume in the air), and so forth.

**Figure 1.1—Transactional Communication Model**

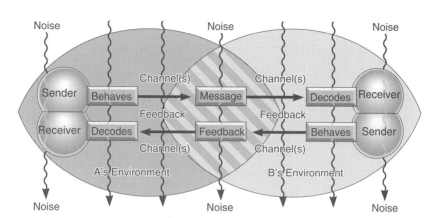

Although the elements in the communication process are described individually, they all occur simultaneously when people communicate. Speakers and listeners concurrently send and receive messages. They are, at once, both receiver and sender. As one individual speaks, the other still communicates via smiles, facial expressions, nods, posture (visual communication) and/or through sighs, uh hums, gasps (vocal communication). This continuous, uninterrupted view of communication is known as the **transactional model of communication**. See Figure 1.1 for a visual depiction of how the model works. While the transactional model is usually used to describe interpersonal communication, or communication between two individuals, it can also be applied to public speaking contexts as well. This is described in the next section.

## A Transactional Approach to Public Speaking

### *Speakers*

Regardless of the type of presentation being made, an awareness of the communication process can help speakers to be more dynamic. For instance, in public speaking contexts, people typically think of speakers as message senders and audience members as message receivers. This is a faulty assumption. Because of the feedback process, both speakers and listeners (the audience) become simultaneous senders and receivers. The difference between the two is in the number of channels each possesses through which to convey messages. Good public speakers use all three channels—visual, vocal, and verbal. That is, they might use various facial expressions and gestures (visual), use their voice to place emphasis on a word or reduce their volume to a whisper (vocal), or include vivid descriptions, stories, or humour in the content (verbal).

## *Audience Members*

On the other hand, audience members are more likely to convey their response to the public speaker (feedback) by using the visual channel (nods, smiles, even the "finger") and the vocal channel (laughter, hoots, gasps). When audience members do those sorts of things, they are engaging in feedback and they essentially become the senders. In public speaking contexts, audience members are not as likely to use their verbal channel (words) unless they are invited to pose questions or make comments. (The interruptions by a heckler would be the exception to this.) It is up to the receiver (the public speaker) to interpret and respond to the messages. What goes on during a presentation is that both the speaker and the audience are simultaneously interacting and communicating with one another.

---

### THE 3 V'S (CHANNELS) OF COMMUNICATION

Use the 3 V's (visual, vocal, and verbal) to improve your public speaking presentations.

**VISUAL CHANNEL**
Visual communication is what you do with your body—what the audience sees. It includes facial expressions, gestures, posture, clothing, use of space and movement, etc.

**VOCAL CHANNEL**
Vocal communication refers to how the voice is used to convey messages. It includes volume, tone, pitch, rate, articulation, emphasis, and odd sounds such as sighs, humphs, whistles, grunts, groans—anything that is not actual language.

**VERBAL CHANNEL**
Verbal communication refers to words and content. Examples include organization of messages, types of support material used, jokes, stories, grammar, and so on.

---

## *Transaction between Speakers and Listeners*

Excellent speakers also try to respond to all members of the audience. Or, as Donna Moulton, a former student, so aptly put it, they develop their audience relationships. However, there is a general inclination to think that there are just two parties in the public speaking process—the speaker and the audience as a whole. In some respects this is true, but lively speakers try to relate to and connect with as many individual audience members as possible; to almost communicate interpersonally with them. Perhaps referring to Figures 1.2 and 1.3 (page 12) can clarify this notion.

### *The One-to-Many Approach*

Figure 1.2, showing a one-to-many approach to public speaking, suggests that the communication occurs in just one way: The speaker sends messages to the audience. As noted earlier, this would not be effective communication because the speaker

**Figure 1.2—The One-to-Many Approach**

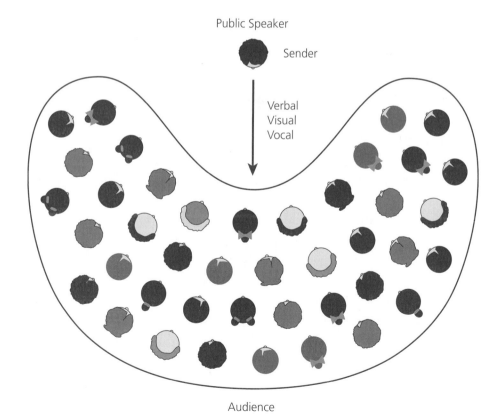

would not be reading and responding to the feedback being sent by the audience. Poor speakers operate like this—they are concerned only with getting out what they have to say.

The one-to-many approach to public speaking also suggests that the audience is extremely powerful in relation to the speaker. Little wonder people who think of public speaking in this way are reluctant to speak in front of large groups. They are apt to perceive public speaking as a performance—that is, those speakers focus on how they speak, move, sound, use their hands, etc., as if the audience is judging them and they have to do everything correctly.

### The One-on-One Approach

The best public speakers take a transactional, or one-on-one approach. Figure 1.3 suggests that speakers have a one-on-one relationship with each member of the audience. As noted earlier, they see the audience as individuals with whom they exchange messages. If they see

**Figure 1.3—The One-on-One Approach to Public Speaking**

Public Speaker

S = Sender     M = Message     VVV = Visual / Vocal / Verbal
R = Receiver     F = Feedback

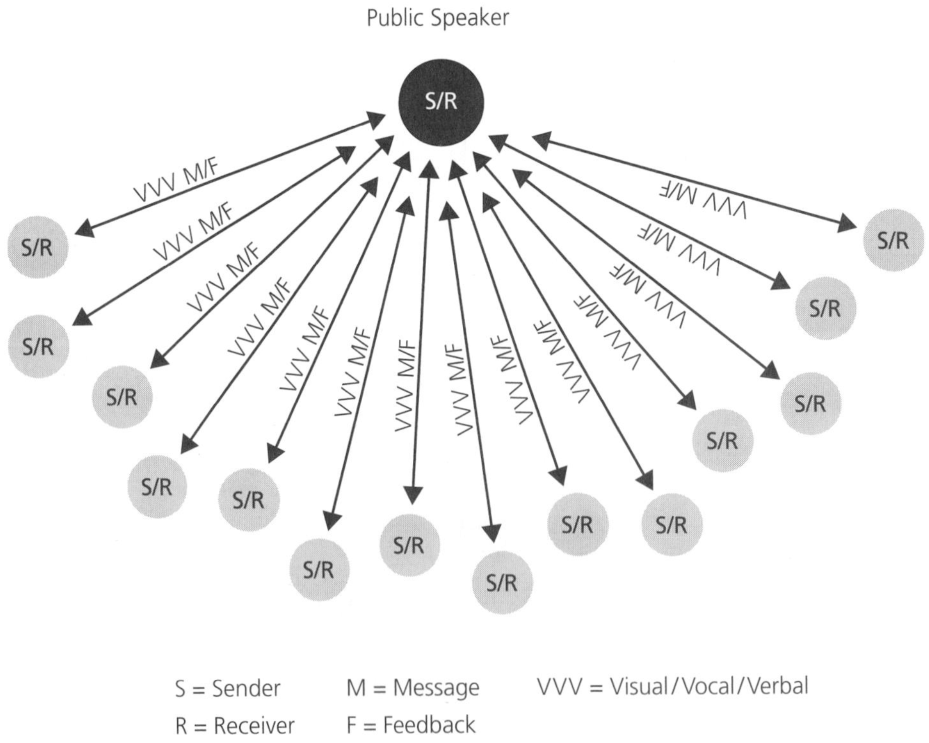

a look on one listener's face that suggests she or he does not comprehend something, such speakers reword the message right on the spot.

This one-on-one approach is in keeping with Motley and Molloy's (1994) research that speakers who take a communication orientation (that is, as if they were in one-on-one, interpersonal communication) as opposed to a performance orientation (as suggested by the one-to-many theory) are less apprehensive. They are also more dynamic. Therefore, to use the communication process to its fullest, try to think of the audience not as one huge entity but rather as individuals with whom you have some interesting things to share.

## Listening

The one-on-one, or transactional approach to public speaking, also puts responsibility on the audience to listen. Sometimes audience members pay little attention to the speaker. They look around the room, shuffle through papers, or whisper loudly to the people around them. These messages do not go unnoticed by speakers. There is a tendency for audience members to assume that speakers cannot see them. On the contrary; if speakers pay attention to the audience and have good vision, they have a bird's eye view of the room. They see everyone and know everything that is going on.

### *Improving Listening*

In addition to the notion that paying attention to a speaker demonstrates common courtesy, listening is hard work and people are not very good at it. There are several reasons for this. For the most part, we are exposed to very little information on listening in the educational system. Further, discrepancies between speaker rates and our ability to process information also contribute to the problem. People speak at approximately 100–150 words per minute but we have the ability to process information at rates up to 600 words per minute (Wolvin & Coakley, 1988). This leaves extra "head space" that can result in our thinking about other things. On top of that, we have bad listening habits. We "pseudolisten," or pretend to listen as we nod our heads, jot down notes, or appear interested. We engage in selective listening where we tune in for certain items, or use insulated listening where we automatically stop listening to certain topics the minute they are broached. Then there is insensitive listening. That means that a speaker's words are taken at face value. We do not observe the nonverbal cues or read "between the lines" (Adler, Towne, & Rolls, 2004). Listening can be greatly improved merely by eliminating any or all of these bad habits.

Getting rid of distractions, trying not to judge prematurely, trying to seek out key ideas, posing questions, and trying to paraphrase what the speaker is saying are strategies that can be used to help us listen for information (Adler, Towne, & Rolls, 2004). But the sad thing is that even if we pay attention and understand speakers, there is no guarantee that we will remember their messages. In fact, the prognosis is not good at all. Researchers suggest that immediately after hearing a message we forget 50 percent of it and after eight hours we recall only 35 percent! After two months, only 25 percent can be remembered (Adler, Towne, & Rolls, 2004). When speaking in front of local audiences, I used to be concerned that perhaps part of my presentation would have overlapped with one I had previously given. However, in light of the statistics cited above, even if that did occur, the likelihood that audience members might recall my words is slim.

If you want to become a more active audience member, try to eliminate your bad listening habits. Make an effort to listen for content and read between the lines of a speaker's message for a fuller understanding. You might also try a technique that one audience member offered. I was making a presentation on listening and invited the audience to share strategies they used. One man told me that he first wrote out the letters of the alphabet on a piece of paper. Then he attempted to

"I gave a presentation today but I only pretended to know what
I was talking about. Fortunately, my audience was only pretending to listen."

Randy Glasbergen

identify significant words to correspond with the letters as I spoke. Apparently he was waiting for me to say a word beginning with *j* when he provided his suggestion. When I noted that the process might be somewhat distracting, he said that he actually listened more carefully when he did this. Further, when the presentation was over, he had both an alphabetical and a chronological record of the speech that he could refer to later.

How would you rate your listening skills? Check out the listening test (Kreitner, Kinicki, & Cole, 2003) on pages 24 and 25 at the end of the chapter.

---

### LISTENER DO'S AND DON'TS

#### DO
- Sit up and look like you're interested in the presentation.
- Keep eye contact with the speaker or look at the visual aids.
- Offer positive feedback by smiling, looking attentive, responding to humour, or nodding.

#### DON'T
- Slouch back in your seat with a "just try and connect with me" attitude.
- Read materials such as newspapers, books, or other papers not intended for the presentation.
- Make asides or remarks to those around you.
- Look around the room, adjust clothing, or shuffle needlessly.

---

## STRATEGIES USED BY DYNAMIC, EXCITING SPEAKERS

It is well known that strong, assured speakers who are popular with their audiences think a certain way and engage in specific behaviours. One way to work toward your public speaking ideal is to try to implement some of the strategies that such exciting presenters use. Three that reinforce the transactional model of communication include speaking extemporaneously, providing interesting and relevant content, and having a good delivery. I reinforce these in my classes and students have met with excellent results. They give intellectually stimulating, well-delivered speeches that hold their audience's attention. These strategies are described below.

## EXPERT ADVICE

My advice to students is, "Don't use canned words." I suggested to one bright, creative student who set up her notes in full sentences to use just main points. That way, she could establish more of a connection with the audience. Instead, she memorized! While she used picturesque, creative language, you could see that each word was planned ahead of time. Although she was good, she was not nearly as enjoyable as students who were less "perfect."

When a speaker uses words that come naturally, audience members become a part of the conversation. They will respond with a nod, a laugh, a visual response of some kind—but they will feel part of whatever is happening. My best speakers, those who are anticipated with great pleasure by their classmates, are able to create a chemistry with the audience. They may not be perfect, but they're real!

*Michelle Strenkowski*
*Vancouver Community College, Vancouver, B.C.*

# Dynamic Presenters Speak Extemporaneously

Dynamic speakers typically engage in extemporaneous speaking. That is, they work from a prepared outline, one that is either in their heads or in note form in front of them. For example, Brian Rogers, with KPMG Calgary and a member of the board of directors for the Canadian Institute of Chartered Accountants, says he can speak for half an hour from seven topics scribbled on the back of a business card. He can do this because he is adept at extemporaneous speaking. When people possess a strong subject expertise, this approach allows them to interact on an interpersonal level with the audience. They know in advance how the presentation will proceed, but they can be spontaneous and respond to unexpected events that may occur during the speech. Audience interaction is high. This type of freedom is not available when a speech is read to an audience.

Extemporaneous speakers also avoid memorization. Unless a person is a skilled actor, it is difficult to deliver a dynamic presentation when every word is laid out in advance. Most often, memorizers sound mechanical and staid, as if they are more interested in finishing the presentation than communicating with the audience.

There are times when memorization or reading may be encouraged, but this would not be considered extemporaneous speaking. Snyder (1983, p. 69) suggests that manuscript reading may be appropriate in those situations when "every word will appear in permanent form in an official record," and Osborn and Osborn (1994, p. 298) hold that, "Reading from a prepared manuscript may be necessary when accurate wording is imperative or when time constraints are severe. Official proclamations, legal announcements, professional papers, or mass media presentations that must be timed within seconds usually call for manuscript presentations."

The first speeches I ever had to give were in my grade 8 English class. For the first one, I actually memorized an article on Alexander Graham Bell, right from the *Reader's Digest*! (We didn't know about plagiarism then.) It went fairly well; I got through it. A couple of weeks later, when it was time to do the next speech, I wasn't nearly as committed in terms of how much work I was prepared to put into it. Instead of researching and memorizing information, I quickly outlined and organized on a slip of paper a presentation about why women should have the same opportunities as men. Well, I learned a great lesson. My preparation time for speech number two was greatly reduced, my audience feedback was very positive, and I actually enjoyed making the presentation. I was speaking extemporaneously and didn't know it. In all, I learned that when speaking from the heart, there's less prep time and better communication with the audience. On top of that, I got better grades when I used the second approach. I have taken this strategy into my adult life.

*Colette, Former Communication Student*

## *Provide Interesting and Relevant Information*

Good speakers are not boring. This does not suggest that they are funny or offer us a stand-up comic routine, but rather that they engage us by organizing their material in a manner appropriate for the topic and by incorporating material we can relate to. For example, most young teens would probably find stock market fluctuations boring, but references to a few pop icons could grab and hold their attention. According to Edward Greenspan, a well-known lawyer, "A good speech must entertain. It is pointless to make an important point in a boring fashion because it may be lost. It has to be made in an entertaining and dramatic way" (Barnard, 1996, p. 3).

## FOUR BASIC PUBLIC SPEAKING RULES—FACT OR FICTION?

Read over the four public speaking rules listed below and decide if or how they would work for you. Are they too harsh? Would they work in all circumstances? Should others be added? Should any be deleted? What are the pros and cons of each rule? Should there be such a thing as rules to govern public speaking? Discuss the rules with a partner or a small group to get other opinions.

- Never write out a speech word for word.
- Never memorize a speech.
- Never read a speech to the audience.
- Never be boring.

**66 99**

When I was studying at a large university, I was very excited at the prospect of taking a course from a famous sociologist. His work was controversial, he was often "the talk" at student gatherings, and I was thrilled to get into his class. But unfortunately, that rapture was short-lived. The classes were dead boring, and not because this renowned scholar lacked knowledge or subject expertise, but simply because he was such a poor speaker! His idea of a lecture was to pace back and forth across the front of the classroom, stare down at the floor, and mumble incoherently. I ended up hating the class and I lost a lot of respect for him.

*Yu-Fun, Sociology Student*

### Make the Material Come Alive

Most topics can be made interesting by using engaging and relevant examples, statistics, or narratives (stories) to make the material come alive. Making any kind of an emotional connection with the audience also makes a presentation more interesting. For instance, people love to hear stories, and they can be lured and captivated by employing this rhetorical technique. Further, speeches are more appealing if speakers select a topic they feel strongly about. Chatel, a student working on a special biology project, informed us about the mating habits of ducks. Because of her delight in the topic, that enthusiasm and curiosity transferred to us. The very next weekend, a good number of students were at the park to witness firsthand what those ducks were up to.

*Make The Delivery Shine*

How a presentation is delivered has a strong effect on audience attention. Two individuals can present very similar speeches, and while one might seem tedious and monotonous, the other will shine. The difference is a matter of delivery! Like Chatel, stimulating speakers bring enthusiasm and poise to the podium—they have an appreciation for their topic and convey their ardour through their voice and body language. They alter the pitch and tone of their voice, and use emphasis and vocal variety. In other words, their attitude is expressed not only through the words they select but also through their vocal qualities. Further, good speakers communicate with their whole bodies. They are not afraid to "talk with their hands," use a variety of facial expressions, move about, make eye contact, or show their emotions. They speak their minds with conviction and rhetorical style.

When I work with clients we look for a presentational style that's right for them and their comfort level. There is no one way of doing things. Some presenters prefer notes with bullet points, others are guided by a multimedia presentation. I help them to find their own way, their own performance preference. That's what will make them successful.

*Laura M. Peck, Vice President*
*Barry McLoughlin Associates Inc., Ottawa, Ontario*

# ▨ FEAR OF SPEAKING IN PUBLIC IS NORMAL

## You Are Not Alone in Your Nervousness

Most people do not have an easy time with public speaking. In fact, according to a popular publication, *The Book of Lists* (Wallechinsky, Wallace, & Wallace, 1977), Americans' number one fear is making a speech in public. I suspect this is true for Canadians as well. So, when public speaking students, professionals, participants in training seminars, nurses, businesspeople, and even graduate students about to defend their theses and dissertations tell me that they would rather die than make a speech or presentation, they are probably not kidding. The fear of death is ranked number six!

Regardless of whether you are extremely apprehensive about speaking in public or you just experience momentary fear, both responses are normal. Richmond and McCroskey (1995), two communication scholars who have done extensive research on this phenomenon, report that at least 70 percent of the population experiences moderate to high levels of anxiety when it comes to public speaking.

Obviously, people who love doing public presentations are clearly a minority, and you would be surprised to learn the number of rock singers, actors, and public figures who are terrified of being on stage. Some teachers and trainers are quite comfortable in front of their classes, but put them in other environments and their stress levels rise. Even your public speaking instructors experience nervousness.

When I first started presenting my research at the National Communication Association conferences, I was very nervous. It was one thing to offer my work up for scrutiny, it was quite another to do so in front of individuals whose work I was actually citing in my papers. I think those early presentations were my worst. But instead of letting my fears and intimidations stop me, I persevered. And, with practice and experience, I now present with ease and poise . . . and even with an occasional dash of humour. In the next chapter you will learn several strategies to help you control your fears. Meanwhile, note that even though speakers may not look nervous, they usually are.

## Nervousness Is Good

Nervousness isn't bad, it just feels bad. In fact, nervousness can actually enhance a presentation because of the extra energy it gives the speaker. Think of speakers who possess a ho-hum, have-to-be-there kind of attitude. They usually lack energy and excitement and bring little enthusiasm to their presentations. For nervous people, the added adrenaline pumping through their bodies allows them to be more vibrant and animated than they would be in interpersonal contexts. Being nervous and anxious works well for public speakers. The next time you feel apprehensive before having to do a presentation, think of it as a positive rather than a negative attribute. Energy and enthusiasm are infectious—so one could reason that nervousness can be a key element in your success. How to deal with communication apprehension is discussed in the next chapter.

When I get up in front of the class, it excites me and makes me feel important, like what I'm saying matters not only to me, but also to somebody else. It gives me a feeling of gratification and confidence in that I know I can achieve things not only in this class, but also in life!

*Benita, Former Communication Student*

# AN EXPERIENTIAL LEARNING APPROACH

This text is designed to take an experiential learning approach to help readers improve their public speaking skills. Experiential learning means learning by doing. Research shows that such direct participation promotes better long-term learning (Specht & Sandlin, 1991). Further, students using experiential learning strategies report that they prefer it to traditional forms of learning and they gain insight into their public speaking strengths and weaknesses (Rolls, 1993). Experiential learners also make better classroom presentations (Rolls, 1993), and both females and males respond favourably to this learning approach (Rolls, 1997).

The experiential learning philosophy advanced in this text holds that learning to master public speaking requires the integration of three learning dimensions: the cognitive, affective, and behavioural.

## The Cognitive Dimension (Knowledge)

The *cognitive* dimension refers to the theoretical comprehension of public speaking. Gaining an understanding of how to organize material, present persuasive arguments to friendly versus hostile audiences, or enhance credibility will exemplify some of the rudiments of public speaking theory that will enable you to present strong, professional speeches.

## The Affective Dimension (Emotions)

Knowledge of public speaking theory, however, does not necessarily ensure that individuals will make fine, informative presentations when they actually have to stand in front of a group of people. It is one thing to know something intellectually (cognitively), quite another to actually do it. This is often because of the feelings that are experienced before, during, or after a speech. These are referred to as the *affective* dimension and speakers usually have to deal with nervousness before they can do their best presentations. For example, one student said that on the days of her communication course, she woke up at 4:00 a.m. and worried until her 8:30 a.m. class. Debilitative feelings such as embarrassment, fear of forgetting or looking stupid, hypersensitivity, resentment, and a host of others can hinder speakers' ability to realize their potential. On the other hand, facilitative emotions such as confidence, comfort, or optimism can actually help. Often, the difference between debilitative emotions (those that obstruct) and facilitative emotions (those that assist) is only a matter of degree. For example, a little fear can actually energize a speaker, while an extreme amount can be crippling.

Given the influential and complicated role that emotions play in the public speaking process, it is important to recognize and understand how feelings affect your public speaking proficiency.

 **EXPERT ADVICE**

In communication class, I feel things that I have never felt before. I am frightened of the thought of expressing myself, yet so satisfied with my achievement when I am finished. It is one of those occasions in life when my nerves and mind are in conflict. Every part of me is scared and wants to leave the room, but my brain knows that if I go and do this brief presentation, I will have a self-reward that will forever benefit me.

*Chin-Feng, Former Communication Student*

## The Behavioural Dimension (Skills)

The final element in the experiential learning approach is the *behavioural* dimension, which refers simply to skill acquisition—how well speeches are delivered. The focus in this component is on identifying and assessing your presentational strengths and weaknesses. One effective way to do this is by recording yourself on video. Although this prospect may make you nervous, research shows that students benefit from this pedagogical tool (Quigley & Nyquist, 1992; Rolls & Strenkowski, 1994). As one student put it, "After I delivered my speech, I felt it had been a failure. However, after viewing it, I found that the opposite was true. I don't think it will go down as one of the great orations in history, but I was surprisingly pleased" (Rolls, 1993, pp. 192–93). Students generally report that their presentations are better than anticipated. You might ask your instructor to record your speeches so you too can engage in this reality-testing exercise.

In all, this experiential learning approach to public speaking will help you to gain an understanding of relevant concepts and theories, to feel confident and competent in your abilities, and to improve upon and acquire new delivery skills. To help you plot your success, you might consider keeping a communication journal. Questions that focus on each area are included at the end of each chapter.

Finally, this text is written with the assumption that the course you are presently taking is preparing you not only for in-class presentations, but also for those you do, or will do, in your personal and professional lives. Although your course will end, you will continue to strengthen your skills and further enhance your strengths as you participate in real-life public speaking events.

# CHAPTER AT A GLANCE

- It is important to develop public speaking skills to succeed in education, increase employability and business success, deal better with new media, be a responsible citizen, and improve critical thinking abilities.
- The communication process consists of senders, receivers, messages, channels (3 V's), feedback, and noise.
- Both public speakers and audience members simultaneously send and receive messages.
- Top public speakers adopt a transactional, one-on-one approach.
- The audience shares in the transactional approach to public speaking by listening and responding visually and vocally.
- Excellent speakers use an extemporaneous speaking approach, provide interesting content, and have a good delivery.
- While a fear of speaking in public is normal, that same fear can make speakers more energetic.
- In an experiential learning approach to improving public speaking skills, an examination of three learning dimensions is required: cognitive (thoughts), affective (feelings), and behavioural (skills).

# APPLICATION AND DISCUSSION QUESTIONS

1. Assess your listening skills by taking the following listening test (Kreitner, Kinkicki, & Cole (2003).

## Assess Your Listening Skills

**Instructions**

The following statements reflect various habits we use when listening to others. For each statement, indicate the extent to which you agree or disagree with it by selecting one number from the scale provided. Circle your response for each statement. Remember, there are no right or wrong answers.

**Listening Skills Survey**

1 = Strongly disagree

2 = Disagree

3 = Neither agree nor disagree

4 = Agree

5 = Strongly agree

1. I daydream or think about ot.her things when listening to others.

   1  2  3  4  5

2. I do not summarize the ideas being communicated by a speaker.

   1  2  3  4  5

3. I do not use a speaker's tone of voice or body language to help interpret what he or she is saying.

   1  2  3  4  5

4. I listen more for facts than overall ideas during classroom lectures.

   1  2  3  4  5

5. I tune out dry speakers.

   1  2  3  4  5

6. I have a hard time paying attention to boring people.

   1  2  3  4  5

7. I can tell whether someone has anything useful to say before he or she finishes communicating a message.

   1  2  3  4  5

8. I quit listening to a speaker when I think he or she has nothing interesting to say.

   1  2  3  4  5

9. I get emotional or upset when speakers make jokes about issues or things that are important to me.

   1  2  3  4  5

10. I get angry or offended when speakers use offensive words.
    1  2  3  4  5
11. I do not expend a lot of energy when listening to others.
    1  2  3  4  5
12. I pretend to listen to others even when I'm not really listening.
    1  2  3  4  5
13. I get distracted when listening to others.
    1  2  3  4  5
14. I deny or ignore information and comments that go against my thoughts and feelings.
    1  2  3  4  5
15. I do not seek opportunities to challenge my listening skills.
    1  2  3  4  5
16. I do not pay attention to the visual aids used during lectures.
    1  2  3  4  5
17. I do not take notes on handouts when they are provided.
    1  2  3  4  5

Now add up your total score for the 17 items, and record it in the space provided.
Refer to the norms below to evaluate your listening skills.

**Total Score =** _____

**Norms**

Use the following norms to evaluate your listening skills.
17–34 = Good listening skills
35–53 = Moderately good listening skills
54–85 = Poor listening skills

How would you evaluate your listening skills?

2. Answer the following questions in your communication journal:
    a. *Cognitive dimension:* Explain, with examples, the difference between the one-to-many approach to public speaking and the one-on-one approach. How can you personally become a better public speaker by adopting the one-on-one approach?
    b. *Affective dimension:* Say you were asked to make a public presentation in the next day or two. Describe the range of feelings you would experience as a result of such a request.

    c.   *Behavioural dimension:* Of the rules that top speakers use, which one is the most difficult for you? Develop a three- or four-step plan that could help you to abide by that specific rule.

3. Think about some of the best and the worst presentations you have witnessed. What speaker characteristics made them either way?

4. On a scale of 1 (no fear) to 10 (extreme, debilitating fear), rate your anxiety level when you must give a speech. Have you ever seen a good speaker who was also nervous? Explain and give examples.

5. In a small group, share with one another why you are taking this course and what you hope to gain. Even if it is a compulsory class, express what you might possibly get out of it.

6. Prepare a mini-speech (not to be written out or memorized!) for your next class. The topic will be your most irritating pet peeve. The speech should include your specific pet peeve (what it is), a description of how it works, how/why it bothers you, and what you think could be done to eliminate it. There are no length requirements or restrictions.

7. Play the Commonalities Game. Meet in groups of five to seven individuals and come up with 15 weird things that you have in common with one another. They cannot be things such as you are all taking a public speaking course, are BBA students, or like to watch *Corner Gas*. The commonalities must be truly unique—something like you all have a dog with a white mark on it's left hind leg, you were all born in December, or you all have the same tattoo in the same place. Afterwards, have each group introduce members to the class and disclose what peculiar things they have in common with one another.

## REFERENCES AND FURTHER READINGS

Adler, R.B., & Elmhorst, J.M. (1996). *Communicating at work: Principles and practices for business and the professions* (5th ed.). New York: McGraw-Hill Ryerson.

Adler, R., Towne, N., & Rolls, J.A. (2004). *Looking out: Looking in* (2nd Canadian ed.). Scarborough, Ont.: Thomson Nelson.

Barnard, S. (1996). *Speaking our minds: A guide to public speaking for Canadians* (2nd ed.). Scarborough, ON: Prentice Hall.

Berns, F. (2004). Blow your own horn. *Kitchen & Bath Business, 51*(10), 28.

Friesen, C., & Markman, S. (2004). Talk your way into the practice you want. *Consulting to Management, 15*(1), 49–54.

Gaut, D.R., & Perrigo, E.M. (1998). *Business and professional communication for the 21st century.* Boston: Allyn and Bacon.

Gittlen, S. (2004). The public side of you. *Network World, 21,* 61, 63.

Kreitner, R., Kinicki, A., & Cole, N. (2003). *Fundamentals of organizational behaviour.* Toronto: McGraw-Hill Ryerson.

McLaughlin, M.A. (1995). *Employability skills profile: What are employers looking for?* (Report No. EDO-CG-95-44) East Lansing, MI: National Center for Research on Teacher Learning. (ERIC Document Reproduction Service No. ED399484).

Motley, M.T., & Molloy, J.L. (1994). An efficacy test of a new therapy ("communication orientation motivation") for public speaking anxiety. *Journal of Applied Communication Research, 22,* 48–58.

Osborn, M., & Osborn, S. (1994). *Public speaking* (3rd ed.). Boston: Houghton Mifflin.

Quigley, B.L., & Nyquist, J.D. (1992). Using video technology to provide feedback to students in performance courses. *Communication Education, 41*(3), 324–334.

Richmond, V.P., & McCroskey, J.C. (1995). *Communication: Apprehension, avoidance, and effectiveness* (4th ed.). Scottsdale, AZ: Gorsuch Scarisbrick.

Rolls, J.A. (1993). Experiential learning as an adjunct to the basic course: Student responses to a pedagogical model. *Basic Communication Course Annual, 5,* 182–199.

Rolls, J.A. (1997). Gendered evaluation responses to experiential learning as an adjunct to the basic communication skills course. *Canadian Journal of Communication, 22,* 41–60.

Rolls, J.A., & Strenkowski, M. (1994). Rationale and description of the video resume model. *The Journal of Cooperative Education, 29,* 77–83.

Snyder, E. (1983). *Speak for yourself—with confidence.* New York: New American Library.

Specht, L.B., & Sandler, P.E. (1991). The differential effects of experiential learning activities and traditional lecture classes in accounting. *Simulation and Gaming, 22*(2), 196–210.

Toastmasters International. (2004/2005). *Online reports*. Retrieved June 15, 2005, from http://www.toastmasters.org/artisan/member.asp?CategoryID=1&SubCategory ID=51&Pag...

Wallechinsky, D., Wallace, I., & Wallace, A. (1977). *The book of lists*. New York: Bantam Books.

Wolvin, A., & Coakley, C.G. (1988). *Listening* (3rd ed.). Dubuque, IA: W. C. Brown.

Wood, J. (1997). *Communication in our lives*. New York: Wadsworth.

# Chapter 2
## Dealing with Nervousness

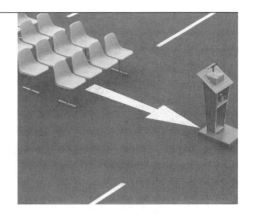

## CHAPTER GOALS

In this chapter, you will learn
- what communication experts say about nervousness
- the type of apprehension you may personally experience
- how to control physical and mental manifestations of nervousness
- how and why to think positively about the audience
- how to prepare for success

# ■ INTRODUCTION

I once developed and taught a course for extremely shy adults who wanted to improve their public speaking skills. Called *Freeing Your Personality,* we met weekly in a small communication lab. On the first night, only three of the 12 individuals who registered for the course showed up. As we waited for possible latecomers, I couldn't help but notice that people would approach the door, look in, and then continue on their way. Some of them did this more than once—they were too overwrought to enter the lab. I literally had to go into the hallway, introduce myself, and persuade them to join us. In fact, it took two weeks for one particularly shy man to enter.

But once everyone was in, and the course was up and running, they all worked hard to deal with their fears, and to identify and acknowledge skills they did not even know they possessed. Every person left the course feeling more confident and less nervous about speaking in public.

Why are people apprehensive when they speak before groups? Why is it that students feel comfortable speaking from their seats, yet experience discomfort when talking from only a few feet away, in front of the class? It does not seem to make sense. However, Hamilton Gregory (1999, pp. 25–26), a public speaking professor, suggests at least four good reasons why students may be scared: they fear being stared at, they fear failure, they fear rejection, and they fear the unknown. Whenever they are in front of an audience, they essentially put their credibility on the line—good reason to be a little tense.

While such concerns regarding public speaking are valid, many things can be done to manage anxiety. In fact, public speaking anxiety has received considerable attention by researchers and there is agreement that it can be reduced (Ayres & Ayres, 2003). While a variety of treatments have shown to be effective, programs that use a multidimensional approach result in the highest success rates (Allen, Hunter, & Donohue, 1989; Ayres & Ayres, 2003; Dwyer, 2000; Rossi & Seiler, 1989; Whitworth & Cochran, 1996). In keeping with this research, the chapter is designed to review the causes of nervousness and to offer a variety of suggestions that can alleviate or reduce the tension associated with making presentations. If you follow some or all of the suggestions, you too should become less nervous.

To make the strategies work, experiment with and practise until you find the ones that best meet your needs. For instance, perhaps you are only nervous because you are unsure of how to organize a speech. Or, you may have to rethink how you perceive your role in the public speaking process. If you possess a phobic fear of public speaking, you might consider professional counselling, although the percentage of people in this category is extremely low.

---

**EVERYBODY'S BUSINESS**

Although business professionals have always recognized that communication skills are critical for business success, their focus on *communication apprehension* (CA) is a relatively new phenomena and their research is uncovering an educational gap in this area. For example, studies have found that MBA students score high in public anxiety, although those MBA students who had math undergraduate degrees had significantly lower CA (Burk, 2001). Two professors from Concordia University, Drs. Aly and Islam, reported that while accounting students overall had high CA levels, females' levels were higher than their male counterparts (2005). Nick Huber (2005) reported the findings of a British survey that found, of 200 business leaders, 58 percent said public speaking was the most daunting part of their work, and presenting to the board made 41 percent of them nervous. Golden's (2004) study of health care CEOs suggested that skills training in public speaking is essential if they are to be comfortable in their roles. As a result of these and other studies, trade magazines regularly contain articles that provide public speaking tips. In an attempt to try to remedy the CA problem, many business schools now require students to enrol in public speaking classes. Perhaps you are reading this book for that very reason.

The chapter begins with a brief overview of the causes of nervousness because understanding the root of your anxiety can go a long way toward reducing it. The remainder of the chapter is organized around the three major factors that contribute to speech anxiety: the audience, the material, and you.

# ■ CAUSES OF NERVOUSNESS

Communication scholars have long been interested in understanding the fear associated with public speaking, and they have typically labelled it according to what they thought caused it. Which of the descriptions below best describe the nervousness you feel?

## Stage Fright

Theodore Clevenger (1959) reasoned that people had misgivings about forgetting material, performing poorly, or sounding stupid merely because they were on stage, in front of people. Thus, he called it *stage fright*, a term still used today. He thought it was something you either did or did not experience—there was no in between.

## Communication Apprehension

James McCroskey (1977) explained the condition in terms of *communication appre-hension* (CA) and asserted that there were two types: trait and state. *Trait CA* refers to shyness that is experienced in both interpersonal (one-on-one) and public speaking settings. People who label themselves shy or bashful would experience trait CA. They are only comfortable conversing with people they know well.

*State CA* refers to the fear that is *only* associated with public speaking, and most people experience it to some degree—it is a normal condition. Some people endure high levels while others have only mild symptoms that disappear as the presentation progresses. Because people can feel nervous speaking in groups or in a host of other contexts, state CA is often now referred to as *contextual CA*. You can assess the degree to which you experience CA by taking the Personal Report of Public Speaking Anxiety (PRPSA) test that appears at the end of this chapter. Record your score and retake it at the end of the term to obtain a numerical verification of how much your CA level dropped as a result of taking a public speaking course.

## Reticence

Gerald Phillips (1968) thought that people feel anxious because they do not possess the skills associated with doing a speech. He referred to this as *reticence* and reasoned that if people were taught how to, and given an opportunity to practise making presenta-tions, they would feel less apprehensive. He also thought that if students could be taught to think differently, or turn their negative thoughts into more positive ones, then that might help as well. He referred to this as *rhetoritherapy* (Phillips, 1977). For example, assuming that if you make just one mistake in a speech you will be consid-ered stupid exemplifies irrational, negative thinking. It would be much more produc-tive—and realistic—to assume that everyone makes mistakes. Phillips (1997) referred to this type of thinking as *myths*. Other examples of the irrational mindset include thinking that speakers are born, not made, or thinking that it is better to be quiet and have people think you are stupid than to open your mouth and prove it.

## Personality and Audience Factors

Peter MacIntyre and his colleagues (1995a, 1995b, 1997) found that speaker per-sonality traits and audience characteristics also affected the nervousness that stu-dents feel. For example, while you might not be comfortable presenting the results of a research project to your marketing class, you might actually enjoy giving a speech on that topic at a junior achievers meeting. MacIntyre's work is featured later in the chapter.

Having read what can cause nervousness, to what do you attribute any awkwardness you may feel: stage fright, trait CA, state CA, contextual CA, reticence, personality factors, or audience factors?

# YOU AS A CAUSE OF NERVOUSNESS

Sometimes nervous speakers can be their own worst enemies in that they maintain a negative attitude about speaking in public. In those and other cases, one of the best ways to reduce communication apprehension is to think differently about your role in the phenomena. Several options are outlined in this section.

## SPOTLIGHT ON SPEAKERS

### ROWLING NERVOUS ABOUT READING

Toronto (CP)—J.K. Rowling is terrified.

The outrageously successful author of the Harry Potter children's books has arrived in Toronto for Tuesday's historic "intimate" reading to an estimated 20 000 of her young fans at the city's SkyDome sports cathedral.

"I try not to focus on that," Rowling told a Sunday news conference. "Thanks for reminding me."

The Edinburgh-born writer said she agreed to the Dome venue at a time when she was fending off a blizzard of requests for personal appearances. She thought saying yes to the reading idea would be a way of conducting a one-on-one with a large number of Potter fans all at once. But she didn't think of the implications until it was too late.

"I'm so terrified!" she confessed. "I'm not the Rolling Stones. How's that going to work?"

Rowling said the largest reading audience she's had to date was 2000 in Germany and she found it a lot of fun, even with an interpreter.

Asked if the Dome mega-reading is a good idea, she said to ask her afterwards. But she added that she has been assured it will be very intimate, even if the SkyDome has a 60 000-seat capacity.

*Canadian Press/Cape Breton Post, October 23, 2000, p. 27*

# Identify and Rationalize Symptoms

Regardless of the causes of CA, symptoms manifest themselves in predictable ways, although symptoms may vary from person to person. The accompanying box contains a list of ways in which CA is typically felt. Review the sensations and check off the ones you have experienced. You may even have felt some of these while being interviewed, giving a reading at a religious service, or introducing yourself. Richmond and McCroskey (1985) claim that in addition to public speaking anxieties, people can suffer high levels of apprehension when speaking in small groups, attending meetings, singing, or even writing!

Does your body or mind behave in any of the ways mentioned in this box? Occasionally, a person who has especially high communication apprehension reports having experienced all of the symptoms! However, when public speaking classes generate their own list, students are relieved to hear the broad array of feelings experienced just within their class. They draw comfort in knowing that other students suffer in similar ways, and this seems to help reduce their communication apprehension. Another way to reduce CA is to think differently about the symptoms. If you look at yourself as a cause of nervousness, you can actually begin to deal with it by changing how you think about yourself. One way to do this is described in the remedy below.

---

## SYMPTOMS OF NERVOUSNESS

The following is a list of frequently felt physical and mental manifestations of public speaking anxiety generated by students in introductory communication courses. Check off the ones you have experienced.

_____ Your mind races ahead of your mouth.

_____ Your mind lags behind your presentation.

_____ You feel flushed and think that everyone can see that you are red.

_____ Your mouth is so dry you can hardly utter the words.

_____ You stammer.

_____ You get tongue-tied.

_____ You forget words.

_____ You do not articulate, or you omit, parts of words.

_____ You lose your place in the presentation.

_____ You forget important sections.

_____ You use distracting vocal fillers like "um."

_____ You feel there are too many eyes looking at you.

_____ Your vision is blurred and you cannot focus on the audience.

_____ Your armpits itch.

_____ You have butterflies in your stomach.

_____ Your palms sweat.

_____ Your hands shake.

_____ Your legs (sometimes just one) tremble.

_____ Your entire body quivers.

_____ You sway back and forth.

_____ You sway from side to side.

_____ You pace back and forth.

_____ You develop nervous tics and twitches (some of which you know the audience can see).

_____ You shuffle or tap your feet.

_____ You fidget with body parts.

_____ You play with your clothes or jewellery.

_____ You adjust your glasses or notes.

_____ You rub your hands together.

_____ You hug and caress the podium.

_____ You crinkle and fold your notes.

_____ You feel sick to your stomach.

_____ Ripples of fear and panic filter through your entire body.

_____ You get dizzy and think you may fall over.

_____ Your heart pounds so badly you can feel it in your ears.

_____ You experience heart palpitations or flutters.

_____ You feel weak and think you may pass out.

_____ You have to go to the bathroom.

_____ You purposely omit parts of the presentation just so you can sit down.

_____ You leave the podium and end up saying the final words on the way to your seat.

_____ You can't remember anything once you sit down.

_____ You giggle nervously.

_____ Your upper lip gets sweaty.

_____ You get hyper.

## *A Remedy*

The following is a remedy to help you deal with and even eliminate your symptoms. The first step is to identify specifically how speech anxiety is usually manifested in your body. (A review of the list in the box above can help.) For instance, perhaps your knees shake, or you start to stammer. When these symptoms appear during a presentation, you likely obsess about them. Rather than concentrating on the presentation or the audience, the focus is shifted to the manifestations of nervousness. This leads you to feel nervous about being nervous, and then even more fearful as you think you are becoming too anxious. Thoughts like the following exemplify this process: "Oh no, my knees are starting to tremble. I'm getting too nervous and losing control. Uh-oh, here goes my presentation down the tube." This process is very uncomfortable, especially when such thoughts and responses begin to spiral out of control. The more you tremble, or whatever your particular symptom is, the more nervous you become.

If you have experienced any of this, you are ready to proceed with the second step in the remedy. When the symptoms first appear, rather than become alarmed, recall that nervousness is manifested in many different ways. Shaky knees are just how it is displayed in your particular body. No big deal—your knees have shaken before, and they will likely do so again. In other words, try to minimize rather than maximize the manifestations by changing the panicky thoughts into rational, constructive ones, such as, "Oh, there go the old knees starting to do their thing again. This is so crazy, and even uncomfortable, but it's not going to stop me."

When students are asked to reshape their thinking in this way, some claim that the symptoms actually disappear. This is not surprising given that communication and psychology scholars assert that cognitive restructuring is helpful when it comes to allaying a wide variety of fears. By understanding and accepting how nervousness is manifested in your body, you too will find that such emotional displays either begin to dissipate or that you are no longer alarmed by them (Rolls, 1998).

---

 **EXPERT ADVICE**

If you're the type of person who gets sweaty palms, keep a tissue in your pocket. Right before you do an interview, presentation, or even make an announcement, put your hand in your pocket and give the tissue a squeeze. This takes away some of the perspiration.

*Shannon Farrell, Research Officer*
*Maritime Provinces Higher Education Commission, Fredericton, N.B.*

---

## Know That Nervous Speakers Can Be Successful

A commonly held misconception is that nervous speakers are poor speakers. This is simply not true. Because anxious students often overcompensate for their apprehension through increased effort, they can actually become superior speakers. In other words, they ensure that they are well prepared, they thoroughly research and organize their material, and they practise the presentation until they feel comfortable with its flow. Reticent, well-prepared students report that preparation reduces their worry load—they have one less thing to be concerned about.

An accountant once remarked that real-life listeners in business settings prefer nervous speakers who know their material over big-time talkers who offer little of use. There is also a tendency to think that calm, confident speakers will automatically lead good sessions. However, it is possible to be too cocky and not give the presentation enough attention. When this happens, speakers lose their credibility.

Even if you have a very high level of anxiety, you can still be a successful speaker. Remember, many symptoms of anxiety are internal, and if you prepare for the presentation you will be effective.

## Strive for Excellence, Not Perfection

Many students operate under the assumption that they have to be perfect when speaking in public—nothing less satisfies them. Such an attitude can only lead to failure because there is *no such thing as a flawless performance*. Everyone makes mistakes, and anyone expecting perfection is headed for disappointment. Perfectionists are often terrified to try anything new for fear they will not do an exemplary job. Little wonder they fear speaking in public.

Do not worry about being perfect. Because mistakes are inevitable, take them in stride. If you forget part of a speech, mispronounce a few words, lose your place, or fumble, put it into perspective: in the big scheme of things, it is really no big deal. Keep in mind, too, that most people do not expect perfection from speakers, and in fact, many actually enjoy when speakers err. These speakers appear more human and audience members are more likely to relate to them. Think back to some of the best speakers you have heard—if you were to analyze their presentations, I'd bet you would find many imperfections.

## Lighten Up

Having a sense of humour can help you deal with most situations. Often, we take things too seriously, as did one of my former students, Jo-Anne. After class she was complaining about the poor job she had done in her videotaped classroom speech. I was quite surprised because I thought it had gone well. She had a good rapport with the audience, and the speech was well organized with relevant support material and examples the class could relate to. She received an overall positive evaluation, and even the class seemed impressed with her work. Jo-Anne's concern and focus, however, was on the fact that she had paused to think of another example. As a result, all she could recollect of the speech was that interruption, and she felt the pause had ruined the entire presentation. No matter what I said I could not convince her otherwise.

It was only after she reviewed her videotaped performance that Jo-Anne began to assess her success more realistically. She was amazed to discover the pause that had grown in magnitude in her head was actually rather brief. It certainly did not detract from the overall performance. Clearly she was striving for perfection, and when she did not achieve it, she needlessly berated herself for what she thought was a second-rate performance. While you should strive to do your best, do not cheat yourself by aiming only for flawlessness—it does not exist.

## Develop Your Self-Confidence

Confident individuals are less likely to have speech anxiety and there is a correlation between confidence and perceived competence (MacIntyre & Thivierge, 1995a). If you think you have expertise in a particular subject, then you are less likely to feel nervous during a presentation on that subject.

Your self-concept is how you generally feel and think about yourself and one way that it is developed is through reflect appraisal (Adler, Towne, & Rolls, 2004). For instance, if you have been told by family members, significant others, or teachers that you are not a good public speaker, you are likely to see yourself as incompetent. Or, perhaps you had one negative experience and now you generalize that to believe that you lack good speaking skills.

Because the self-concept is subjective, it is often difficult to change, and there is a tendency to cling to old, obsolete information about yourself. In fact, "once communicators fasten on to a self-concept—whether it is positive or negative—the tendency is to seek out people who confirm it" (Adler, Towne, & Rolls, 2004, p. 53). This leads to the self-fulfilling prophecy problem, where your own notions or expectations influence your behaviour. For instance, if you continually tell yourself that you will do a bad job on a speech, there is a good likelihood that you will indeed give a poor speech. Your self-fulfilling prophecy is negative, and so is your output.

Two psychologists, Robert Rosenthal and Lenore Jacobson (1968), conducted an interesting study on teacher expectations. They informed elementary school teachers that 20 percent of the children (who were randomly selected by the researchers) would show a significant increase in their intellectual growth. The teachers knew which children were supposed to be the late bloomers. What happened? Those very children showed considerable gains in their IQs, not because they were any brighter but because teachers expected that to happen.

The results of this study can help you in two ways: (1) expect that you will do well and you will; and (2) you can probably do much better than you think you can. If you apply the concepts and principles in this text and give yourself plenty of practice, you will become a skilled speaker.

You can also develop general self-confidence and a better self-concept by focusing on the positive aspects of your life. Give yourself a pat on the back for your accomplishments. Begin to accept compliments. There is nothing worse than praising someone and having him or her shrug it off—this insults the individual giving praise. Remember too that people generally do not go out of their way to flatter others, so accept compliments graciously and incorporate the sentiment into your new optimistic sense of self.

Finally, people who possess personality traits such as emotional maturity, self-control, and tolerance for ambiguity also tend to feel less apprehensive in public speaking situations (MacIntyre & Thivierge, 1995a). Therefore, it makes sense to try to develop such characteristics. You may want to embark on a journey of self-improvement.

---

 **EXPERT ADVICE**

When people come together at work, they usually do a little social chat before they get down to the business at hand. For me, it's the same with public speaking. If I have to get right into the business of the presentation, it can make me feel uncomfortable, or even a little nervous. But, if I can take a moment to say something of a social nature, then it tends to ease both me and the audience into the business or goal of the talk. It adds a personal touch.

*Wanda Harbin, Ombudsperson and Training Officer*
*Marine Atlantic Corporation, North Sydney, N.S.*

---

## Practise Systematic Desensitization

While systematic desensitization is a procedure used to help people overcome phobias, it is also widely used to treat communication apprehension. Developed by Joseph Wolpe in 1958, its goal, according to Dwyer (1998) is "to help you develop a new relaxation response to a feared or anxiety-provoking event, such as public speaking" (p. 73). There are three steps in systematic desensitization parts: (1) create a hierarchy of public speaking fearful events; (2) train yourself to relax your entire body; and (3) visualize your body relaxing in response to each step in the hierarchy of fears you developed (Dwyer, 1998).

To create a public speaking hierarchy of fears, develop a list of fears and arrange them from the least to the most threatening. These might range anywhere from asking a question in class to giving a presentation for the instructors in the communication department. In step 2, train yourself to relax your entire body. One way to do this is to tighten and contract every muscle and body part, beginning with your toes and finishing with the top of your head. In step 3, starting with the least frightening situation (such as asking a question in class), visualize yourself doing this. Continue visualizing until you feel comfortable. Then move to the next item on your list—like answering a question in class. Imagine answering a question and feeling good about it. Maybe see your professor giving you positive feeldback about what you said. Continue in this vein through each step until you feel you could make a presentation for communication faculty. However, do not expect this technique to work overnight—the greater the depth of your fears, the longer it will take to ease them.

## THINK YOUR WAY TO SUCCESS: A COGNITIVE APPROACH TO REDUCING NERVOUSNESS

You can actually reduce your nervousness by keeping the following in mind:

- Everyone feels some degree of nervousness when speaking in public. To feel apprehensive is to be normal.
- Just because you know you are nervous does not mean that everyone else knows it too.
- Many top-rated speakers categorize themselves as highly apprehensive speakers. This shows that nervous speakers can also be excellent speakers.
- No one expects speakers to be perfect. Instead of striving for perfection, strive for excellence.
- Instead of thinking that "experts" in the audience are out to criticize your presentation, think of them as individuals who are truly interested in your topic. They will provide positive feedback.
- When instructors are writing during your presentation, do not assume they are making negative comments. Instead, think that they are saying positive things about you and your presentation.

# ■ THE MATERIAL AS A SOURCE OF NERVOUSNESS

## Be Prepared

If you are confident that you are well prepared, this will transfer into a belief in yourself. Communication scholars have demonstrated that there is a negative correlation between self-confidence and nervousness. This means that the more confident you feel, the less nervousness you will endure.

Sometimes students do not prepare because they are unfamiliar with the requirements of the assignment or the mechanics of how to prepare the speech. This type of behaviour would be unacceptable in the workplace. If you find yourself in this category, get the information from your instructor. If you are not prepared, you will definitely feel nervous.

Other students do not prepare because the mere thought of the presentation scares them so much that they engage in avoidance behaviour. In their minds, making the speech becomes such an onerous task that it literally becomes unmanageable for them. These can be the same students who maintain A averages in other courses. Here is where guidance from communication instructors can help, most of whom welcome the opportunity to assist. They can help and/or provide reassurance that your topic is appropriate.

If you feel overwhelmed when you have to do a speech or presentation, try to take it one step at a time. Worrying about everything all at once is unproductive. Instead, start by learning the assignment specifications, then select and research your topic, adapt the material to the required format, and finally, practise until you feel ready.

---

### ✍ EXPERT ADVICE

How much preparation time should you put in? Laura Stack (2004), a professional speaker and trainer, recommends that for new presentations, speakers put in 10 hours of researching and outlining a presentation for every hour on the platform! She also recommends that you should have 45–50 minutes of material per hour so that there is time for questions and answers. Although your individual classroom presentations might not be that long, Stack's comment underscores the importance of preparation and practice.

---

# Practise

In a review of our course evaluation forms, when asked what students would change if they could do their speeches again, the most common reply was that they would practise more. They write that additional preparation would have allowed them to more effectively gauge the time, become better acquainted with the content, and deliver a more refined presentation. There are two ways to practise: physically and mentally.

I remember the presentation I did in my organizational behaviour class. I practisced beforehand and it really made a difference. I knew what I was going to say, when I was going to say it, and how I was going to say it. I was way less nervous because I felt I was in control of the situation.

*John, BBA Student*

## *Practise Physically*

Practising out loud until you feel comfortable with the overall rhythm and delivery of the speech diminishes nervousness. However, there are several phases in the preparation process. First, make sure you have a thorough understanding of the topic. You need to know the material "inside out," and not just the specific information you will share with your audience. You should possess additional data and facts that go well beyond the scope of the presentation so that you feel confident as a subject expert.

Once you have established a strong knowledge base and outlined the speech, proceed to step 2, the physical practice. Recite the speech in front of a mirror or video camera. This gives you an idea of what the audience will see. Some students prefer to say their speech for a friend. However, this strategy can reduce rather than boost their confidence levels if they are not yet ready for an audience.

The goal of practice is to repeat the speech until you feel positive about the potential performance. This means that you have to go through it many times. For each practice round, start at the beginning and proceed right to the end without stopping. If you forget or fumble parts, correct yourself and continue. This approach more accurately simulates the actual presentation. While you are speaking, also envision an audience in front of you. If you concentrate on this, you may begin to feel nervous, which is a good thing. Do not stop practising until your nervousness has transformed into excitement. Only then have you rehearsed enough. If this does not happen, and you start to worry that the content is not good enough, enhance and change it until it meets your standards.

One word of caution, though: do not over-train, because you may end up memorizing the material. Another problem with over-practise is that you may offer your peak performance without an audience. You do not want this. Also, it is important to practise with the actual note card you will use during the presentation. This familiarity creates a psychological bond that goes with you to the performance. Some people colour-code their outlines with markers, coloured pens, or highlighters for easy access. Speakers who write out new note cards just before their presentations are often astonished to find that they do not offer the same level of security as the old ones did. Chapter 6 discusses in more detail how to make and use notes effectively.

---

I like to present my speech a number of times. Once I'm comfortable with it, I do it for a friend. Then I will say it for my family, and finally, I will perform it again for some of the people in class. By the time I get to class I will have done it for so many people already that it won't bother me to do it for a few more. By that time I will have all the kinks worked out.

*Gordon, Communication Major*

---

Practice is not only a must for the apprehensive speaker, it should be routine for everyone. Some bright, outgoing students give mediocre speeches because they do not go through the material beforehand. As a result, they do not meet time requirements, they are disorganized, and the speech's content has little depth. In all, they lack polish. Such students receive lower grades than the more nervous speakers who attend to the mechanics of the presentation. That is, they meet time requirements, present their work in an organized fashion, and make poised, professional presentations.

## *Try Not To Memorize*

Some students equate preparation with memorization. They feel that they do not know a speech unless they can repeat it verbatim every time they practise it. But memorized presentations leave no room for speakers to react to unexpected events that may occur during a presentation. There is no leeway when one, and only one, specific way to deliver a message is planned. Further, speakers can sound mechanical and staid, as if they are more interested in finishing rather than connecting with the audience. But the worst

## EXPERT ADVICE

Practising out loud rather than just in your head has several advantages: it will not only allow you to become comfortable with the topic, but it will also refine your timing. It will also provide you with a physical memory of delivering the speech that will reduce nervousness when you step in front of your actual audience. Go through the speech aloud several times to master your timing, your command of your material, your delivery, and your use of visual aids.

*Dr. Jennifer MacLennan, Associate Professor and D.K. Seaman Chair*
*University of Saskatchewan, Saskatoon, Saskatchewan*

thing about memorization occurs when students, due to nervousness or whatever, go blank. They often repeat sentences or phrases a couple of times, as if trying to get themselves jump-started. While audience members might be sympathetic, this does little to enhance a speaker's credibility.

Rather than memorize speeches, try to speak extemporaneously. This will allow you to react to the moment. Should you lose your place, or become momentarily confused, just refer to you outline . . . and do not rush yourself. Remember, pauses always seem longer to speakers than they do to listeners. Overall, memorized speeches are stiff and artificial at best, and awkward and embarrassing at worst. They are not accepted in the everyday business world and they do not make for transactional communication where the speaker and the audience are on the same wavelength, creating meaning together.

### Practise Mentally with Positive Visualization

As odd as it may seem, it is equally important to practise in your head as on your feet. Referred to as positive visualization, this technique is used successfully by athletes. Maltz (1969) reports the results of a study of three groups of tennis players. Before the match, one group practised on the court, a second practised only in their heads, and the third practised both on the court and in their heads. As you may have suspected, the group that practised both physically and mentally fared the best.

The technique can also be applied to making speeches. In a review of the literature, researchers Joe Ayres and Tracy Ayres (2003) report that it is highly effective in reducing communication apprehension in public speaking contexts (Ayres & Hoph, 1985; Beyers & Webber, 1993; Halvorson, 1994). It also works to reduce CA in interview situations (Ayres et al., 2001), and the system is effective over time (Ayres & Hoph, 1990).

"Don't disturb Daddy. He's busy visualizing unparalleled success in the
business world and, by extension, a better life for us all."

To implement the technique, you might use the same visualization process that was used by Ayres and Hoph (1985) with the subjects in their study. You begin by getting into a relaxed state. Then you imagine what would happen to you on the day of a speech. As you go through the following steps, eliminate all negative thoughts and reactions. Try to visualize yourself in a positive frame of mind. See yourself as you get up, select what you will wear, go to class, greet classmates, walk to the front of the class, begin the speech, deliver the body of the speech, end the speech, field questions, receive congratulations from audience members, and then see yourself in some relaxing scene (Ayres & Ayres, 2003, p. 49). If you are the type of person who has a difficult time with visualization, you could supplement the process by creating pleasant pictures or photographs to accompany the scenes noted above. Although the latter may seem like a time-consuming activity, it is a worthy investment in your anxiety reduction as it is another way to reduce CA.

When you are doing this exercise, try to include as many details as possible. For instance, you might visualize different people in your class responding positively to your presentation. You see them nodding, showing an interest in what you are saying, or laughing when you intend to be humorous. Think for a moment that you begin to feel apprehensive, that you are getting a little mixed up (or however CA is manifested by your body). Even as you feel this way you keep speaking and get yourself back on track. The feeling does not affect the speech. Look over at your instructor and see him or her enjoying your examples and anecdotes, and generally being satisfied with your presentation.

---

## PRACTISE YOUR WAY TO SUCCESS: A BEHAVIOURAL APPROACH TO REDUCING NERVOUSNESS

Try the following tips to improve your practise sessions:

- When you begin to practise, do so in private by saying the speech out loud. Pretend that you are in front of an audience, and envision that audience responding positively to you.
- Always say the speech from beginning to end. If you mess up, correct yourself and move on.
- When you feel more comfortable, practise in front of a mirror or record yourself on video.
- Practise using the actual notes that you will have during your presentation.
- Only when you feel confident should you practise your speech in front of anyone else.
- Practise until you feel comfortable with your speech and actually feel positive and somewhat excited about your upcoming presentation.

---

# THE AUDIENCE AS A SOURCE OF NERVOUSNESS

The third source of nervousness comes from the audience. Here are a couple of things to consider that might ease some of that tension.

## Remember that the Audience May Not Know You are Nervous

Many apprehensive speakers assume that their nervousness is always obvious to the audience. But, unless symptoms are external (the speaker faints, hands shake so badly that notes flop about), audience members have no way of knowing what speakers think or feel, or if indeed they are nervous at all. This is because most indicators of communication apprehension are internal and listeners simply cannot see them.

Here are some examples of internal manifestations of CA. One student noted that he had butterflies in his stomach so badly that he thought he was going to lift off, and his heart pounded so hard that he was sure his chest must be heaving in and out. But, listeners cannot know this because they cannot see such symptoms. Here is a variation. Your mind might be racing so much that you omit parts of your speech. However, audiences do not attend all that closely to speakers, so they may not even notice the omission. At most, a few people might think the presentation did not flow particularly well.

The basic point to remember is that just because you feel such sensations, it does not mean that the audience is aware of them. This is why exceptionally anxious people can appear calm, cool, and collected. Immediately following a speech, I sometimes ask students how they felt during their presentation. As a class, we are often surprised to learn that individuals who looked poised and professional, and who presented engaging speeches, actually hated the experience. Because their anxiety

---

### THE RED/HOT FACE PHENOMENON

A common internal response to communication apprehension is a hot face, which is often mistaken for a red face. This leaves many students complaining that they blush when they speak, but we as audience members know this to be untrue. These students automatically assume that if their face feels flushed, it is also red. If you are such a person, you may want to restructure your thinking. If you were sitting comfortably watching a video and you began to feel warm, it is unlikely that you would assume that your body was changing colour—you would be more inclined to take off your sweater or turn down the heat.

However, some people actually do blush when they speak—about 1 in 400 students, according to my estimates. Professor Celeste Sulliman advises her blushers to wear red or pink clothing to help camouflage the condition. Another way to handle the dilemma is to quit fighting it! Why spend time worrying about something that is completely out of your control? And, in many instances, blushing is not that obvious to the audience. The situation can be further rationalized by noting that people are considered more attractive when there is a little colour in their face. In fact, women spend millions of dollars a year on cosmetics to achieve the same effect!

was manifested internally and they were well prepared for the presentation, their uneasiness went undetected.

## Think and Feel Positively about the Audience

MacIntyre and Thivierge (1995a) have shown that audience pleasantness affects public speaking anxiety. If, for example, you think the audience is friendly and supportive, you are less likely to be apprehensive than if you perceive the audience as critical or hostile. But, sometimes, just one person can put off a speaker, as the following story demonstrates.

A communication trainer described a public speaking seminar he was conducting for a national company. Throughout the session, one woman paid rapt attention but provided little in the way of positive audience feedback (like nods or smiles). Further, she did not speak much when called upon. Overall, she looked very poised in her navy suit and she communicated in a precise, formal fashion. As a result of these factors and her nonverbal communication, the trainer became intimidated by her. He began to weigh everything he said in terms of how he thought she might perceive his message.

When the session was over, she headed directly for him. He assumed she was going to suggest how he might improve future workshops. To his surprise, however, she complimented him on being so open and relaxed. He was taken aback when she remarked that she wished she could speak as freely as he did. She went on to say that she was a very shy person who avoided speaking in public and that she was only attending the session because her boss insisted that she do so. This narrative suggests that we must be careful when we interpret audience cues and not jump to negative conclusions about the messages they are sending.

In relation to your classroom speeches, remember that fellow students want you to succeed. Most empathize with you because they have been, or will be, in the same situation. Have you ever felt embarrassed for a speaker? Most of us, on occasion, have experienced this phenomenon and it implies that people are sensitive to speaker needs.

Keep in mind too that instructors are also rooting for you because your success is their success; they take pride in your accomplishments. Sometimes public speaking students become nervous when they notice professors looking at them and then glancing away to write on an evaluation sheet. Like the trainer mentioned above, students jump to the false conclusion that instructors are recording unsatisfactory aspects of the presentation. Try not to think this way. Most professors assess both communication strengths and weaknesses, and they are more likely to be logging the positive dimensions of your performance.

## Know Your Audience

Some speakers are uneasy when they know people in the audience. They may be apprehensive about not meeting the expectations of friends or acquaintances. For others, seeing some familiar faces puts them at ease.

Regardless of whether or not you are acquainted with the audience members, it is important to know about the collective audience. If you are aware in advance that you will speak to 18- to 25-year-olds, you can craft your presentation to contain subject matter and examples relevant to that group. If you learn that they are avid golfers, you can further refine the material to include content that a more diverse audience might not understand. The better you know the audience, the better you can fashion your speech to meet their needs. Further, the better you know your audience, the better you can predict their responses. Finding out all you can about the audience is an effective way to reduce your tension. Audience analysis is discussed in Chapter 4, "Researching the Speech."

---

 **PUBLIC SPEAKING IN THE 21ST CENTURY**

**TALK TO ME**

Need additional, hands-on help dealing with your CA? Perhaps an interactive, Internet program called *Talk to Me* (Botella et al., 2000) can provide some assistance. Facilitated by an amiable cartoon character, Dr. Net, and using a variety of media applications, the program takes a therapeutic approach to CA reduction. It is designed to help users identify their negative thinking about speaking in public and to change that thinking. *Talk to Me* can also be tailored to meet your specific needs. You can check it out at *http://www.internet meayuda.com* but if you choose to sign up, it will cost 50 euros (Cdn$69 as of January 25, 2006).

---

## Communicate with Rather Than Perform for the Audience

### *A Communication Orientation*

Another valuable tool that helps to relieve speech anxiety is the approach you take toward the audience. Motley and Molloy (1994) recommend that you take a communication orientation rather than a performance orientation to your presentation. In the communication orientation, you approach the situation as if you are in conversation with the audience and have some important, interesting information you want to share. Their study shows that people who adopt this outlook think more positively about the situation and experience less apprehension.

For example, one student planned to do her major speech on ecosystems because she had easy access to information on the topic. But, she wasn't inspired; she was more interested in depression. She explained that she had studied this topic in her psych classes and lived with a family member whose depression was so severe that hospitalization was required on several occasions. With a little encouragement, the student gladly switched her topic and her entire attitude toward the speech immediately changed. She became excited at the prospect of sharing her knowledge and experience with the disease. She felt her speech would be a success if anyone in the audience who suffered from the disease would seek help.

---

 **EXPERT ADVICE**

Don't think about yourself—think about the audience and what you are trying to say. If you're singing, think about the song. That's the way to get over stage fright.

*Buffy Sainte-Marie, Ph.D.*
*Singer, songwriter, activist, former Sesame Street regular, and educator*

---

### A Performance Orientation

On the other hand, a performance orientation tends to make speakers feel more uncomfortable because they put so much pressure on themselves. Here is how Peter MacIntyre and his colleagues put it (MacIntyre, Thivierge, & MacDonald, 1997, p. 158):

> [A] speaker with a performance orientation would believe that success primarily depends on her/his oratorical behavior (eye-contact, vocal range, vocabulary use, etc.). Believing that s/he is being scrutinized for performance flaws, this speaker would suffer considerable anxiety about making even minor mistakes. On the other hand, a speaker with a communication orientation places emphasis on the speech content, information-gain, and attitude change, which is more similar to everyday, interpersonal communication. The communication oriented student should experience less public speaking anxiety.

In other words, be audience-centred rather than self-centred. Many speakers, in their nervousness, become self-focused, and according to Daly, Vangelisti, and

Lawrence (1989), this can be very distracting for the audience. Speakers who are self-focused and possess a performance orientation give poorer speeches.

## A Communication Orientation Example

One of the most powerful speeches I ever heard came from a person who adopted the audience-centred approach. I was driving to the university and scanning the radio stations when a male voice caught my attention. I gathered that he was from Alcoholics Anonymous, and his message was so intense that I ended up sitting in the car in the parking lot trying to hear as much as I could before having to run, last minute, to class. The speaker's communication orientation was clear. He spoke from the heart and shared personal details of his life. He lured his listeners with tales of his descent into alcoholism and caught us with candid descriptions of the grimy world he inhabited throughout his alcoholic haze. Then he warmed our hearts as we silently encouraged him in his struggle with sobriety and recovery. The speaker had a very cordial, interpersonal approach. I felt as if I was sitting in a living room with a group of friends and one was relating a fascinating story.

What an excellent presentation. Although the man had poor articulation, his grammar was wanting, and he continually used vocal fillers, it did not matter because he focused on connecting with his audience. He was there not to perform but rather to describe what he had endured. Without doubt, he presented one of the most engaging speeches I have ever heard (I figure at this point in my career I have witnessed some 5325).

To adopt a communication orientation, it helps to be committed to your topic—choose subjects that are important to you so you bring conviction to the presentation.

---

**66 99**

In our Problem Centred Studies 300 course, our group had to do a presentation for seven advisors. One of them, we knew, had written many articles, and even a book, on the very topic our group researched. Needless to say, we found this a little intimidating. However, this advisor turned out to be our biggest supporter. He wrote a lot while we were speaking, but almost everything was positive. During the discussion part of the presentation, he asked questions that allowed us to show the other professors just how much our group knew about the topic. We all left there feeling really good.

*Shauna, Former Problem Centred Studies Student*

---

## Do Not Be Put Off by Audience Expertise

Most speakers are threatened when they believe that the audience possesses a greater expertise than they do. This is understandable. However, by the same token, it suggests that such listeners will be very interested in your presentation. And when an audience shows interest, it reduces tension in speakers (MacIntyre, Thivierge, & MacDonald, 1997). Often, students report feeling nervous at the onset of a speech or interview, but start to loosen up and relax as they receive positive feedback from the listeners. Feedback can come in the form of nonverbal cues such as smiles, nods, forward leans, and other displays of interest. Watch for these signs in audience members and try to give speakers this type of feedback when you are sitting comfortably in your seat.

## ■ DEEP ABDOMINAL BREATHING

Regardless of whether your CA is self-based, content-based, audience-based, or a combination thereof, there is a final technique that can relax you and reduce the physical symptoms of anxiety. It is deep abdominal breathing, which is the enemy of anxiety and it works for speech anxiety as well.

The following is the technique used by Karen Kangas Dwyer. She is a researcher who specializes in communication apprehension and she has written a book devoted specifically to that topic. Dr. Dwyer has kindly agreed to allow us to print her Deep Abdominal Breathing Exercise as it appears in *Conquer Your Speech Fright* (1998). Check out Figure 2.1 on the opposite page and give it a try.

## CHAPTER AT A GLANCE

- It is normal to feel nervous about public speaking.
- Do not let your body's response to nervousness make you more uptight. Instead, identify your symptoms and think about them rationally.
- The audience does not necessarily know that you are nervous.
- You can be a nervous, yet successful, speaker.
- You do not have to be perfect.
- Being prepared helps reduce nervousness.
- Practise for excellence.
- Communicate with your audience as if you are conversing with them as individuals.
- Do positive visualization.
- Think good thoughts about yourself and expect that you will succeed.

### Figure 2.1—Deep Abdominal Breathing Exercise

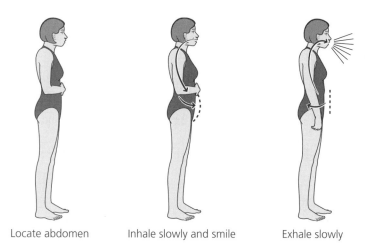

Locate abdomen      Inhale slowly and smile      Exhale slowly

## DEEP ABDOMINAL BREATHING EXERCISE

You can train yourself to use deep abdominal breathing by practising this exercise daily for three to five minutes at a time. You can choose to stand or sit during the exercise. It is more relaxing if you practise it while sitting. (Actually, you can practise this exercise lying down with knees bent and your feet spread comfortably. But if you are tired and fall asleep, you will miss the practice session!) Follow these steps:

1. First scan your body and note if you are feeling any tension or anxiety.
2. Next, find your rib cage and place one hand directly below your rib cage—that is, your abdomen.
3. Now, concentrate on your breathing. Inhale *slowly* and *deeply* through your nose, feeling your abdomen expand and your hand rise for a count of four (1—2—3—4—). Your chest should barely move.
4. Pause slightly and smile for a count of four (1—2—3—4—). Smiling releases endorphins (natural mood elevators) into your blood.
5. Then, exhale slowly and fully through your mouth, making a "whoooo" sound like the blowing wind, for a count of four (1—2—3—4—).
6. Relax and take a few normal breaths. Tell your muscles to go loose and limp. Make an effort to let all the tension drain away from every part of your body.
7. Continue taking at least 15 to 20 deep breaths with slow, full exhales for about three to five minutes.

When you practise deep abdominal breathing, try to keep your breathing smooth and regular. Try not to gulp the air. If you get a little lightheaded at first, from the increased supply of oxygen, simply return to regular breathing for a minute or two and the lightheadedness will subside.

You will want to practise deep abdominal breathing every day for at least two weeks in order to train your body to master the technique. After the initial training, you will find it an indispensable tool to use whenever you feel anxious or tense. It will trigger relaxation and especially help you feel calm right before you give a speech. You can adjust the deep abdominal breathing exercise so it can be performed without others noticing. Simply follow the same procedures, except exhale slowly and fully through your nose, instead of making the wind sound through your mouth.

# APPLICATION AND DISCUSSION QUESTIONS

1.  Take the Personal Report of Public Speaking Anxiety (Richmond & McCroskey, 1985, pp. 113–14) and record your score. Does it represent the degree of nervousness that you think you feel? Check out the scores of others in your class. Do their scores represent the degree of awkwardness you see in their presentations? What do you think accounts for differences in the scores and what you actually observe in individuals?

## Personal Report of Public Speaking Anxiety (PRPSA)

### Directions

This instrument is composed of 34 statements concerning feelings about communicating with other people. Indicate the degree to which the statements apply to you by marking whether you (1) strongly agree, (2) agree, (3) are undecided, (4) disagree, or (5) strongly disagree with each statement. Work quickly; just record your first impression.

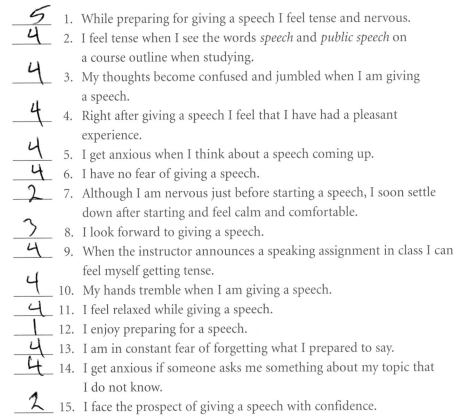

__5__   1. While preparing for giving a speech I feel tense and nervous.

__4__   2. I feel tense when I see the words *speech* and *public speech* on a course outline when studying.

__4__   3. My thoughts become confused and jumbled when I am giving a speech.

__4__   4. Right after giving a speech I feel that I have had a pleasant experience.

__4__   5. I get anxious when I think about a speech coming up.

__4__   6. I have no fear of giving a speech.

__2__   7. Although I am nervous just before starting a speech, I soon settle down after starting and feel calm and comfortable.

__3__   8. I look forward to giving a speech.

__4__   9. When the instructor announces a speaking assignment in class I can feel myself getting tense.

__4__  10. My hands tremble when I am giving a speech.

__4__  11. I feel relaxed while giving a speech.

__1__  12. I enjoy preparing for a speech.

__4__  13. I am in constant fear of forgetting what I prepared to say.

__4__  14. I get anxious if someone asks me something about my topic that I do not know.

__2__  15. I face the prospect of giving a speech with confidence.

_4_ 16. I feel that I am in complete possession of myself while giving a speech.

_2_ 17. My mind is clear while giving a speech.

_2_ 18. I do not dread giving a speech.

_4_ 19. I perspire just before starting a speech.

_5_ 20. My heart beats very fast as I start a speech.

_2_ 21. I experience considerable anxiety while sitting in the room just before my speech starts.

_4_ 22. Certain parts of my body feel very tense and rigid while giving a speech.

_4_ 23. Realizing that only a little time remains in a speech makes me very tense and anxious.

_3_ 24. While giving a speech I know I can control my feelings of tension and stress.

_4_ 25. I breathe faster just before starting a speech.

_4_ 26. I feel comfortable and relaxed in the hour or so just before giving a speech.

_4_ 27. I do poorer on speeches because I am anxious.

_4_ 28. I feel anxious when the teacher announces the date of a speaking assignment.

_4_ 29. When I make a mistake while giving a speech, I find it hard to concentrate on the parts that follow.

_5_ 30. During an important speech I experience a feeling of helplessness build up inside me.

_5_ 31. I have trouble falling asleep the night before a speech.

_5_ 32. My heart beats very fast while I present a speech.

_2_ 33. I feel anxious while waiting to give a speech.

_5_ 34. While giving a speech I get so nervous I forget facts I really know.

## Scoring

To determine your score on the PRPSA, complete the following steps:

1. Add the scores for items 1, 2, 3, 5, 9, 10, 13, 14, 19, 20, 21, 22, 23, 25, 27, 28, 29, 30, 31, 32, 33, and 34.   = 90

2. Add the scores for items 4, 6, 7, 8, 11, 12, 15, 16, 17, 18, 24, and 26.   = 35

3. Complete the following formula:

   PRPSA = 132 *minus* the total from step 1 *plus* the total from step 2.

Your score should range between 34 and 170. If your score is below 34 or above 170, you have made a mistake in computing the score.

77

**Interpreting Your Score**

You can interpret your score by following the key below. (Richmond and McCroskey's (1985, p. 35) words have been modified from a paragraph format to the form below.)

The percentages reflect the number of college students who fall into each category. It is interesting to note that the majority of students (70 percent) were either in the *moderately high* or the *very high* categories. This suggests that it is normal to be highly anxious when it comes to public speaking.

*Score:* 34–84 (5%)
*Category:* Very low anxiety about public speaking.
*Description:* Very few public speaking situations would produce anxiety in people who score this low.

*Score:* 85–92 (5%)
*Category:* Moderately low level of anxiety.
*Description:* While some public speaking situations would be likely to arouse anxiety in people with such scores, most situations would not be anxiety-arousing.

*Score:* 93–110 (20%)
*Category:* Moderate anxiety in most public speaking situations.
*Description:* The level of anxiety is not likely to be so severe that the individual cannot cope with it.

*Score:* 111–19 (30%)
*Category:* Moderately high level of anxiety.
*Description:* People with such scores will tend to avoid public speaking because it usually arouses a fairly high level of anxiety in them.

*Score:* 120–70 (40%)
*Category:* Very high level of anxiety.
*Description:* People in this range feel very high anxiety in most, if not all, public speaking situations and are likely to go to considerable lengths to avoid such situations.

2. Answer the following questions in your communication journal:
   a. Cognitive dimension: Review the section on theories of nervousness due to speaking in public. Which one most accurately reflects your situation: stage fright, trait communication apprehension, state communication apprehension, reticence, personality factors, or audience membership? If your particular feelings do not fit into any of these categories, how would you label your nervousness?

    b.   Affective dimension: Describe the types of speaking situations that make you nervous. Give examples and reasons for why you feel the way you do.

    c.   Behavioural dimension: Develop a hierarchy of the fears you have regarding public speaking. Use them to practise systematic desensitization.

3.   Working in small groups, make a list of how nervousness is manifested in the minds and bodies of your group members. Have groups share their symptoms with the rest of the class. Finally, as a class, discuss how your feelings about nervousness have changed as a result of this exercise.

4.   If you could have coached J.K. Rowling before her mega-reading at the SkyDome, what advice would you have given to help her deal with her nervousness?

5.   Of the various techniques described in this chapter, which ones have you used intuitively to help control public speaking anxiety? Which ones will you experiment with now?

6.   Prepare and deliver a mini-presentation on the following topics:

    a.   How you feel about making presentations.

    b.   Your business, educational, or political role model. Select an individual who you would like to pattern your professional life after. Describe the qualities that make that person so appealing to you.

    c.   Your brush with fame. Name a famous person you met, describe the circumstances under which the meeting occurred, and give your overall impression of the person. If you have not met a celebrity, indicate who you would like to meet and explain why.

7.   Based on the "Fear in a Hat" exercise for children and youth to identify their fears (*http://www.wilderdom.com/games/exercises/FearinaHat.html*), this exercise can be adapted to online public speaking classes.

    a.   Have online students privately submit three fears they or someone they know has when called on to deliver a speech.

    b.   Assemble and post the submissions (eliminating duplications).

    c.   Assign or ask students to select a couple of fears (other than their own) and to offer suggestions for handling or reducing those fears.

    d.   Suggestions can be submitted privately or done in real time in a full-class interactive session.

    e.   If suggestions are submitted privately, post the list.

    f.   Conduct an interactive session to discuss each fear and solution. Invite students to offer additional ideas to allay the fears.

    g.   After each fear is reviewed, eliminate it from the list.

# REFERENCES AND FURTHER READINGS

Adler, R.B., Towne, N., & Rolls, J.A. (2004). *Looking Out/Looking In* (2nd Canadian ed.). Toronto: Thomson Nelson.

Allen, M., Hunter, J., & Donohue, W. (1989). Meta-analysis of self-report data on the effectiveness of public speaking anxiety treatment techniques. *Communication Education, 38,* 54–76.

Aly, I., & Islam, M. (2005). Factors affecting oral communication apprehension among business students: An empirical study. *The Journal of American Academy of Business, 2,* 98–102.

Assagioli, R. (1973). *The act of will.* New York: Viking Press.

Assagioli, R. (1976). *Psychosynthesis: A manual of principles and techniques.* New York: Penguin Books.

Ayres, J., & Ayres, T. (2003). Using images to enhance the impact of visualization. *Communication Reports, 16,* 47–55.

Ayres, J., & Hoph, T.S. (1993). *Coping with speech anxiety.* Norwood, NJ: Ablex.

Ayres, J., & Hopf, T.S. (1990). The long-term effect of visualization in the classroom. *Communication Education, 39,* 283–291.

Ayres, J., & Hopf, T.S. (1985). Visualization: A means of reducing speech anxiety. *Communication Education, 34,* 318–323.

Ayres, J., Wongprasert, T., Silvia, J., Story, T., Hsu, C., & Sawant, D. (2001). Effects of performance visualization on employment interviews. *Communication Quarterly, 49,* 160–171.

Beyers, P. Y., & Weber, C. (1993, November). *The timing of visualization treatment and its effects of public speaking anxiety.* Paper presented at the annual meeting of the Speech Communication Association, Miami Beach, Florida.

Botella, C., Banes, R.M., Guillen, V., Perpina, C., Alcaniz, M., & Pons, A. (2000). Telepsychology: Public speaking fear treatment on the Internet. *Cyberpsychology and Behavior, 3,* 959–968.

Botella, C., Hofmann, S.G., Moscovitch, D.A. (2004). A self-applied, Internet-based intervention for fear of public speaking. *JCLP/In Session, 60,* 821–830.

Burk, J. (2001). Communication apprehension among Master's of Business Administration students: Investigating a gap in communication education. *Communication Education, 50,* 51–58.

Canadian Press. (2000, October 23). Rowling very nervous about reading. *Cape Breton Post, 27.*

Clevenger, T., Jr. (1959). A synthesis of experimental research in stage fright. *Quarterly Journal of Speech, 45,* 134–145.

Daly, J.A., Vangelisti, A.L., & Lawrence, S.G. (1989). Self-focused attention and public speaking anxiety. *Personality and Individual Differences, 10,* 903–913.

Dwyer, K.K. (1998). *Conquer your speech fright.* Fort Worth, TX: Harcourt Brace.

Dwyer, K.K. (2000). The multidimensional model: Teaching students to self-manage high communication apprehension by self-selecting treatments. *Communication Education, 49*(1), 72–81.

Golden, M.S. (2004). Not just healthcare. *Marketing Health Services, 24*(2), 48.

Gregory, H. (1999). *Public speaking for college and career* (5th ed.). Boston: McGraw-Hill College.

Halvorson, S.K. (1994, November). *A comparative analysis of relaxation techniques on state anxiety in public speaking classes.* Paper presented at the annual meeting of the Speech Communication Association, New Orleans, LA.

Huber, N. (2005, February). Most senior managers fear public speaking. *Computer Week, 20.*

MacIntyre, P.D., & Thivierge, K.A. (1995a). The effects of speaker personality on anticipated reactions to public speaking. *Communication Research Reports, 12,* 1–9.

MacIntyre, P.D., & Thivierge, K.A. (1995b). The effects of audience pleasantness, audience familiarity, and speaking contexts on public speaking anxiety and willingness to speak. *Communication Quarterly, 43,* 456–461.

MacIntyre, P.D., Thivierge, K.A., & MacDonald, J.R. (1997). The effects of audience interest, responsiveness, and evaluation on public speaking anxiety and related variables. *Communication Research Reports, 14,* 157–168.

Maltz, M. (1969). *Psycho-Cybernetics.* New York: Pocket Books.

McCroskey, J.A. (1977). Oral communication apprehension: A summary of recent theory and research. *Human Communication Research, 4,* 78–96.

Motley, M.T., & Molloy, J.L. (1994). An efficacy test of a new therapy ("communication-orientation motivation") for public speaking anxiety. *Journal of Applied Communication Research, 22*(1), 48–58.

Phillips, G.M. (1997). Reticence: A perspective on social withdrawal. In J.A. Daly, J.C. McCroskey, J. Ayres, T. Hopf, & D.M. Ayres (Eds). *Avoiding communication:*

*Shyness, reticence, and communication apprehension* (2nd ed., pp. 129–150). Cresskill, NJ: Hampton Press.

Phillips, G.M. (1968). Reticence: Pathology of the normal speaker. *Speech Monographs, 35,* 39–49.

Phillips, G.M. (1977). Rhetoritherapy versus the medical model: Dealing with reticence. *Communication Education, 26,* 34–43.

Richmond, V.P., & McCroskey, J.C. (1985). *Communication: Apprehension, avoidance, and effectiveness* (4th ed.). Scottsdale, AZ: Gorsuch Scarisbrick.

Rolls, J.A. (1998). Facing the fears associated with professional speaking. *Business Communication Quarterly, 61*(2), 103–106.

Rosenthal, R., & Jacobson, L. (1968). *Pygmalion in the classroom.* New York: Holt, Rinehart and Winston.

Rossi, A.M., & Seiler, W. J. (1989). The comparative effectiveness of systematic desensitization and an integrative approach to treating public speaking anxiety. *Imagination, Cognition, and Personality, 9,* 49–66.

Stack, L. (2004). Ten time-management tips to aid presenters. *Presentations, 18*(11), 50.

Whitworth, R. H., & Cochran, C. (1996). Evaluation of integrated versus unitary treatments for reducing public speaking anxiety. *Communication Education, 45,* 306–314.

Wolpe, J. (1958). *Psychotherapy by reciprocal inhibition.* Palo Alto, CA: Stanford University Press.

# Chapter 3

## Nonverbal Communication: Using Your Voice and Body

## CHAPTER GOALS

In this chapter, you will learn
- to make presentations that are nonverbally stimulating
- to eliminate distracting gestures and movements
- to use your voice as an instrument to further enhance your message
- to recognize and eliminate common articulation problems that detract from a speaker's credibility

# ■ INTRODUCTION

We have all witnessed speakers, professional or otherwise, who continually use repetitious movements like adjusting glasses or clothing. Typically, these distracting gestures become the focus of our attention. For example, one student speaker, Katie, began by scratching herself. At first she rubbed her nails up and down her arms and the audience could observe the long white lines that were imprinted with each sweep. Shortly after, Katie began to scratch her thigh, which made a rustling, distracting noise as her hand rubbed against her windbreaker pants. Just when it seemed like she would proceed in a more professional manner, she started to scratch and massage her shoulder and then her cheek, and finally her hand climbed up to her ear. All the while, Katie presented her speech in a slow, quiet voice. She later recounted that while she was aware of rubbing her arm, she had absolutely no recollection of the other intrusive nonverbal behaviours.

Have you ever considered how your nonverbal communication influences the meanings listeners get from your messages? Or how your nonverbal communication will influence the overall impression you will make as a speaker? Some communication scholars hold that up to 93 percent of emotional content is conveyed through nonverbal messages. I tend to agree with the more conservative estimates of scholars such as Birdwhistell (1970) and Burgoon (1994), who suggest that about 65 percent of the message in face-to-face communication comes from nonverbal behaviours. Even at 65 percent, this suggests that more than half of the meaning you convey comes not from the message content, but rather from your voice and body, both of which provide clues to listeners about how to interpret your message. Clearly, attention to nonverbal communication is important.

The overall goal of this chapter is to enhance your awareness of the strong influence that nonverbal communication plays in creating a successful speaking outcome. Your nonverbal communication should help you create a "meeting of meaning" between you and the audience. You will learn ways to make your voice and body contribute in a positive way to your delivery. While more on delivery is presented later in the text, it is important to identify visual and vocal strengths and weaknesses early on. This way, you can immediately begin the improvement process so that by the time you are making presentations, you will have turned negative mannerisms into positive ones.

This chapter is divided into two major sections: visual nonverbal communication and vocal nonverbal communication. After reading it through, you will be able to assess your nonverbal communication. A great way to do this is to videotape yourself doing a short, informal presentation. You might just introduce yourself and tell a little about your program. As you view the playback, select one or two areas that need improvement and begin working on them. But, make sure to watch the playback at least five times. Otherwise, you might be overly critical and focus only on your faults. When you get used to seeing yourself, however, you will be more objective and better able to recognize both your strengths and weaknesses.

# ■ NONVERBAL COMMUNICATION

## The Basics

Because of the major role that nonverbal communication plays in the public speaking process, it is helpful to have a basic understanding of this persuasive force. Nonverbally, speakers communicate through their general body build and looks, the clothing they wear, their facial expressions, their gestures, how they use space, and how they deal with their notes. And, based on these nonverbal variables, listeners make judgments about speakers (often before a word is even uttered). For instance, speakers who use more animated gestures and nonverbal communication are thought to possess more credibility.

During interviews for management positions, I like to invite along a female colleague whose job is not to participate in the interview process, but rather to observe the candidates. This process allows us to gain insight that we might likely miss if someone was not watching so closely.

*Janet, Senior Ottawa Human Resources Manager*

## Reliability of Nonverbal Communication

In many situations, nonverbal communication can be more reliable than verbal communication. For example, how many times have you had the feeling that a person was lying? Perhaps it wasn't anything that the person actually said or did, but you just did not believe in the speaker's sincerity. You may have been responding to the speaker's *micromomentary nonverbal behaviours*, those brief movements that are barely visible, and mostly, of which you are not even consciously aware. As Liska and Cronkhite (1995, p. 290) note, they are "fleeting expressions that cross the face so swiftly that they can only be identified when videotaped and then played back in slow motion." However, these cues are still processed by listeners, so they affect listeners' judgments. In circumstances when you feel a person is lying, your perceptions could very well be accurate if the individual demonstrates a series of cues. See the accompanying box for a list of *deceptive* cues typically associated with lying.

The reliability of nonverbal communication depends on who is decoding, or reading, it. Research indicates that females, in general, are better decoders than males (Hall, 1978; Henley, 1977; Stewart et al., 1996), and females at all stages of development are better than males when it comes to interpreting emotional expressions (Trotter, 1983). However, males who work as counsellors, actors, or therapists tend to be as good as or better than women in their interpretations of nonverbal messages (Rosenthal et al., 1974). Interestingly, success in these professions requires a strong sensitivity to nonverbal messages. When it comes to decoding deceptive cues, or knowing if a person is lying, younger people are better than older individuals (Lieberman, Rigo, & Compain, 1998) and women are better than men (McCormack & Parks, 1990).

## Ambiguity of Nonverbal Communication

Readers should recognize that nonverbal communication can be ambiguous. A single gesture or movement can be interpreted differently depending on the culture, the context, or whether or not the observer can hear the accompanying dialogue. For example, when people fold their arms across their chests, it is generally accepted that they are not open to communication. While this may be accurate, such individuals might be concealing a stain on their clothing or preventing a jacket front from opening to reveal a little extra girth. They might simply be cold. It is always important to read nonverbal communication within the context it is offered and to look for several indicators of a meaning. Interpretation based on just one gesture or movement can lead to confusion and even conflict.

### *Emblems*

There is also a series of gestures that has a direct, translatable meaning within a specific culture. Known as emblems (Ekman & Friesen, 1969), speakers can get into trouble when audiences interpret an unintended meaning. For example, the common "OK" sign used throughout North America to signify that things are good has an entirely different meaning in other parts of the world. If you use it in France or Belgium, you'll be communicating that a concept or audience is worthless. In Greece or Turkey, the same gesture will be interpreted as an insulting sexual invitation (Ekman, Friesen, & Baer,1984). A former student from Japan explained to our class that the gesture used by Canadian adults (with their thumb between their index and middle fingers) to say playfully to children, "I've got your nose," has distinct, sexual undertones in his country. You can see how doing business in a global economy or living in multicultural centres makes it important to be aware of cultural nonverbal differences. This accounts for why many businesses provide intercultural communication training for their employees. Further, we need to be tolerant of culturally determined nonverbal communication.

---

## TYPICALLY EXPRESSED DECEPTIVE CUES

Below is a list of nonverbal cues typically associated with deception. Such nonverbal communication is usually unintentional on the prevaricator's part and is referred to as *leakage*. These cues are not communication in and of themselves; when you see people shuffle their feet, do not automatically jump to the conclusion that they are lying (they could have a foot cramp). Cues must be read in context. If, for example, you sense that someone is not on the up-and-up, and he or she also demonstrates several of the deceptive cues below, then there is a strong likelihood that the speaker is attempting to deceive you.

### FACE
Look for pupil dilation, eyebrow flashes, averted gaze, perspiration, lip biting, excessive frowning or inappropriate laughing, excessive and inappropriate smiling.

### BODY
Look for hair grooming, foot shuffling, posture shifts, leg crossing, playing with rings or pencils.

### VOICE
Look for breathiness, restricted pitch increased or decreased pitch breaks and variety, speaking frequency, quavering (muscle tension).

**Source:** Liska & Cronkhite (1995, p. 289).

---

# Implicit Personality Theory

Humans seem compelled to fill in missing information about others, often by assuming that one set of traits, such as size, relates to others. For example, Jim, a Winnipeg communication consultant, told me he was inspired to lose 23 kilograms (50 pounds) after he invited a group of insurance workers to share their perceptions of him when they first saw him enter the training room, before the session had begun. One participant confessed that he did not expect Jim to be very smart or energetic, although he was pleasantly surprised by Jim's knowledge base and his seemingly boundless energy. Jim attributed such an attitude to his size—he weighed in at some 136 kilograms (300 pounds). In our society, inaccurate, negative connotations associated with being overweight include fat and lazy, fat and ugly, fat and slow, and so on.

This notion of associating one set of characteristics with others is referred to as *implicit personality theory* (Rosenberg & Sedlak, 1972), and the example shows how listener interpretations can be incorrect. Public speakers should possess a knowledge of how they might be perceived by others so they can offset potentially inaccurate or confusing perceptions—although such a step need not require changing their body size or shape. Listeners, in turn, need to be more aware of some of the not-so-accurate assumptions made about individuals.

As part of my volunteer work for the 2000 federal election, I attended a short session on Election Day protocol. We were a relatively small group of about 20 to 25 individuals housed in a small hall. Because I was seated behind a man substantially taller and wider than me, I was unable to see the session leader at the front of the room. I continually shifted from one side of my seat to the other, trying to get a glimpse of our trusty leader. Then the following occurred to me: it is not only a given that competent speakers make eye contact with the audience, it is their responsibility to do so. Had the facilitator been an experienced, adept presenter, she would have positioned herself or moved into spaces so that she could address and connect with each audience member. I know I would have been better able to concentrate on what she was saying.

*Bernie, Election Worker*

## Paralanguage

Not only is meaning conveyed through the more obvious nonverbal behaviours, but it is also sent through the speaker's vocal cues, or *paralanguage*. Such "language" includes the speaker's tone, accent, pitch, rate, articulation, emphasis, use of pauses, and so on. Each contributes to the meaning that is placed on the general, face-to-face message. Think of the many different interpretations that could emerge from the simple sentence: "Please turn off the photocopier before you leave" merely by altering the tone of voice or changing where the emphasis is placed. Say the sentence five or six times out loud, changing its intent by accentuating a different word each time.

# VISUAL COMMUNICATION

 **EXPERT ADVICE**

Obviously, there are different levels and comfort zones when it comes to public speaking. For me, the key is "eye contact" and speaking in a "one to one" frame of mind. Once you become comfortable speaking in public, I believe the more you can do off the cuff, or at least with just "thoughts" on paper versus an actual text speech, the more attentive your audience will be. By not breaking eye contact as much, you keep them engaged. You can see reactions and you're able to react accordingly. "One to one" simply means that you should speak to an entire audience the same way you would speak to just one person in a room. This way, you don't fall into a habit of talking too loudly or over-emphasizing a point.

*Jeff Hutcheson*
*Canada AM*

## Eye Contact

Speakers have an obligation to connect with the audience, and one of the strongest ways to do so is through the eyes. Those speakers who look audience members in the eye find such communication rewarding and reinforcing. They tend to perceive their presentations as interpersonal communication with every single person in the audience. Such contact gives speakers a sense of connection, control, and power as they read the positive feedback they receive. Audience members like it too.

### An Eye Contact Strategy

Many apprehensive speakers find it difficult to make eye contact. Even people who speak to groups for a living can fall into this category. If you are such a person, designate three friendly individuals to whom you will speak during a presentation—one on each side of the room, and one in the centre. As you present your speech, look from one to the other. This should help you to feel more comfortable looking at your audience. This strategy might also benefit individuals from co-cultures where avoiding eye contact demonstrates respect. For instance, Adler, Towne, and Rolls (2004) write that Mi'kmaq students avoid eye contact with elders in deference to them. "However, when this same behaviour is directed toward non-Aboriginal authority figures such as university professors, deans, judges, and so forth, it may be perceived as insolence rather than the courtesy and deference they mean to convey" (p. 29). Choosing three specific listeners to look at during a speech may help such speakers.

It worked for Phoenix Wan, a business student from China, when she tested the strategy. Phoenix's presentations were always well prepared, well documented, and interesting. Further, she was enthusiastic and students liked her. However, because she was afraid to make eye contact, Phoenix had no idea how popular she was. She tried the strategy and was so delighted with the results that she expanded it to encompass all students. That too worked and Phoenix was both moved and amazed by the positive feedback she received from her classmates.

---

 **EXPERT ADVICE**

When you look above the heads, you are speaking to an audience. When you look at eyes, you are speaking to people. Nothing can substitute for genuine eye contact, and imitators will never be as convincing, or impressive, as those who do the real thing.

*Professor Tanya Brann-Barrett, Department of Communication*
*Cape Breton University, Sydney, Nova Scotia*

---

## Facial Expressions

Making an emotional connection with your audience is important and using facial expressions, rather than offering a "monotone" face, is a good way to do that. As Fripp (2004) notes, "How you deliver your material has a lot to do with the enjoyment of your audience. If they have a good time, they are more likely to like you and your ideas" (p. 18). Keep in mind that 65 percent of meaning is transmitted through nonverbal communication, and that facial expressions are particularly useful for relating emotional content.

Nonverbal displays of emotion are called *affect displays* (Ekman & Friesen, 1969). Although they occur mainly in the face, they are also conveyed in other ways. If you won $5 million, you would likely let out a whoop, jump around, hug someone near you, and have a large smile on your face. Tears of amazement might also well up in your eyes. Such demonstrations of emotion are all examples of affect displays.

In public speaking contexts, it is critical that facial expressions reflect the verbal message. For instance, when television announcers report tragic news stories, their faces reflect the gravity of the situation. Smiling during such newscasts would be inappropriate. Sometimes emotions leak out, as is the case when students, disappointed with their presentations, leave the podium with a grimace on their face. Such behaviour is unprofessional, and in most instances, speeches are much better than the presenters think.

My life was changed so dramatically by the birth of my son that when we were required in our public speaking class to relate a person, place, thing, or event that had an impact on our lives, I thought this would be the perfect topic. However, the speech did not turn out like I had hoped. I became so overwhelmed with emotion that I began to cry. See, I used to be heavy into drugs and alcohol, but once I got pregnant, I knew I had to give them up, and I have been clean ever since. But explaining this was way harder than I thought. My life is so wonderful now, and that little boy is so gorgeous; it was he who got me my life back, and I am so thankful. But, what I want to say to you is to make sure that you pick topics that don't make you too emotional. It's not cool to lose control when you're speaking in front of people.

*Colleen, Reentry Business Student*

## Gender and Facial Expressions

There are gender differences associated with facial expressions. For instance, women are more expressive and better at conveying emotions. They also smile more than men (Pearson, Turner, & Todd-Mancillas, 1991). Both men and women are more attracted to others who smile (Lau, 1982). Based on this research, men are urged to be more expressive and smile more often. Women, on the other hand, have a tendency to smile even when they are not happy. They should be cautioned against inappropriate grinning as it can reduce their credibility.

> ## FIVE TIPS FOR PODIUM USE
>
> 1. Place and organize your notes on the podium before you begin. Do not hold them.
> 2. If there is a computer screen on the podium, adjust everything so that any paper notes can be viewed with ease.
> 3. Avoid gripping the podium, especially when the *whites of your knuckles* are visible.
> 4. Use gestures and avoid leaning on, hanging over, rocking, or moving the podium from side-to-side.
> 5. If you are using the podium just to hold a brief outline but you plan to speak beside it, turn the podium on a slant so you can glance comfortably at your notes.
> 6. If you are presenting most of your speech from behind the podium, you might be able to move away every once in a while, depending on the nature of the presentation.
> 7. Stand up straight and do not hide behind the podium. If it is too large for you, request a platform on which to stand.

# Gestures

A frequently asked question in public speaking classes is "What do I do with my hands?" The answer is simple: Use them, but do so in a natural way. Communication scholars agree that nonverbal communication in general can repeat, contradict, substitute for, complement, accent, or regulate verbal messages, and much of this is done with gestures. Thus, speakers who hold their hands behind their backs miss valuable opportunities to augment their verbal messages.

While gestures can be divided into several subcategories (Ekman & Friesen, 1969), the most relevant to public speakers are illustrators and adaptors.

## *Illustrators*

*Illustrators* are positive nonverbal behaviours that enable speakers to add to or enhance their message. If, for example, you were referring to a huge snowball, you might use your hands to carve out a circle in the air. That circle would be interpreted by listeners as the size of the snowball. You would not necessarily have to verbalize its dimensions—they would be communicated via your hands. Knapp (1986, p. 72) points out that illustrators "may be movements that accent or emphasize a word or phrase, sketch a path of thought, point to present objects, depict a spatial relationship, depict the rhythm or pacing of an event, draw a picture of the referent, or depict a bodily action."

Exciting speakers incorporate many illustrators into their presentations. However, to be effective, these must occur naturally during the spoken message. I once judged a high school public speaking match, and it was clear how one contestant had practised both verbally and nonverbally for the presentation. Just after uttering the phrase "And I say unto you," he pointed at the audience. This tardy gesture resulted in an unintended humorous effect.

---

 **EXPERT ADVICE**

I used to be an awfully fidgety speaker. I'd remove imaginary lint from my clothes, tap my feet, wring my hands, and God knows what else. Then I had a speech teacher who gave me a great hint. He said that when I got nervous I should scrunch my toes together inside my shoes. I have to say that it's not as good as playing with my notes or something, but it does relieve some of the stress. And, they tell me that toe grinding inside footwear is far less conspicuous to the audience. You should give it a try.

*Paul, Information Technology Student*

---

## *Adaptors*

While illustrators add spice and colour to presentations, adaptors are distracting. *Adaptors* are those nonverbal behaviours that help people cope with stress. The anxiety is not so severe or threatening as to require counselling or drug therapy, but rather it relates more to the moment.

For example, have you ever noticed how some older speakers make their presentations with their hands in their pockets, rattling their change, and rocking up and down on the balls of their feet? Or recall Katie, from the beginning of the chapter, who scratched her way through her presentation. I am sure you have all seen nervous speakers who crumple their notes, adjust their eyeglasses, or play with their jewellery. These nonverbal behaviours are adaptors.

To curb the use of adaptors, try to avoid the object that you tend to manipulate. For example, if you have a tendency to play with a pen during your presentation, do not hold one when you speak. If you fiddle with your earrings or adjust your ring, do not wear them. Those individuals who play with their clothing could be in for real trouble!

Adaptors not only detract from the speaker's overall impression, but audience members also begin to concentrate more on those gestures and movements than on the message. Sometimes they even count them! Adaptors should also be avoided because they convey uneasiness to the audience. Instead, you want to appear capable and skilled.

---

### WHAT TYPE OF ADAPTORS DO YOU USE?

Ekman and Friesen (1969) identified three types of adaptors. Which ones are you most prone to using?

#### SELF-ADAPTORS
Actions where you touch yourself. Examples include kneading your hands, rubbing parts of your body, scratching, pinching, or curling your hair around your finger.

#### OBJECT-ADAPTORS
Articles that are manipulated. Notes pens, pointers, jewellery, glasses, or visual aids are all common targets. So too are podiums when speakers hang over them, grip them, or use them in other creative ways.

#### ALTER-ADAPTORS
Body shifts. Swinging your leg, shifting position, tapping your foot, or pacing all exemplify alter-adaptors.

---

## Posture

Confidence, self-esteem, enthusiasm, nervousness, and a host of other personal factors and emotions can be discerned through your posture. To communicate professionalism and expertise, maintain an open posture as opposed to crossing your arms in front of your body. This pose suggests defensiveness even though you may not feel that way. Keep your head held high and facing the audience. Sometimes speakers tilt and hold their head to one side, but this nonverbal pose denotes a subordinate stance, and may even be interpreted as a preening or courtship gesture, those nonverbal behaviours that signal a romantic interest in someone!

Postures to avoid include leaning against the wall (or on other objects such as a table or desk), putting your hands in your pockets, sitting on a desk, putting your foot up on a desk or chair, or hanging over the podium. While these postures may be considered cool in informal settings, they are generally thought to be unsuitable in formal public speaking situations.

In general, however, it seems that when speaking in public, it makes the most sense to do what your mother probably told you years ago: "Stand up straight, don't pick at yourself, and pretend you're having a good time."

---

### THE CHALLENGE OF TECHNOLOGY

While technology offers a host of public speaking aids such as overheads or PowerPoint presentations, it also presents some challenges. For instance, when speakers present behind a podium with a computer screen in front of them, it detracts from their body language and limits their movement. In situations where speakers are in a spotlight while the audience is in darkness, eye contact is limited or impossible. It is no wonder, then, that many speakers prefer to stay in place and read from the computer. But they do so at the cost of not connecting with their audience.

There are several things that can be done to offset these problems. First, speakers can know their material well enough so they need only limited use of slides that contain only key words. Then the audience is forced to look and listen rather than read along with the presentation. Wireless microphones can be requested in advance, thus increasing speaker mobility. Petite persons can ask organizers for a small platform to stand on so that their gestures won't be hidden by the podium. If the lights cannot be turned up for the presentation, speakers can still look at all audience members. While speakers won't be able to see the audience, listeners will see them looking their way. Each of these adjustments will help to create a more dynamic presentation.

---

## Movement

Read "Dave's Use of Space" on page 74. Dave made two of the most common movement errors: they were too patterned and too predictable. Instead of keeping the audience interested and creating nonverbal diversity during the presentation, his activity became distracting. There should be neither too much nor too little movement. Dave's was too much.

So too would be the type of manoeuvre that Jason, a trainer with the federal government, related to me. He shared that he sometimes moves away from the front of the room and walks among his trainees. He thought this was a good way to relate to them. However, upon assessment, he was surprised to learn that they felt uncomfortable, as if their territory, or personal bubble, had been invaded.

This makes sense in light of anthropologist Edward T. Hall's (1969) notion of the four types of distances that we use in our daily lives: intimate, personal, social, and public. Public distance ranges from about 3.6 m to 7.5 m. When Jason moved close to his students, he essentially entered their personal space (from 45 cm at its closest to 1.2 m). Such a distance, considered within range at a party among old, close friends, for example, would be far too intimate in educational settings. Jason may even have inadvertently communicated at a personal distance (less than 45 cm away), reserved for lovers and for parents with their children.

## DAVE'S USE OF SPACE

Part of my job as a communication lab coordinator was to videotape classroom speeches. I recall one student in particular, Dave, a grade 5 teacher taking courses to increase his licence level. The reason I remember him so well was because he paced back and forth across the room when he spoke. When he got to one side of the room, he turned toward the class, spoke for about 45 seconds, and then proceeded to stroll to the other side of the room. He must have been musical because he moved with absolute, regular frequency.

Video cameras were heavy and awkward in those days, and it took a great deal of exertion to stay focused as Dave continually changed position. I followed him for a time, then resolved to point the camera at the middle of the front of the classroom, a place where this particular teacher never stayed for very long.

Students in that class were required to watch their presentations afterward in a communication lab. That's when I realized that my alternative taping strategy turned out to be a good learning experience for Dave. To see what he viewed, imagine the TV screen showing the front of the classroom. Dave saw himself pace across the room and then out of view, and then he heard himself speak from that position. He then saw himself pace across the screen, with perfect timing and rhythm, this time in the opposite direction, then out of sight to the other side of the room. He would have witnessed this several times. Had the instructor told Dave that he was pacing back and forth too much, he may not have interpreted his pacing as ineffective and distracting. However, on viewing the videotaped performance, it was clear just how disruptive and nonproductive Dave's "use of space" was.

To demonstrate these distances in one of my classes, I approached a student very closely and asked if I was too near. As she replied, "No," in a strained, uncomfortable voice, she simultaneously moved her head as far back as she could get it in order to move into a more comfortable zone. Keep in mind that people differ somewhat in their perceptions of distance levels. However, while public speakers may occasionally move into the audience's space, most people are more comfortable when the speaker remains at the public range.

Many students wonder if they should move away from the podium and the answer is yes. Audience members are often impressed when lecturers move toward them. It relays a message of confidence and interest, and serves to keep their attention. Even if technological aids prevent straying too far, use strong, large, and timely gestures. Good speakers employ an assortment of spontaneous and instinctive movements, while poorer speakers appear bolted or frozen in one position.

---

### EDWARD T. HALL'S DISTANCE ZONES

1.  Public distance (3.6–7.5 m): This is the typical space used in public speaking situations.
2.  Social distance (1.2–3.6 m): You would see this distance in business settings.
3.  Personal distance (45 cm–1.2 m): This would be the distance most couples would stand in relation to each other in public.
4.  Intimate distance (less than 45 cm): Although sometimes inevitable in crowded elevators or subway cars, this zone is reserved for people with whom you are very close—lovers, children, family members, or pets.

**Source:** Hall (1969).

---

# Beginnings and Endings

## Clean Beginnings

How many times have you been at a conference, workshop, or meeting where someone, seemingly out of the blue, begins to make an announcement or convene a session? Such speakers just plow ahead without first ensuring that they have everyone's attention. This leaves listeners missing important information and speakers looking nonprofessional. They have not started with a clean beginning.

A clean opening is one in which speakers summon the audience's attention and wait until everyone is focused on them before they begin. In my public speaking course, clean beginnings are practised during the second class. Students come prepared to give a short, informal presentation. They are directed to stand on an X (which is marked on the floor), pause, take a breath, and then begin to speak. This type of clean opening allows the audience to prepare for and anticipate the presentation and enables the speaker to relax a little.

## Clean Endings

A clean ending, surprisingly, is similar to the clean beginning. When speakers demonstrate clean endings, they finish what they are saying, thank the audience (if appropriate), and only then do they leave the podium or place from which they are speaking. A dirty ending is one where speakers leave before they are finished. In the worst cases, their final words trail off as they move toward their seats (a filthy ending). A more subtle demonstration of this leave-taking behaviour is when speakers rearrange their notes during the final wrap-up, or move away from the podium on the last syllable of the final word. Even more subtle are mild shoulder movements leaning towards where the speaker is headed next, even before the presentation ends.

Most people have some sense of good public speaking behaviours, and many are not even nervous. But, awareness of the subtle nuances of these movements differentiates between amateur and expert speakers.

---

### NONVERBAL GUIDELINES FOR USING YOUR BODY

- Dress in comfortable, suitable clothing.
- Have a clean beginning.
- Attend to your posture.
- Make eye contact.
- Use facial expressions and smile when it's appropriate.
- Use natural gestures but avoid adaptors.
- Move away from the podium on occasion.
- Make use of space but do not pace or rock back and forth.
- Be skilled at using microphone and visual aids.
- Have a clean ending.

# Dress

Because clothing is often the basis on which first impressions are made, and because it heavily influences the judgments made about speakers, it is critical to dress in a way that meets audience expectations. I recall the contrasting attire of two student debaters: one wore a suit and tie, the other sweats and sneakers. Even though the sweatsuit-clad speaker was the superior debater, the formally suited speaker actually garnered more general credibility. Although defining others by their clothing is superficial and shallow, it still occurs, and speakers need to be aware of this.

Hillman (1999) offers several good suggestions to keep in mind when you select the clothing you will wear for a public presentation. He urges speakers to dress according to the situation, to dress comfortably (nothing too tight or distracting), to think of your attire as part of your visual aids, to dress in good taste, to dress with the temperature in mind, and to choose something that you feel good in (pp. 162–163).

---

## BUSINESS AND PROFESSIONAL SPEAKING DRESS CODE CHECKLIST

### WOMEN
- dark two-piece suit, or contrasting skirt and jacket
- dark, professional-looking dress
- neutral, solid-coloured blouse
- unobtrusive jewellery (plain gold or silver are good)
- dark-coloured pumps (not sling-backs)
- neutral or taupe stockings

### MEN
- dark two-piece suit, with the jacket buttoned while speaking
- contrasting trousers and sports jackets
- dark, plain, or small-print tie
- long-sleeved shirt
- dark shoes

In the classroom setting, you might choose more casual clothing. For instance, if you wear a formal, two-piece suit, it may distance you from your audience.

**Source:** Brody (1998, pp. 117–118).

From an idea by Tanya Brann-Barrett.

We had a great speaker at our diversity awareness conference. She hooked us right away by asking pertinent questions and she waited to hear the responses. Then she used our answers throughout the presentation to support her material. But what I really liked was how she connected with us. She was animated and used lots of gestures and facial expressions. You could see her enthusiasm as she moved about in order to see everyone. She had a very personable approach and she was a fine contrast to a couple of the speakers who seemed to drone on in a lifeless fashion.

*Kyle, Student Diversity Centre*

When I suggest that students dress the part for their presentations, sometimes their notion of "dress up" is different from mine. I am thinking of professional wear; some female students confuse this with party or bar apparel (short skirts, tight tops, imaginative hair, innovative jewellery, and high heels). When making professional presentations, keep in mind that speakers of both sexes are thought to be more persuasive when they wear a jacket with pants (or skirts) and that navy blue tends to enhance a speaker's credibility. Further, if you select clothing that looks good and feels good, you will be better able to focus on the audience.

# ▨ VOCAL COMMUNICATION

Thus far in the chapter, the focus has been on how facial expressions, posture, clothing, and gestures (to name a few) can help to create an image of a credible speaker. Besides apparent and obvious nonverbal communication, meanings are also conveyed through vocal communication—what you do with your voice. This includes your rate, volume, tone, pitch, and so forth.

## Rate

How quickly or slowly a person speaks is referred to as vocal rate. Vocal rate is altered according to several factors: the audience's expertise or knowledge level, the topic's complexity, and the mood you wish to create. Rate is used also for emphasis, and in most instances, is based on the speaker's natural speaking tempo.

Typically, more serious or sombre subjects are presented slowly. However, there is some disagreement over ideal speaker rate. Some communication scholars adopt a deliberate, even rate with many pauses, arguing that this gives audience members time to comprehend and digest the material. Others think a more rapid pace helps keep the audience's attention.

Unless dictated by the nature of or the circumstances surrounding the speech, I prefer a quicker rate. As noted earlier in the text, speakers generally talk in the vicinity of 125–175 words per minute while listeners process information at 300–400 words per minute, and some up to 600 words. So, what happens in the heads of quick processors when they listen to a speaker presenting at an average or slow rate? They start thinking about other things—they cannot help themselves.

In an interesting study conducted by Paul Cameron at a large American university, students were asked to record, at sporadic intervals, what they were thinking about while sitting through a lecture. The results indicated that 20 percent were reminiscing about something, 20 percent were actually paying attention, 12 percent were actively listening, and 20 percent were having erotic thoughts! Another 20 percent were daydreaming, worrying, or thinking about lunch, and the remaining 8 percent had religion on their mind (as reported in Adler, Towne, & Rolls, 2004). Based on this study, if you want your audience to listen to and keep up with you, you had better present your material in a lively, brisk fashion. But, do not speak at such a clip that you will not be understood.

Inexperienced speakers need to be aware that, due to nervousness, their pace will likely increase when speaking in front of a group. This has timing implications. If you clocked your speech at five minutes in the comfort of your home, you may find that with the increased rate, and the possibility of omitting a few things, the speech may take only three-and-a-half to four minutes to deliver. I have never heard a student report that his or her classroom speech was longer than anticipated, but I have been told repeatedly that the presentation was much shorter than anticipated, even if it was rehearsed beforehand.

## Time Restrictions

Regardless of how engaging speakers are, they need to adhere to time restrictions. Even if the presentation is going exceptionally well and audience feedback is excellent, speakers must end on time. More is not better. This is especially salient in business and professional settings where "time is money" and people are juggling several commitments. They simple do not have the freedom to indulge gabby speakers.

Learning to work within a minute of the time frames set for your classroom speeches can help you prepare for real-life speeches in that you become adept at selecting a topic, organizing it, practising it, and delivering it when you must deal with time restrictions. The best way to meet your time requirements is through practice. Given that you will speak more quickly during your actual performance, allow your speech to run a little longer during the run-through session. It is always easier to eliminate information on the spot than it is to add it.

## SPOTLIGHT ON SPEAKERS

### STUTTER DIDN'T HALT KELLY'S ATTAINMENT OF POLITICAL GOAL

One of the most traumatic episodes of Halifax Mayor Peter Kelly's life happened when he was asked to read in front of his grade 3 class.

"I didn't do very well," he recalls, sitting in his spacious City Hall office.

Struggling with a speech impediment, the eight-year-old Mr. Kelly got to the second word before his stutter stopped him from continuing. The laughter of his classmates brought him to tears.

"That's the stuff that you don't forget," he says.

"I just accepted it as a part of the challenge and shied away from speaking a lot and getting up in class to speak."

That's common behaviour for people who suffer from stuttering, he says.

"Some consider it to be a disability—I suppose it depends on the extremity of the stutter." But he didn't let it hold him back.

Mr. Kelly says he worked hard at minimizing his stutter, seeing speech therapists for help throughout his school years.

The tenacity paid off—his speech improved and he took on roles that involved a lot of public speaking.

He became editor of his high school newspaper and was vice-president of his student union while attending Nova Scotia Community College.

Then he embarked on a career as a politician. He served as councillor and mayor in the former Town of Bedford before amalgamation in 1996. Then he represented the district on the new regional council until elected mayor in October 2000.

"For a stutterer, politics is a strange field to get involved in," he says.

Mr. Kelly says he still gets nervous whenever he has to speak publicly— but it's not something he can avoid.

"It's part of the job and part of what is expected of the mayor," he says.

"It comes with the territory—it just makes the job that much more challenging."

Despite still having a stutter, he doesn't avoid any of his responsibilities, he says.

He chairs council meetings, gives state of the municipality speeches, and even receives invitations to speak before audiences in other parts of the country.

He says his stutter often becomes more pronounced, especially when he's tired or nervous.

Words that begin with *s* or *e* are especially troublesome.

"When you get up to speak in front of a big crowd, you hope that you'll always be able to follow through to the end, because you don't want to start something and not be able to get through it."

He says he refuses to let that happen.

"I will always get through anything—whether I have to stop and rethink, regroup and move forward," he says.

"And I don't let it get to me as much as it did before. It's just that it's part of me, it's part of who I am and it just adds to my challenge to make sure I'm understood to make sure that I do the best for the municipality."

Mr. Kelly says his stuttering is also difficult for other people to deal with.

"It may be uncomfortable for some," he says. "People try to help you when you are a stutterer. When you're trying to say the word, they'll try to say the word for you."

"As a stutterer, that's not always the best thing you want to hear, although it's all done with good intention."

Councillor Jerry Blumental (Halifax North End) says Mr. Kelly hasn't let the disability stand in his way.

"It doesn't make him a bad mayor because he has a stutter," he says. "He's smart—he overcomes the problem."

"When he relaxes, he makes a good speech."

Mr. Kelly says one source of inspiration for him has been Winston Churchill, who also stuttered but persevered to become an accomplished politician.

But the mayor also gets calls sometimes from parents looking for help with children who stutter, he says.

"I'd be more than pleased to meet with them and explain to them what I've gone through and what I've done over the years to try to get to where I am today."

His advice?

"Do what you want to do and do it the best you can and don't let it ever hold you back."

The Chronicle-Herald/The Mail-Star, *January 7, 2002, p. A4*

# Volume

Regardless of how interesting, well documented, relevant, or entertaining a speech is, it will mean little if it cannot be heard. A low *volume* gives the impression of apprehension and lack of confidence. On the other hand, speakers with great resonant voices are thought automatically to be more assertive and intelligent, and people pay more attention to them. A good volume is one that every person in the room can hear without having to strain.

Public speaking voices should be substantially louder than standard, conversational voices. However, you need not be so thunderous that your volume becomes distracting. Any part of a delivery that calls attention to itself is not good. Further, the appropriate volume depends on the competing noises, the dimensions of the room, and whether you are using a microphone. In classroom speeches, the first speaker can sometimes set the volume level for the others. This can be particularly annoying if the person could hardly be heard. Speakers whose voices drop at the end of their sentences can also irritate audiences.

## *How to Increase Your Volume*

If you speak in a small, low voice, try speaking louder. Volume can be increased by standing up straight, breathing from your diaphragm, and projecting your voice around the room.

To practise, choose one or two paragraphs from this text to read aloud. Then find a room where you will not be interrupted, and set up a tape recorder with the volume set at a level about halfway between the lowest and highest settings. Your mission is to read the selected passage several times, each time increasing your volume. Afterward, replay the tape without changing the volume setting. You are improving if you notice a definite increase in volume with each reading. Repeat this exercise every couple of days until you speak at an appropriate volume—the one that can be heard most clearly from the back of the room (get a friend to listen to you).

 **PUBLIC SPEAKING IN THE 21ST CENTURY**

Using your voice as the instrument it is intended to be requires proper breathing, relaxation, and tongue dexterity. The Private Voice Exercises offered at the following Web site provides relaxation, skeletal, diaphragm, breathing, articulator, and resonator exercises. Go to *http://www.usao.edu/ mvliet/private_voice/voice_exercises.htm.*

## *Projection*

Related to volume, or loudness, is projection. Projection can be described as a "controlled energy that gives impact, precision, and intelligibility to spoken sounds" (Mayer, 1988, p. 261). To project your voice, open your mouth wider than you normally would. When you do this, your articulation will become more "energetic and nimble" (Mayer, 1988, p. 33). You can improve your projection by chanting the following vowel sounds. As you do so, "aim your tones forward against the upper front teeth" and "give the *oh* and *aw* sounds the same frontal placement and luster of *ee* (Mayer, 1988, p. 33).

    1. ee-ee-ee-ee  2. oh-oh-oh-oh  3. aw-aw-aw-aw  4. lee-loh-law  5. bee-boh-baw
    6. bee-boh-baw  7. dee-doh-daw  8. wee-woh-waw  9. mee-moh-maw  10. tee-toh-taw

## Tone

*Tone* is the vocal characteristic that conveys meaning or emotion. Children are often accused by parents of being disrespectful or impolite based not on what they have said, but how they say it. That is tone. This same phenomenon can occur in public speaking contexts. Because tone helps to set the mood of the message, watch that your voice does not, either intentionally or unintentionally, have a sarcastic or patronizing tone. It could distort your meaning and confuse the audience.

---

### ✍ EXPERT ADVICE

Stop and really listen to a conversation between two people. What you'll notice is that broken grammar and sentence fragments abound. Thoughts stop in mid-flight, veer off in new directions, or get reiterated in a different way. Several sentences combine into a long string or get chopped into pieces. Educated or not, this is how we talk.

If you use this same conversational style in your presentations, your audience members will tune in. Remember, our brains are hardwired to process intuitively this type of information. Without even consciously realizing it, your audience members will analyze your speech and conclude that you are having a conversation with someone. A few seconds later, human nature being what it is, they will also arrive at the conclusion that the person you are having a conversation with is them.

Conversation, by definition, is a two-way street. When you speak in a conversational style, your audience realizes you're providing one half of it. Even though they may never actually speak, in their heads they will intuitively participate in your presentation to complete the dialogue.

*John Miers, Chair*
*Black Isle Consultants*

---

## Pitch

*Pitch* refers to how high or low a tone or sound is. Pitch is determined by sex, age, and emotional state. For example, men typically develop and speak in a low pitch, while women generally have a more moderate one. Younger girls and teens have a tendency to speak in higher-pitched voices. When women are nervous, excited, or angry they sometimes raise their pitch. This happens to some female students when they are making presentations.

Everyone has an optimum, or natural pitch level and this is where an individual's voice functions most efficiently and dramatically (Mayer, 1988). There is also a habitual pitch level, or the one used most often by a person. You can find your habitual pitch by sitting comfortably in a chair, inhaling two or three times, and then sighing several times. The sigh pitch that comes out approximates your habitual pitch level (Mayer, 1988).

To produce a pleasing voice, speak at your optimum and habitual pitch levels. A pitch that is too high for you can sound shrill and squeaky, while a low pitch can sound growly.

## Inflection

When pitch is changed with a single, uninterrupted sound, it is referred to as inflection. Mayer (1988) describes three types of inflection—upward, downward, and double. In an upward inflection, the voice glides from a lower to a higher pitch. In a downward inflection, the voice glides from a high to a low pitch. In a double inflection, both upward and downward pitches are used. For further clarification, Mayer (1988, p. 171) uses arrows to signify the inflections. These are offered in Figure 3.1 below.

A change in pitch can alter meaning in that it denotes whether a sentence will be interpreted as a statement or a question. Take the sentence "The cat is on the roof and we can't get her down." If it is intended as a statement, the pitch will not be altered. However, if it is meant as a question, the pitch is raised on the word that is questioned. Say the cat sentence as a statement, and then repeat it as a question by raising your pitch on the word *down*. Now repeat the sentence and raise your pitch on the word *cat*. The meaning of the sentence will likely change a little. For the most part, public speakers do not have difficulties with pitch. Still, some people have a habit of raising their pitch at the end of almost every sentence, making their conversations sound like lists of questions instead of statements. This in turn makes them sound unsure of themselves, as though they are seeking validation for everything they say.

### Figure 3.1—Types of Voice Inflection

Upward Inflection      Downward Inflection      Double Inflection

**Source:** Adapted from Mayer (1988, p. 171).

# Articulation

*Articulation,* enunciation, and diction all refer to the same thing: the manner in which individual speech sounds are produced. Mumblers do not have good articulation because they add, delete, substitute, or overlap sounds. This is why it is difficult to understand them. A person with good articulation, for example, would attend to the *ing* in *going* while a poor articulator might say *goin'*. People who enunciate all the individual units within a word are thought to have good articulation. They would say "*what | are | you | doing*?" rather than "*what'r'ya doin'*?" or "*black | and | blue*" instead of "*black 'n' blue*" (Mayer, 1988, p. 59).

Other common articulation errors include *filum* instead of *film*, *pitcher* instead of *picture*, *genelmen* instead of *gentlemen*, or *tree* instead of *three*. Some individuals say *dis*, *dat*, *dese*, and *dose* for *this*, *that*, *these*, and *those*. In the Newfoundland dialect, *h* is often eliminated from the beginning of words so that *head* becomes *'ead*, *hole* becomes *'ole*, and *hint* becomes *'int*. See the quiz below for articulation errors that are embedded within sentences.

---

### MINI ARTICULATION QUIZ

Read the following sentences written in poor articulation and see if you can determine what is being said. Repeat the sentences using good articulation. Check page 95 for the answers.

1.  You gwin first.
2.  Jeet yet?
3.  No, jew?
4.  Swennyway.
5.  Whatimezit?
6.  Wassup?
7.  Gonexra beer?
8.  Tekedezy.

---

66 99

I didn't think articulation was important until I moved to an urban centre where everyone seemed to speak so precisely. It took me a while, but I eventually improved and now I'm more confident when I give reports. But I also notice when others speak poorly. Poor articulation is only a habit. If I can improve, so can you.

*Ryan, Accountant*

---

## How to Detect and Correct Articulation Errors

If you have poor, sloppy *articulation*, you will not suddenly speak clearly during a public presentation. Instead, you must address the articulation problems beforehand.

The first step is to identify your particular problems. You can do this by audio- or videotaping yourself as you read a passage, do a short presentation, or chat about what is going on in your life. Afterwards, listen carefully and critically to isolate any errors. According to DeVito (1997), there are three types of articulation problems: *errors of omission*, *errors of addition*, and *errors of substitution*. Examples are listed in the accompanying box; use them as a guide to assess yourself. You might also ask a friend to help you.

---

## THREE COMMON TYPES OF ARTICULATION ERRORS

### ERRORS OF OMISSION
Occur when parts of a word are eliminated
- *goin'* instead of *going*
- *dint* instead of *didn't*
- *an'* instead of *and*
- *wit'* instead of *with*
- *wanna* instead of *want to*
- *libary* instead of *library*
- *'ammer* instead of *hammer*

### ERRORS OF ADDITION
Occur when sounds are added to words
- *haudit* instead of *audit*
- *hice* instead of *ice*
- *acrost* instead of *across*
- *filum* instead of *film*

### ERRORS OF SUBSTITUTION
Occur when one sound is exchanged for another
- *swedder* instead of *sweater*
- *ya* instead of *you*
- *ah* instead of *of*
- *te* or *ta* instead of *to*
- *thum* instead of *them*
- *genelmen* instead of *gentlemen*
- *ax* instead of *ask*
- *dis* instead of *this*

---

Because it takes time to identify and remedy articulation problems, start by selecting one or two errors that you continually make, and begin correcting them immediately. For instance, if you catch yourself dropping the final *g* (saying *goin'* or *waitin'* instead of *going* and *waiting*), correct yourself by repeating the word and articulating the sound. And note too that your aim is not to sound artificial. As Mayer (1988) puts it: "Natural articulation avoids either of two extremes: sloppiness and artificiality. It's neither *undercooked* nor *overcooked*. It's simply speech that is as clear and sharp-edged as it's apparently easy and unforced. It doesn't distract the listener" (Mayer, 1988, p. 58).

Why attend to your articulation? Because individuals who speak well are thought to be better educated, more intelligent, and more credible. Good articulation projects a more professional image.

"Keep out! Keep out! K-E-E-P O-U-T."

# Pronunciation

So, what's the difference between articulation and pronunciation? Pronunciation refers to the "correct production of words" and correct is based on the speaker, the area, and the audience. For example, Americans typically pronounce "Z" as "zee" while Canadians say "zed." What is accepted pronunciation in one place may be quite different in another. When telemarketers call my husband and ask for Mr. "McClean," I know immediately that they are not from eastern Canada. Otherwise, they would know that the accepted pronunciation is MaClaine (with emphasis on Claine). The name is actually spelled MacLean.

When using new technical terminology, language peculiar to a certain discipline (argot), or names, it is important to have the accepted pronunciation.

---

 **PUBLIC SPEAKING IN THE 21ST CENTURY**

You can listen to a host of speeches at the following Web sites. Go to them, select a couple of speakers, and analyze their vocal styles. Assess their volume, tone, pitch, inflection, articulation, pronunciation, and their use of vocal fillers and vocal variety. For example, check out Robert Munsch and hear him read his books at *http://www.avonmaitland.on.ca/~esl/listen1.htm.*

Access a variety of American speeches at *http://www.americanrhetoric. com/speechbank.htm.* For instance, you might follow the text as Laura Bush speaks and discuss any discrepancies.

---

## *Accents*

Student discussion often focuses on whether or not accents, or dialects, should be eliminated. Some are proud of their accents and certainly having a Newfoundland and Labrador accent has not hindered the careers of individuals such as Mary Walsh, Rex Murphy, Rick Mercer, Gordon Pinsent, or Shaun Majumder.

Ultimately, the decision to speak more conventionally is up to the individual. However, people who speak with a heavy dialect might want to consider accent reduction. Woolf (2004) writes that, "When listening to someone who has a thick accent, people routinely miss 10–30 percent of what is said" (p. 12).

Overall, there does exist a standard English, typically used by news announcers. However, while nonstandard English speakers are considered less credible than standard speakers, they are also thought to be more warm and kind.

## TONGUE TWISTERS

To sharpen your articulation and pronunciation, try saying the following tongue twisters. You can see these and more at The Online Communicator: It's Hard to Say at *http://www.online-communicator.com/hard2say.html*.

1.   I need a box of biscuits, a box of mixed biscuits, and a biscuit mixer.
2.   Friday's five fresh fish specials.
3.   Imagine an imaginary menagerie manager imagining managing an imaginary menagerie.
4.   Twixt this and six thick thistle sticks.
5.   The sixth Sikh Sheik's sixth sheep's sick.
6.   Three free thugs set three thugs free.
7.   Charles deftly switched straight flange strips.
8.   She stood at the balcony inexplicably mimicking him hiccupping and amicably welcoming him in.
9.   Six sick slick slim sycamore saplings.
10. Peter Piper picked a peck of pickled peppers.

A peck of pickled peppers Peter Piper picked.
If Peter Piper picked a peck of pickled peppers,
Where's the peck of pickled peppers Peter Piper picked?

Say the following phrases five times in a row and see what happens.

• Unique New York
• Toy boat
• Blue black bugs blood

## Vocal Fillers

*Vocal fillers*, sometimes referred to as *vocal segregates*, are those *um*s, *ah*s, *like ah*s, and *an' da*s that are interjected throughout presentations. When used extensively, they are extremely distracting and affect a speaker's believability. Most speakers who use fillers are unaware that they are even doing so. One reason they seem compelled to add an *ah* or *um* instead of just pausing is because pauses tend to seem much longer to speakers than to listeners. However, pauses that are carefully placed can be used to great dramatic effect. To listeners, this might be considered the effective use of the pause.

### How to Reduce the Use of Vocal Fillers

If you have a habit of using fillers, try this exercise with the assistance of a friend. Your assistant's job is to say any noun that comes to mind and then to time you for 30 seconds. Your mission is to speak for 30 seconds on that particular topic without using any fillers. As soon as your assistant says the word, begin at once to speak—without even thinking. It does not matter what you say—it can be stupid, funny, or not even make sense. The goal is just to have you speak. Every time you use a vocal filler, your friend should knock on a table or wall (ringing a hand bell or pressing a buzzer is even more effective). Try this exercise for several days so that you begin to hear your own fillers. From then on, every time you catch yourself using one, lightly pinch yourself. If you continue in this way, you will soon be filler free.

## Vocal Variety

As Osborn and Osborn state, "The importance of vocal variety is most evident in speeches that lack it" (1994, p. 307). It is through your vocal variety that you bring your enthusiasm to the podium and make the material come alive. To use *vocal variety* means to alter the loudness, pitch, tone, and emphasis within your presentation. You can also vary your rate and incorporate pauses for further effect. You might stress and accentuate certain words to provide additional variety. The goal, above all else, is to avoid speaking in a monotone as it can be very boring.

## Using a Microphone

While using a microphone looks easy enough, unskilled speakers often have a difficult time with it. They do not talk directly into it, they move around so much that the audience misses some of their comments, or they look intimidated by the whole ordeal.

### Tips for Using a Microphone

If you will be speaking with a stationary microphone, you can do a number of things to ensure your success. First, request a time before the presentation to check out the mike. If it is a podium mike, adjust it so that when you stand comfortably; it is neither too high nor too low, neither too close, nor too far away. If you are using a floor stand, adjust the height of the stand and turn the microphone toward you. Become adept and proficient at handling the mike.

Depending on its sensitivity, you may or may not need to lean into the mike. If it is highly sensitive, you can be freer with your gestures and head movements. However, if the mike is a cheaper model, try not to move too far away or shift your head from side to side. Otherwise, it won't pick up your voice.

Remember that bumps and bangs on the mike are greatly amplified. So too are "p" and "b" sounds, which tend to pop. Be careful of heavy breathing—this is not an inviting sound to listeners. The best way to learn to use and become comfortable with a microphone is to practise—preferably before the audience arrives.

## Vocal Hygiene

Many people take their voices for granted, as I did until I contracted viral laryngitis that caused total voice loss for almost five weeks. It was only through voice therapy sessions with a speech-language pathologist, Kelly Roberts, that I was able to eventually recover. She also taught me a lot of valuable information about vocal hygiene. Check out her recommendations for keeping your voice in good working order.

 **EXPERT ADVICE**

How can you practise good vocal hygiene? Do vocal warm-ups before you speak to an audience. If the room is large or has noisy ventilation, make sure to use a microphone. Drink plenty of water—get hooked on it. Finally, give yourself lots of voice rest. If you are going to be talking for an extended period of time, incorporate periods of voice rest throughout your day. Should your voice become hoarse or tired, rest it. And if such problems persist, do not hesitate to see an otolaryngologist to assess the status of your vocal cords.

To keep you in good vocal working order, do not drink excessive amounts of caffeine or alcohol. Do not speak in a loud voice or yell from room to room in your home. Do not engage in excessive throat clearing. Instead, swallow or drink sips of water. Should you lose your voice, immediately put yourself on voice rest. Never whisper—it only does further damage.

*Kelly Roberts, Speech-Language Pathologist*
*Cape Breton Victoria Regional School Board, Sydney, Nova Scotia*

# CHAPTER AT A GLANCE

- It is estimated that 65 percent or more of face-to-face communication comes from nonverbal communication.
- Nonverbal communication can be more reliable than verbal communication.
- Effective speakers have an animated visual and vocal communication style.

- Effective speakers try to avoid the use of adaptors, those gestures, movements, and objects that distract listeners.
- While it is good to move away from the podium, do not invade the listeners' personal space.
- Speak at an appropriate rate and do not exceed time limits—no matter how good your presentation is.
- Start improving your articulation now; do not wait until the day of your speech.
- If you are going to use a microphone, practise beforehand.
- Practise good vocal hygiene.

# APPLICATION AND DISCUSSION QUESTIONS

1.  Answer the following questions in your communication journal:
    a.  *The cognitive dimension:* From the topics covered in this chapter, which ones are the most important to your success as a public speaker? Why?
    b.  *The affective dimension:* How do you feel when you are making a presentation, and how does that affect your nonverbal communication? Give specific examples.
    c.  *The behavioural dimension:* One way to assess your nonverbal and vocal communication is to videotape yourself as you give a short presentation. Watch the replay at least five times before you begin your assessment. The reason is that most people do not like seeing themselves. They think they are too fat, their noses are too big, or their ears stick out too much. Others do not like the sound of their voice. This is why it is good to watch your presentation several times—only then will you be able to do an objective self-assessment. Using the assessment guide below, select one or two areas that you will work on.

## Nonverbal Assessment Guide

Rate yourself using the following scale:

4 = excellent, 3 = good, 2 = needs some work, 1 = needs a great amount of work

**Visual Communication**

_____ Eye contact
_____ Facial expressions
_____ Illustrators
_____ Adaptors

_____ Posture and clothing

_____ Use of space and movement

_____ Use of notes

_____ Use of visual aids

_____ Clean beginnings

_____ Clean endings

**Vocal Communication**

_____ Volume

_____ Rate

_____ Tone of voice

_____ Pitch

_____ Articulation

_____ Pronunciation

_____ Vocal variety

_____ Vocal fillers/segregates

2. When speakers avoid eye contact during conversations, there is a general tendency to suspect that they are lying. How do you think this belief translates into public speaking contexts? Which speakers hold more credibility for you: those who make eye contact or those who do not?

3. Review Ekman and Friesen's categories of gestures. Then ask for volunteers to do two-minute speeches on what they did last weekend. As they speak, watch and record the types of gestures they use. Note the content in relation to the use of illustrators and adaptors (self, object, alter see box on page XX). If you are unable to find volunteers, ask your instructor to speak. Afterward, discuss which category was used most often. Offer suggestions as to why this may be, and think of other contexts where other types of gestures might be more prominent.

4. Which is more important to you: a speaker's content or his or her nonverbal delivery? Why?

5. Which voice qualities do you think contribute most to an effective speech? Which ones are the biggest detractors?

6. What vocal qualities should a speaker use in the following situations: presenting a eulogy, giving a bridal toast, making a science presentation, doing a reading in a place of worship?

7. Play charades. It is interesting to see how much can be conveyed and interpreted through nonverbal behaviours.

8. Use the article featuring Mayor Peter Kelly as a starting-off point for a small group discussion on how stuttering, heavy accents, speech impediments, and nonverbal tics impact both speakers and listeners.

**Mini Articulation Quiz Answers (see box on page 86)**

1. You go in first.
2. Did you eat yet?
3. No, did you?
4. So anyway.
5. What time is it?
6. What's up?
7. Got an extra beer?
8. Take it easy.

## REFERENCES AND FURTHER READINGS

Adler, R.B., Towne, N., & Rolls, J.A. (2004). *Looking Out/Looking In* (2nd Canadian ed.). Toronto: Thomson Nelson.

Birdwhistell, R. (1970). *Kinesics and context.* Philadelphia: University of Pennsylvania Press.

Brody, M. (1998). *Speaking your way to the top: Making powerful business presentations.* Boston: Allyn and Bacon.

Burgoon, J.K. (1994). Nonverbal signals. In M.L. Knapp and G.R. Miller (Eds.), *Handbook of interpersonal communication* (2nd ed., pp. 229–285). Thousand Oaks, CA: Sage.

DeVito, J.A. (1997). *The elements of public speaking* (6th ed.). New York: Longman.

Ekman, P., & Friesen, W.V. (1969). The repertoire of nonverbal behavior: Categories, origins, usage, and coding. *Semiotica, 1,* 49–98.

Ekman, P., Friesen, W.V., & Baer, J. (1984). The international language of gesture. *Psychology Today, 18,* 64–89.

Fromkin, B., Rodman, R., Hultin, N., & Logan, H. (1997). *An introduction to language* (1st Canadian ed.). Toronto: Harcourt Brace & Company.

Fripp, P. (2004). Exciting speeches: Make an emotional connection. *Executive Excellence, 21*(5), 18.

Hall, E.T. (1969). *The hidden dimension.* Garden City, NY: Anchor Books.

Hall, J.A. (1978). Gender effects in decoding nonverbal cues. *Psychological Bulletin, 85,* 845–857.

Henley, N.M. (1977). *Body politics: Power, sex, and nonverbal communication.* Englewood Cliffs, NJ: Prentice Hall.

Hillman, R. (1999). *Delivering dynamic presentations: Using your voice and body for impact.* Needham Heights, MA: Allyn and Bacon.

Ivy, D.K., & Backlund, P. (2004). *Exploring gender speak: Personal effectiveness in gender communication* (3rd ed.). Boston: McGraw Hill.

Knapp, M.L. (1986). Nonverbal communication: Basic perspectives. In J. Stewart (Ed.), *Bridges not walls: A book about interpersonal communication* (4th ed., pp. 68–84). Toronto: Random House.

Lau, S. (1982). The effect of smiling on person perception. *The Journal of Social Psychology, 117,* 63–67.

Lieberman, D.A., Rigo, T.G., & Compain, R.F. (1988). Age related differences in non-verbal decoding ability. *Communication Quarterly, 36,* 290–297.

Liska, J., & Cronkhite, G. (1995). *An ecological perspective on human communication theory.* Fort Worth, TX: Harcourt Brace College.

Mayer, L.V. (1988). *Fundamentals of voice and diction* (8th ed.). Dubuque, IA: Wm. C. Brown.

McCormack, S.A., & Parks, M.R. (1990). What women know that men don't: Sex differences in determining the truth behind deceptive messages. *Journal of Social and Personal Relationships, 7,* 107–118.

Miers, J. (2004/2005). The natural. *CMA Management, 78*(8), 13.

Osborn, M., & Osborn, S. (1994). *Public speaking* (3rd ed.). Boston: Houghton Mifflin.

Pearson, J.C., Turner, L.H., & Todd-Mancillas, W. (1991). *Gender and communication* (2nd ed.). Dubuque, IA: Wm. C. Brown.

Rosenberg, S., & Sedlak, A. (1972). Structural representations of implicit personality theory. In L. Berkowitz (Ed.), *Advances in experimental social psychology* (Vol. 6, pp. 235–297). New York: Academic Press.

Rosenthal, R., Archer, D., DiMatteo, M., Koivumaki, R., Hall, J., & Rogers, P.L. (1974). Body talk and tone of voice: The language without words. *Psychology Today, 8,* 64–68.

Stewart, L.P., Cooper, P.J., Stewart, A.D., & Friedley, S.A. (1996). *Communication and gender* (3rd ed.). Scottsdale, AZ: Gorsuch Scarisbrick.

Trotter, R.J. (1983, August). Baby face. *Psychology Today,* 14–20.

Woolf, R. (2004). How to talk so people will listen. *Business Credit, 106*(3), 12.

# Chapter 4
## Researching the Speech

## CHAPTER GOALS

In this chapter, you will learn
- why and how to analyze your audience
- how to deal with homogeneous and heterogeneous audiences
- how to find a topic that works for you and your audience
- how to locate information on your topic
- how to use support material

# ▦ INTRODUCTION

"How to Make 23 Bacon, Lettuce, and Tomato Sandwiches" was the title of a speech presented by a student who actually prepared the 23 sandwiches during the presentation. He did an admirable job as he assumed the role of a TV host: he was organized and well prepared, he interjected humour throughout, and he was adept at sandwich making. After he topped them off with brightly coloured cellophane-tipped toothpicks, he distributed them (along with cold cans of pop) to the class. While the student did an overall good job, his topic was not in keeping with the assignment specifications.

Topic selection is not always easy. In fact, some students report that one reason they do not practise enough for their presentations is because they spend so long searching for an appropriate subject that they run out of time. This dilemma contrasts with real-life situations where speakers are called on to give lectures on specific issues and they either accept or reject the invitation.

The goal of this chapter is to explain how to select and research a topic so it works for both you and your audience. In particular, you will learn how to get a sense of who your audience is, how to select a suitable topic, how to research the topic, and how to integrate the information into your speech so that it is interesting to your audience. Although each of these overlaps at times, for the most part, they are separated in the chapter.

# ▦ ANALYZING YOUR AUDIENCE

## Audience Characteristics and Speech Goal

Before you can begin to research, organize, and develop a speech, you need to have a topic. You also need to have some idea of how you wish to treat that topic. That is, you need to decide if your goal is to entertain audience members, inform them about something, persuade them to change their minds or think differently about something, or take some kind of action. Once you have this in mind, your goal will direct you as you seek out pertinent, interesting information to include in the presentation.

At the same time, it is equally important to have an understanding of just who is in your audience because the audience make-up will influence what information will be pertinent to them. As one reviewer so aptly put it, the speech purpose and the listeners determine all the decisions made with regard to the message. This also plays out in the business world. Huber (2005) sums up Khalid Aziz's (chair of the Aziz Corporation) advice for making boardroom presentations. He writes, "Research the audience. Find the overlap between what you want to say and what the audience wants to hear. . . . Don't bombard your audience with too many facts. Maintain their interest with 'killer information'—something they did not know" (p. 20).

Although speech goal is covered more extensively in Chapter 5, it is helpful to keep it in mind as you begin your research. Having a goal and insight into your potential listeners also makes it easier to decide what information to retain and what to discard.

The process of learning about the audience is referred to as an *audience analysis*, and the attributes you uncover are called *audience characteristics*. This dimension of speech making is important not only for the reason noted above, but because people of different ages, sexes, cultural backgrounds, or education levels (to name only a few variables) possess distinct values and attitudes. Insight into listeners enables you to give speeches that will not bore them. An accountant, for instance, could present the topic "Money Management" to several different groups. While the same finance principles might apply, the type and amount of support material should differ from group to group. For example, what a university student could save or invest monthly would differ from, say, a professional living on a six-figure income. In such a case, the accountant's ability to adapt to the group would be crucial to her or his success.

## Conducting an Audience Analysis

The easiest way to learn about your audience is to quiz the individual who invites you to speak. Ask for estimates regarding age, educational level, gender, background experiences, socioeconomic level, and so on.

You should also inquire about the approximate number of people you will address. It could be daunting to prepare for a small audience of 15 or so, only to find 50 in attendance, especially if you have handouts to distribute.

Hanna and Gibson (1995, p. 99) suggest that, if possible, you analyze your audience directly through interviews and questionnaires. While this is probably the best method, it is not always possible or convenient. Given that you will likely be preparing classroom speeches, you are in an excellent position to analyze your audience because you see classmates on a regular basis.

# Audience Factors

This section explores how different audience characteristics may be relevant to your speech. Please note, however, that not everyone falls neatly into categorical slots. Much of an audience analysis consists of stereotypical notions about your listeners.

## *Age*

As you know, attitudes and interests vary with age. Younger audiences may be focused on developing relationships, choosing a career, getting a job, or learning more about pop icons. Middle-aged people's interests might focus on making ends meet, paying off a mortgage, putting their children through university, or selecting their vacation destination. Senior citizens might be more interested in health issues, social issues, or family.

Knowing the audience age range can help you to adapt your speech accordingly. For example, two presentations on "Gender and Nonverbal Communication" (one to high school students and the other to middle-aged, small business owners) could include the same main concepts but employ different examples. High school students might enjoy learning about preening or courtship behaviours, those non-verbal gestures that are used to attract potential romantic partners. Business owners might benefit more from examples like nodding behaviours: when men nod, it generally signifies agreement, but when women nod, it indicates understanding and

---

### AUDIENCE ANALYSIS AT A GLANCE

You can get insight into your audience by considering the following factors. Keep them in mind by thinking **PROCESS VAC**.

**P**olitical leaning
**R**eligious affiliation
**O**ccupation
**C**ultural background
**E**ducational background
**S**ex
**S**ocioeconomic level
**V**oluntary or captive listeners
**A**ge
**C**lubs and organizations

---

encouragement for the speaker to continue. Because both sexes use and interpret nodding differently, you can imagine the communication confusion that this one movement can cause in the workplace.

## Sex

An awareness of whether the audience will be predominantly female, male, or mixed should also influence topic selection and treatment. It is well documented that females and males communicate and respond to the world differently. Two gender differences that are pertinent to public speaking are humour and persuasion.

### Humour

Women and men use and enjoy different types of humour. Women typically prefer and engage in situational humour. For instance, have you ever seen two women just crack up about something? When you ask them what they were laughing about, they often reply, "Oh, you wouldn't understand. You had to be there." Situational humour refers to something funny that arises unexpectedly out of the context.

Men, on the other hand, are more inclined to enjoy "put down" or aggressive humour (Pearson, Turner, & Todd-Mancillas, 1991). When men insult each other it is referred to as *jocular sparring*, and it is one of the ways they build camaraderie and friendship (Ivy & Backlund, 2004). However, men who insult women as a form of affection or humour can expect rejection. Therefore, the types of humour that work well with a male audience could fall short when the audience is entirely or predominantly female.

### Persuasion

While the research shows that neither sex is more persuasible, each sex is swayed by different types of evidence. Men, it is thought, are persuaded more by the inclusion of facts and statistics in a speech. Women, on the other hand, tend to respond more to empathy, so appeals to sympathy work better for them. Because women are more accepting of compromise, they are also persuaded by arguments of reciprocity—that is, they will agree to do something as a favour or in return for a favour (Johnston, 1994).

For instance, I taught a persuasion course where we missed a class due to inclement weather. To make up the time, I needed one student group to do its presentation a day early. Approaching an all-women group, I asked if they would be willing to help me out. They agreed. The class later joked that I should have used one of the persuasive strategies we were discussing in the course. The fact is, I had. When asked why the group agreed, they said they felt sorry for me! Apparently, appealing to that group of women worked with a strategy I had not so innocently selected.

Since taking my public speaking course, I listen much more critically to speakers. For example, I attended a health conference where most presenters were physician researchers while the audience members were social workers, addictions counsellors, nurses, physiotherapists, speech language pathologists—you know, front line care givers. The presentations contained such detail that many listeners lost interest; they didn't understand or really care about how the studies were done. The presentations would have been much better had the presenters concentrated on the practical implications of their research. I didn't think the presenters adapted very well to their audience.

*Ashley, Former Communication Student*

## *Educational Background*

Knowing in advance the type and level of education the audience has enables speakers to gauge how complicated their presentation should be. For instance, if most audience members have a background similar to the speaker, then more complex issues can be presented. But if the audience is unfamiliar with a topic, speakers should express those issues in everyday language. At the same time, there is no need to talk down to the audience.

## *Cultural Background*

People of different cultural backgrounds will often hold diverse (sometimes even contradictory) beliefs, values, and ways of behaving. The more sensitive you are to differences and similarities, the better you will be able to adapt your message to address their values and this will enhance your credibility. Do not assume that everyone is like you.

If you live in a major urban centre such as Toronto, Montreal, or Vancouver, there is likely to be lots of diversity in your speech classes. Such audiences present a challenge in that you need to be aware of the "culturally based assumptions and predispositions you bring to a speech. It is very common for people to regard as universal values that are actually only the values of a specific culture" (Zarefsky & MacLennan, 1997, p. 93). To help you adapt better to your audience, Joseph DeVito (1997, p. 183) suggests that you answer the following questions. Your responses can enhance your awareness of how the more diverse members in the audience will relate to the material you plan to include in your speech.

1. Are the differences within cultures relevant to your topic and purpose?
2. Are the attitudes and beliefs held by different cultures relevant to your topic and purpose?

3. Will the varied cultures differ in their goals or their receptiveness to suggestions to change their lives?

4. Will the cultures have different views toward education, employment, and life in general?

If your nationality or race is different from most members of your class, use the opportunity to present a speech on some aspect of your culture. Your classmates would find this especially interesting, and it is an appropriate subject for a classroom speech. At Cape Breton University where I teach, there is a large Mi'kmaq student population. Both my students and I have enjoyed speeches on clan mothers (female versions of the male elders), death rituals, Aboriginal self-government, reserve politics, the influence of residential schools, and the federal *Indian Act*. These speeches have helped us to gain a greater understanding of First Nations cultures.

It never occurred to me when I decided to do my speech on "Ways to Reduce the Stress Associated with Christmas" that not everyone in the class celebrated this Christian holiday. It was only afterward, during the question period, when Harold (who was Jewish) and Ahmed (who was Muslim) shared the obligations connected with Hanukkah and Ramadan that I came to realize that I had completely ignored those audience members.

*Joel, Former Communication Student*

## *Political Leaning*

An awareness of political tendencies will also help you to better meet the goals of your speech. If, for instance, you know that audience members happen to vote New Democrat, while you have tended to adhere to the principles of the Conservative Party, then you can expect that your opinions on many issues will likely clash with those of your audience. In such situations, it may be wise not to inject support and examples into your speech that may alienate your audience.

## *Socioeconomic Level*

Socioeconomic levels also affect audience beliefs, attitudes, and concerns. A topic such as "Strategies to Help You Save for Your Winter Southern Vacation" would be less relevant to people in upper income brackets. Students, however, living on student loans or part-time jobs might find the topic pertinent.

## Geographic Location

We need only look at federal election results to see that geographic location influences voting practices across the country. This suggests that individuals from different geographic areas possess different attitudes about various things. They may also have very different communication styles.

Geographic location can also affect interest levels. If you live in Newfoundland and Labrador or in another area of Canada that gets lots of snow, a speech on "How to Adjust Your Driving for Inclement Weather" might prove interesting and helpful. Main points—such as how not to get your car stuck sideways in a sloped driveway, how not to spin out of control, and how to release your car when it is stuck in the snow—would make a good speech. However, if such a speech was offered in Victoria, British Columbia, where extreme winter conditions are rarely experienced, the interest level might not be as high. Phrases such as "pumping your brakes," "rocking the car," or "using weights for traction" might be unfamiliar to the audience.

I was invited to speak to a group of teachers in Ottawa. In comparison with the lively, interactive, East Coast listeners that I was used to, I perceived the rather reserved audience to be somewhat cool. However, I was later informed that they were actually more responsive than usual. I had read the audience feedback incorrectly and thought that my presentation had not gone all that well. Fortunately, I was wrong.

*Natasha, Nova Scotia Educator*

## Clubs and Organizations

Because people generally join associations that are in keeping with their beliefs and values, you can generalize about individuals based on membership practices. If most members in your audience belong to the Sierra Club or Amnesty International, you might assume that they are a more progressive-thinking group. Therefore, topics with a social orientation would work well. If you were invited to speak at a Chamber of

"Good God! He's giving the white-collar voter's speech to the blue collars."

Commerce meeting, topics relating to development or strategies to bring businesses into the community would likely be of interest.

## Occupation

A knowledge of audience occupations allows you to make judgments about income levels, educational backgrounds, values, and types of specialized knowledge audience members possess. All of this can help you adapt your speech in a way that will interest your audience.

## Other Factors

A few other factors can help you generalize about your potential listeners: religious affiliation, whether they are listening to your speech on a captive (have to for a course or as a work requirement) or voluntary (want to be there) basis, and their expectations. Regarding expectations, one student related how disappointed he and most audience members were after hearing a well-known marketing expert speak at a gathering of young entrepreneurs. The presentation topic was marketing strategies, but the speaker's take was somewhat different than what the audience expected. They were hoping to hear specific, low-cost tactics that they could use in their startup businesses. The speaker's approach, although interesting, was focused on how international companies adapt their marketing plans to meet diverse cultural needs.

## Homogeneous and Heterogeneous Audiences

Knowing whether your audience will be homogeneous or heterogeneous can further help you to design your speech. In a *homogeneous audience*, members are similar, at least according to some broad categories. If you were speaking to a group of baseball players, for example, that would be a homogeneous audience. In a *heterogeneous audience*, listeners have different values, backgrounds, or a host of other characteristics. An audience consisting of men and women of various ages, religious affiliations, educational backgrounds, and so on is a heterogeneous audience. Skilled speakers take these differences into consideration.

It is usually easier to speak to a small, homogeneous audience in that your arguments and support material are more likely to pertain to everyone. When you speak to heterogeneous audiences, Zarefsky and MacLennan (1997, p. 86) suggest that you "find general appeals that will be meaningful across the population, rather than . . . select examples and appeals that are highly relevant to some and beside the point for others."

## SELECTING A SUITABLE TOPIC

It is clear that certain topics are better suited for some audiences than others. Completing an audience analysis will help you select an appropriate topic. As Sam "The Record Man" Sniderman says, "I will only speak on topics that I am completely sold on, well acquainted with, and that have no negative aspects." Factors that you might consider when selecting a topic include your own personal background and interests, time factors, technical level of the theme, research availability, and whether you are working from materials such as research papers or reports.

## Interests, Experiences, and Areas of Expertise

One of the best places to begin when selecting your speech topic is with yourself. Start by listing and examining your personal interests, experiences, and areas of expertise. For instance, Eisenberg and Gamble (1991) recommend that students examine their background (where they have lived, types of people they have known, or special interests they have had), their skills (what they do well or special information they

## ✍ EXPERT ADVICE

Students often believe that a speech must be about a serious issue or news story but this is not true. When I was a public speaking student, my extemporaneous speech was about being left-handed. The subject always fascinated me and I share the experience with my students to let them know that as long as they are passionate about a topic, they will succeed. When they get stumped I refer to the word **PICK** and ask the following questions:

**P** – Is there something you are *passionate* about? Is there something you do for a *pass-time*?

_____

**I** – Is there something you are *interested* in? Is there something you are *involved* with?

_____

**C** – Is there something you are *concerned* about? Is there something you *care* about?

_____

**K** – Is there something you already *know* about?

_____

This usually gets the wheels in motion. I've seen many fine speeches grow out of **PICK**.

*Dawn White, Communication Lab Coordinator*
*Cape Breton University, Sydney, Nova Scotia*

have), and their interests (hobbies, what they care about, what they would like to learn more about).

Often, people do not recognize just how engrossing stories from their lives and encounters can be to others. This was how one reentry student in her late twenties felt until she was convinced that her lived experience as a victim of spousal violence gave her a wealth of knowledge that most others simply could not possess. Presenting her speech on that topic, she supplemented general statistics, facts, and particulars with examples and illustrations from her life. It was the latter that made the presentation so memorable. The speech was extremely graphic, even upsetting at times, but also incredibly effective.

The student related in detail how, during one episode, she attempted to escape by running down the stairs, only to be grabbed around her neck by her partner, which caused her to choke as she was pulled backward. Her former mate then proceeded to drag her up the stairs, one by one, by her long, straight, dark-blond hair. Every one of us in that class sat riveted, spellbound, and overwhelmed by the physical misery and mental anxiety that this single event must have produced. The speaker's clear, precise narrative of this and other brutal acts touched everyone, and instructed us in the immense impact that spousal violence has on victims and their lives.

Examples from your life need not be as gruesome as the one above, but do not overlook as possible subjects those that might emerge from your background. Begin with what you know, and then do further research on the topic. Combining your personal background with additional inquiry makes for a well-chosen topic—this is what creates a speech that has depth and insight, as opposed to one that is based merely on opinion and lighthearted banter.

## Time Factors

One of the most important elements to be considered is the time allotment. Formal classroom speeches generally run anywhere up to 10 minutes. This is also a typical time allotment in professional speaking contexts when there is a series of speakers. In such cases, shorter is usually better.

 **EXPERT ADVICE**

### A BRAINSTORMING ACTIVITY

Students often find speech topic selection a difficult process. To help them get past the mental block they may experience, I suggest a brainstorming activity. I ask them to write down as many interests, hobbies, past jobs, travel experiences, skills, talents, etc., that they can think of. Nothing can be too crazy or weird. I then have them look through the list and see what jumps out at them as something they feel they would enjoy talking about. Once they have reduced the size of the list, they can further limit it by narrowing the topics to specific purposes. I also recommend that students then share their ideas with one another. Sometimes we inaccurately assume others will not find our thoughts interesting, and it helps to learn otherwise. By the end of this activity, learners have some possible speech topics and a specific purpose.

*Professor Tanya Brann-Barrett, Department of Communication*
*Cape Breton University, Sydney, Nova Scotia*

While some readers may think 10 minutes is a long time to speak, there are thousands of subjects that are not doable in such a short period. Topics such as "The Role That the Fortress Louisbourg Played in the Protection of North America during the 18th Century," "The Impact of the Global Economy on Local Community Development Initiatives," "The History of Media," or "Canada's Declining Health Care System" are all too broad. A critique of each subject would require so many subtopics that, in all, the speeches would appear to lack depth.

Instead, each topic could be narrowed to a more specific one. For instance, the Fortress Louisbourg topic could be narrowed down to three speech goals or topics: you could provide insight into the social life at Fortress Louisbourg; explain how Louisbourg soldiers sustained themselves during the long, cold winters; or describe how tourists today can actually visit Louisbourg's living restoration project. Or, rather than presenting a history of media, you could narrow the topic to the ethics of downloading free music from the Internet, how the Internet can be used to find and locate birth parents, or how the Internet has changed marketing practices.

Speeches have a specific goal or purpose and follow a structure. Once the goal is established, three topic areas (sometimes more, depending on the topic) are used to

**EXPERT ADVICE**

What would you do if you'd been allotted 60 minutes and the speaker ahead of you goes over by 30 minutes? The client then asks, "Can you wrap it up in 30 minutes?" You'd better be able to deliver. Always have a back up plan as to how you would do the same presentation in half the time.

*Laura Stack, Expert on Employee Productivity and Workplace Issues*
*From* 10 Time-Management Tips to Aid Presenters

support that goal. Keep this in mind as you select and narrow your topic. Always think, what is the main goal, what three major points will achieve that goal, and how can all this be covered in my time allotment? If you were doing a presentation on management communication, your goal would be "how to communicate with subordinates." The three main points could be (1) how to communicate in a respectful manner, (2) how to motivate your team, and (3) how to deal with conflict.

## Adhering to Time Restrictions

Because adhering to time restrictions is so critical, it is important to research a topic well enough that you actually can speak as long as you are required. Speakers who, for example, only talk for three minutes of a seven-minute time specification are thought to be less prepared than those who meet the time standards. For students, this will be reflected in their grades. Or, if you were solicited by a company to deliver a daylong workshop on "Making Effective Presentations," the person hiring you would not be impressed if the session ended at 1:30 p.m. Nor would participants be happy if you kept them past 5:00 p.m. when they expected to wrap up at 4:00 p.m.

 **EXPERT ADVICE**

A public speaker needs to adjust to the audience and if you're at the end of the day and everyone is ready to run and catch a flight or whatever, you need to adjust accordingly. So, you must watch your audience much more than your notes.

*Brian Rogers, Accountant*
*KPMG, Calgary, Alberta*

## Technical Themes

Do not select a topic that is too technical for your audience. For example, if you are a computer science, engineering, or nursing major, topics and terminology that are second nature to you may be meaningless to audience members who lack experience in those areas.

This does not mean that you should avoid scientific themes altogether, just ensure that you explain your terminology. A former student, Kim Liska, who has a master's degree in microbiology, presented a speech showing how prions in animal food sources caused the spread of mad cow disease. Although she employed a lot of unfamiliar jargon, Kim did an excellent job of explaining what it all meant. She simplified a complex topic and presented an interesting speech that truly fascinated the class.

I finally decided that I would do my speech on "How the Rhetorical Strategies Advocated by Ancient Rhetoricians Such as Plato and Aristotle Are Still Relevant in Speech Making Today" because I had done my research paper on that topic in my persuasion course. I was really interested in the topic and had lots of good examples that I could share with the class. Rather than do a normal speech outline, I figured that the best method was to go through the paper and highlight the parts I wanted to talk about, and then read them over several times to make sure I knew them. Big mistake!

Because I didn't do an outline, I had to take the whole report up to the podium. And, it just got worse from there. I thought that I could just talk about the topic, but I ended up reading most of the material. Further, I was only just starting my second point when the timer indicated that there was one minute left. I had to really scramble and figure out what to present and what not to say. I ended up going three minutes overtime, I didn't get to tell the best examples, and I lost a lot of points for reading. I learned the hard way that just because you researched and wrote a paper does not mean it can be presented as a speech. That takes way more work than I put into it. But I think I know how to do it now—even though it's too late for that class.

*Caleigh, Former Speech Student*

## Adapting Written Materials and Reports for a Presentation

Occasionally, students wish do their speech on a research project or paper they are working on in another course. Because they are generally very enthusiastic about the subject, I encourage them to adapt the work for presentation. However, the operative word here is *adapt*. There is so much information contained in a research paper or report that it is virtually impossible to relate everything; hence,

---

### HOW TO ADAPT A WRITTEN PAPER OR PROJECT FOR AN ORAL PRESENTATION

A positive aspect about adapting papers and reports is that you already have a thorough understanding of the topic. This lends itself well to contexts where you have to field questions, plus you have a greater understanding of the topics than what is presented to the audience.

To adapt the work for presentation, you essentially have to redo it as a speech. You start from scratch and create an outline. The guidelines below should help you do this.

- Select a specific goal. Speaking takes longer than reading so while you might be able to read through your paper in seven minutes, it would take much longer to say it out loud. Therefore, select which aspect of the project you are going to present. Then, clarify this as your goal—for example, to inform the audience about *changing vacation destination trends*.
- Select three major points that will achieve your goal. Perhaps they could be (1) what those changing trends are; (2) what may account for the changes; and (3) how the changes influence local economies.
- Decide what you will say about each point and what statistics and sources you will use to support your points.
- Write all this in point form.
- Decide how you will open the presentation.
- Decide how you will end the presentation.
- Practise. Say it all out loud and time yourself. Repeat and modify your points until the presentation is smooth, you feel confident, and the whole thing adheres to the time restrictions.

---

the executive summary. Therefore, written materials must be modified to conform to the oral format. Do not operate under the assumption that both forms of communication are the same. For tips on how to adapt a paper for presentation, see the accompanying box.

---

**" "**

> When speech instructors say that your speeches are not allowed to be boring, they are not referring to topics. *Any* topic can be made interesting with the insertion of relevant, applicable examples, statistics, testimonials, and the like. Audiences love stories, so include a short one. I find that many students skip over meaty, substantive topics that they are excited about merely because they think others will be bored with them. Not so. Remember that your enthusiasm will transfer to the audience.
>
> *Duncan, Former Communication Lab Peer Facilitator*

---

## ■ RESEARCHING YOUR TOPIC

Another major factor to consider when selecting a topic is where to find relevant, up-to-date, and interesting information for the speech. Well-investigated topics lend depth to the speech so that they are both informative *and* engaging. This becomes particularly evident when a lightweight, opinionated presentation is followed by a well-researched one: the lack of effort on the first presentation is emphasized, while the second speaker seems more industrious and interesting.

Topics can be researched in libraries, on the Internet, or through personal interviews and surveys. Take a moment to review the options available to you. If you attend a small college or university, you may need to depend on interlibrary loans for books, which may take a few days to acquire. But, with computer access and a variety of research databases, libraries open the door to the entire world of scholarship. Check out the computer search systems that may be accessible through your library. Find out whether you need to make an appointment and whether there is a charge to access such programs. Many students now do Internet searches from home with just a click of their name and student ID numbers. If you are unfamiliar with how to conduct an online search, find someone who can help you and who will be available for you when you need them.

# Libraries

Libraries house a wealth of information. The best way to access materials is to ask the librarians for help. They can direct you in minutes to indexes and abstracts that will enable you to find up-to-date, interesting information on your topic. Further, they will show you how to use the databases. To help you understand the library research process better, you might categorize your search options in terms of three sources of information: print, CD-ROM, and online or Web searches.

## *Print Publications*

Print materials include books, academic journals, newspapers, magazines, and reference books (such as encyclopedias and handbooks). Sometimes you may find what you need in books. Consult a dictionary or encyclopedia to define a term or read an overview of the subject. If you need statistics, brief factual information, and the latest trends, consult handbooks and yearbooks. Statistics Canada offers a wide array of information. In addition to statistics on many aspects of Canadian life, publications such as *The Daily, Canadian Social Trends*, and *Canada Year Book* are particularly interesting in that they examine the implications of the data. Statistics Canada is also accessible on the Internet (*http://www.statcan.ca*).

---

### REFERENCE BOOKS

Below is a list of just some of the reference books that may be available in your library.

#### DICTIONARIES, THESAURUSES, AND ENCYCLOPEDIAS

*Atlas of Human Anatomy*

*A Bibliography of Canadian Folklore in English*

*Canada Since 1867: A Bibliographical Guide*

*Canadian History: A Reader's Guide*

*Canadian Oxford Dictionary*

*Dictionary of Canadian Biography*

*Dictionary of Canadian Law*

*Dictionary of Genetics*

*Dictionary of the Language of Micmac Indians*

*Dictionary of Superstitions*

*Encyclopedia of Fairies*

*Encyclopedia of Government and Politics*

*Encyclopedia of Indians of Canada*

*Encyclopaedia of Occupational Health and Safety*

*Folklore of Canada*

*Guide to Folktales in the English Language*

*History of Canada: Annotated Bibliography*

*Human Sexuality: An Encyclopedia*

*A Language of Canadian Politics*

*Sport Thesaurus*

*Womanwords: A Dictionary of Words about Women*

*Women's Studies Encyclopedia*

## BIBLIOGRAPHIES, HANDBOOKS, AND YEARBOOKS

*Aboriginal Self Government in Canada: A Bibliography*

*Annotated Canadian Environmental Assessment Act*

*Canada at the Olympic Winter Games*

*Canada Year Book*

*Canadian Electrical Code*

*Canadian Environmental Legislation*

*Canadian Guide to Uniform Legal Citation*

*Canadian Indian Policy: A Critical Bibliography*

*Canadian Parliamentary Guide*

*Canadian Parliamentary Handbook*

*Canadian Women in History: A Chronology*

*Canadian Writers and Their Works*

*Chronology of Women's History*

*The Civil Engineering Handbook*

*Contemporary Authors*

*Dictionary of Literary Biography*

*Electrical Engineering Handbook*

*Electronics Handbook*

*Gender Roles: A Handbook to Tests and Measures*

*Guideline for Canadian Drinking Water Quality*

*International Track and Field Annual*

*Juristat Reader: A Statistical Overview of the Canadian Justice System*

*Methods of Air Sampling and Analysis*

*The Oxford Companion to Canadian Literature*

*Statistics Canada Catalogue*

## CD-ROMs

Libraries also have indexes and abstracts that lead you to sources or articles that you can find in the scholarly journals. Often, they give the full text as well. This means that you may not have to search out the journal and the article, but rather you can print the entire article immediately. Some of the common CD-ROM indexes include *Canadian Business and Current Affairs, Sociological Abstracts, Applied Science and Technology*, and so on. See the accompanying box for a more expanded list.

### INDEXES AND ABSTRACTS ON CD-ROM OR THE WEB

The following list of indexes and abstracts may be found even in the smaller university and college libraries (CD = CD-ROM, W = Web).

*Academic Elite (W)*

*Applied Science and Technology (CD)*

*Biology Digest (W)*

*Canadian Business and Current Affairs (CD)*

*Canadian Case Digest (Abridgement) (CD)*

*Canadian Statute Citations (CD)*

*Consolidated Statutes and Regulations (W)*

> *Environmental RouteNet (W)*
>
> *ERIC (W)*
>
> *MEDLINE (W)*
>
> *MLA International Bibliography (CD)*
>
> *PsycINFO (W)*
>
> *PsychLIT (CD)*
>
> *Sociological Abstracts (CD)*
>
> *UnCover (W)*

## The Internet

Popular Web-based indexes that are available through libraries include *Academic Elite*, *ERIC*, or *UnCover* (see the accompanying box for more). These programs are very user-friendly. However, remember that the librarian's job is to help you, so make sure you ask for help when you need it.

Finally, an incredible amount of information is available on the Internet. Just about every business, organization, government agency, and institution has a Web site. When you do Internet research, beware of the author's credibility. Some students cite Internet information that cannot be checked for authenticity or legitimacy. Make sure you are tapping into reputable Web sites. Also, be aware of any statistics cited— they may be referring to American or other countries' data that do not apply to Canada.

### CHECKING THE RELIABILITY OF INFORMATION ON THE INTERNET

There is always the question of just how reliable the information found on the Internet is. Harris (1997) suggests the use of credibility, accuracy, reasonableness, and support (CARS) to evaluate Internet information. Check out his Web site at *http://www.media-awareness.ca/english/resources/special_initiatives/wa_resources/wa/teachers/backgrounders/harris_evaluating.cfm*. The University of Calgary Library also has a short, effective overview that can be viewed at *http://www.ucalgary.ca/library/netsearch/evaluation.html*.

In combining information from both sites, ask the following questions to check the reliability of your Internet sources:

*Credibility:* What are the author's credentials and institutional affliations? Is the page linked to the institution's home page?

*Accuracy:* How accurate is the information? Is it up to date? Do the links still exist? Is there a bibliography? Is the article comprehensive? Does content seem consistent with what you have found elsewhere?

*Reasonableness:* Is the page biased? Is the purpose of the page for anything other than the dissemination of information? Is the material objective, moderate, and consistent?

*Support:* Is the article supported with sources? Is there contact information?

## Interviews

Experts in your community may be able to provide first-hand information and experiences for you. If, for instance, you were going to do a speech on some aspect of hockey farm teams, and one was located in your hometown, then it would be very helpful to interview one or more of the key individuals associated with the team.

When you conduct an interview, there are several things to keep in mind. The first is that interviewing is both an art and a skill. It is an art in that good interviewers know how to break the ice and put the interviewee at ease, when to push the interviewee with additional probing questions, how to be sensitive to their nonverbal cues, and how to really listen to what the person is saying. It is a skill in that interviewers need to know how to structure an interview, pose a variety of questions, and conduct themselves with the right degree of professionalism.

When someone you have approached has agreed to being interviewed, schedule a time that is convenient for both of you, and select a quiet meeting place where you will not be disturbed. On the day of the interview, arrive early. Bring along a tape recorder so that you can focus on the interviewee rather than on scribbling notes. If the recorder is not battery operated, find a place to plug it in and then put it aside so that it will not be intrusive. Tape recorders that contain internal microphones are good. Finally, test the machine to make sure it is working properly.

The interview consists of three phases: the opening, the middle (with the major questioning), and the closing.

One simple way to conduct an interview is to take a journalistic approach. You simply ask five major questions, listen well, and pose lots of follow-up questions. Whatever your topic, you can always find out *who, what, when, where*, and *why*, and I'd also throw in *how*.

*Anastasia, Former Interview Student*

## The Opening

The opening is very important because this is when you develop a rapport and set the general tone. If you make your interviewees feel relaxed and comfortable, they are more likely to open up to you. Do this by engaging in some small talk about the weather, parking, how busy they are, and so forth. During the opening, tell the person your goal for the interview and what you will do with the information.

## The Middle

You begin to ask your questions in the middle phase of the interview. Prepare an outline in advance of where you want to go in the interview; do not write out every single question you intend to ask. The difference between a good interviewer and a bad one is often a matter of listening. If you prepare some general topics that you would like to probe, then you are better equipped to listen to the responses. It is also a good idea to use a conversational tone to keep interviewees talking.

As you know, questions can be posed in many different ways. One mistake that new interviewers typically make is asking too many closed questions—questions that can be answered with just a yes or a no. For example, if you ask an interviewee, "What's it like living in Winnipeg?" thinking he will describe the city, he may just reply, "Great!" Instead, try "Tell me what it's like living in Winnipeg." See the box on pages 120–121 for the types of questions you could use to help you gain as much information as possible. Then practise using them with a friend in a mock interview.

## The Ending

At the end of the interview, ask whether there is anything the interviewee would like to add. If not, close the interview by summarizing the content and thanking the interviewee for his or her help. Shake hands, gather up your notes and tape recorder, and be on your way. When you use information from the interview, be sure to cite your source. How to do that is discussed later in the chapter.

The interview I did with the mayor was a mess. Things were going well at the beginning because I had written out every question. But halfway though, when I'd ask a question, he'd say that he had already answered it. I hadn't really been listening. This happened a few more times. Then I got mixed up, he lost patience with me, and I didn't know what to do. It was all horribly embarrassing. I'll never do that again.

*Barbara, Former Problem Centred Studies Student*

## TYPES OF QUESTIONS TO ASK IN AN INTERVIEW

Interviews that flow smoothly and unveil an abundance of information generally comprise a variety of questions. Check out the following:

### OPEN QUESTIONS

These questions allow interviewees to answer in a variety of ways. They begin with words like "How do you feel . . . ," "Tell me about . . . ," "What do you think . . . ," "What accounts for . . . ," or "Describe . . . . " For example:
*Describe the skiing at Whistler.*
*Tell me about some of the tourist attractions in Quebec City.*

### CLOSED QUESTIONS

These questions require only short, specific answers. In many instances, a simple "Yes," "No," or other one-word answer will be the reply. These can be useful for getting an interviewer back on track when she or he has gotten off topic. For example:
*How's the skiing at Whistler?*
*What tourist attractions should I see when I'm in Quebec City?*

### PRIMARY QUESTIONS

These questions introduce a topic. For example:
*So, you have described the ski conditions and trails at Whistler. How about telling me about the food and lodging? (open primary question)*

*After I've explored the old section of Quebec City, where would I go to find the best shopping? (closed primary question)*

## SECONDARY QUESTIONS

These probe responses to primary or open questions. For example:

*Tell me about the trails that a beginning skier could use.*

*Tell me about the restaurants in the old section of Quebec City.*

## HYPOTHETICAL QUESTIONS

These are "what if" types of questions: how interviewees would feel, would act, etc. Hypothetical questions focus on the future. For example:

*What would you do if you won a free skiing weekend at Whistler?*

*Where would you go if you had only two days to see all of Quebec City?*

## BEHAVIOURAL QUESTIONS

These questions ask about the past—what the interviewee did in particular situations. For example:

*Tell me about your ski trip to Whistler.*

*What were some of the things you did for excitement in Quebec City?*

## CHALLENGE QUESTIONS

These questions probe previously stated positions or opinions. For example:

*You told me earlier that Whistler is a very popular skiing destination. How does it compare with some of the resorts in Quebec?*

*You said that the Quebec Winter Carnival is really exciting. I once went to New Orleans for Mardi Gras . . . before Katrina. Would it be something like that?*

## MULTIPLE CHOICE QUESTIONS

These provide interviewees with potential answers from which they may choose a response. For example:

*OK, so you know I can afford only one vacation this winter. Do you think I should go to Whistler for the skiing or Quebec City for the carnival, or just stay home and save up for a summer trip across Canada?*

*If I go to Whistler, do you recommend that I stay at a lodge, at a hotel, in a bed and breakfast, or with my friend's family? They have a beautiful chalet and lots of room.*

**Source:** Rolls (2000).

Questions also help interviewers maintain control of the interview. I find that if a person is rambling on and on, I pose a couple of closed, yes/no questions to get the person back on track. Similarly, if the interviewee is not producing much information, I ask them to describe things to me. That usually gets them going.

*Steve, Assistant Basketball Coach*

# Surveys

Some students might like to find support for their secondary research by conducting a survey. Surveys, or questionnaires, are good tools for gathering data on people's knowledge level, attitudes, and practices. However, survey results can be misleading and downright incorrect if they are poorly developed or if respondent answers are dishonest. While there is little you can do to keep subjects from fibbing, the survey can be designed so that instructions are clear and questions probe for the information you seek.

Survey development is not as easy as it seems. Question items have to be precise because the accuracy of the results is related directly to the quality of the question items. The possible answers from which to choose also require considerable attention. The goal of this segment is to provide the basics of survey construction and administration. It is intended only as an introduction to this line of research. If you plan to do a serious study, further reading and study is required.

## *Items*

The questions or statements included in a survey are referred to as *items*. The use of statements allows responses to be collected with a Likert scale; one that could be completed with, for example, *strongly disagree, disagree, undecided, agree,* and *strongly agree*. Statements should be developed so that they assess one piece of information at a time. For example, the following item asks two separate things.

The Canadian government should reduce corporate tax breaks and increase funding to education.

Strongly Disagree    Disagree    Undecided    Agree    Strongly Agree

Some people may agree that chopping corporate tax breaks would benefit Canadians, but they might also think that increased funding should go to health care instead. Or, a person could disagree with the tax break part of the statement but agree that education should receive greater funding. Still, a third individual might agree with both statements in the item, and a fourth might disagree with both statements. The way the question is set up, there is no method to distinguish among the attitudes. To solve this problem, the skilled survey developer would pose two separate items as in the example below.

The Canadian government should reduce corporate tax breaks.
Strongly Disagree     Disagree     Undecided     Agree     Strongly Agree

The Canadian government should increase funding to education.
Strongly Disagree     Disagree     Undecided     Agree     Strongly Agree

Likert scales work well for answering the questions above and the data collected can be coded easily for statistical programs or manual analysis. Other types of items simply ask respondents to check off the appropriate answer. However, all the possible answers must be provided. This style of question works best when there is a limited number of responses, or the potential responses fall neatly into categories, as in the next example.

Your age is

18 or below          [  ]
19–35                [  ]
36–49                [  ]
50–62                [  ]
63–75                [  ]
76–80                [  ]
81 or over           [  ]

If a question is set up like the following, you can see how the accuracy of the results might be suspect.

What do you do during the summer months?

Take classes         [  ]
Work                 [  ]
Travel               [  ]
Relax                [  ]

The first problem with the question is that "summer months" are not defined and thus the term is not clear. As a result, some respondents might think the question is asking what they did on their summer "vacation." And, because "summer" months are not specifically stated, some survey takers might think only of June and July or July and August while others might have entirely different connotations.

The second problem is with the answers; there is nothing that instructs survey takers to complete just one box or more than one. This is important to note because the possible answers are not mutually exclusive. Some survey takers might engage in all four activities during the summer. For example, a hospitality student could very well take a practicum course and do a summer work placement at the Chateau Frontenac in Quebec City. Given that home is a small town two provinces away, this could be considered travel. Further, the student might relax by enjoying the sights and city nightlife with newfound Québécois pals. Other respondents might engage in one, two, or three of the activities listed, and some may not do any. A person could, for example, spend time caring for an aging parent. One way to alleviate these problems is to include an "Other _____" space that subjects may complete.

A third potential problem when developing items is setting them up in the negative. This causes undue confusion and misinterpretation. For example, the following question has a double whammy. It is set up in the negative and the word "exclusive" (versus inclusive) could further muddle the reader. Some subjects will indicate disagreement with the statement when they are actually in favour of it. Those who support the statement in the survey may not agree with it in reality.

The use of exclusive language should not be tolerated in educational settings.

Finally, keep items short and unbiased by avoiding questions that encourage a particular response such as, "and you agree that . . ." This type of question does more to identify the researcher's attitudes rather than the respondents'. To ensure that instructions are clear, give the survey a test run. This will also help to identify the survey's strengths and weaknesses.

## Administering the Survey

Surveys can be administered through personal or telephone interviews or they can be self-administered where subjects complete them on their own. Self-administered surveys are inexpensive and more private but they can result in a poor response rate. Further, if no one is available to answer questions about how to complete the surveys, they may not be completed accurately and some will have to be discarded. Interview surveys can be expensive, but they result in better accuracy and a higher response rate.

Another way to administer a survey is through the Web. Conway (2004) writes that, ". . . several studies indicate that Web surveys produce response rates comparable, if not better than, traditional paper surveys and telephone interviews (p. 1). Check out his Web survey guidelines at *http://www.learningcircuits.org/2004/apr2004/conway.htm* to learn how to develop and administer a Web survey.

For further information about survey construction see Earl Babbie's 1998 book entitled *The Practice of Social Research*. He discusses surveys in a straightforward, clear manner.

# ▇ USING YOUR SUPPORT MATERIAL

So, you know your audience and have chosen an appropriate topic that you will be able to research with relative ease. This final section discusses how you could use your support materials.

## Appropriateness

It is important to consider the appropriateness of your topic and support material. The level of formality of the topic should be in keeping with the audience and the context. A subject that works well in one context could bomb in another.

One student, "Jamie," who was originally going to do his speech on the solar system, decided at the last minute to do it on one planet—Uranus. He had prepared well, and his titles and drawings were neatly presented on a poster board. However, it was immediately clear that his intention was not to focus so much on information regarding the planet, but rather to zero in on the play on words. He made lewd, rude, and crass comments about Uranus, such as "It makes for a good opening at the bar. You could go up to a woman and say, 'I'd really like to see Uranus. . . .' " In a later conversation, he informed me that he had practised the speech several times to make sure it was entertaining. It would have been—on the Comedy Network, but not in a formal classroom speech. The student now works for an advertising agency.

## Definitions

Do not assume that the audience knows what you are talking about. For example, if you think some, but not all, listeners are familiar with a particular term, you could still define it by saying something like "As many of you know, monozygotic twins are twins that come from the same egg. You probably refer to them as identical twins."

## Examples

Examples help people to understand more fully the concepts, theories, or ideas you are presenting. Examples can also make dry topics come alive. In fact, listeners will often recall them long after they have forgotten the main point they support.

## Narratives

Narratives are actual stories that you tell within the speech, and like examples, they too will be remembered when the speech is over. As Peter Bender (2001), one of Canada's most dynamic business speakers, says, ". . . make your talk relevant to your audience. What's in it for them? Why will they care or want to listen? Remember to build that in, and use language and stories to which your listeners can relate" (p. 5). Recall the speech I referred to by the woman who was beaten by her husband. It was her personal stories that made it so powerful. Osborn and Osborn (1994) note that narratives "invite audiences to discover the 'truth' for themselves. With narratives the audience becomes involved in the creation of the message—it becomes their discovery, their truth" (p. 163). Often, personal narratives allow the audience to identify with the speaker.

## Statistics

While a few pertinent, well-placed statistics can provide powerful support for your stance, too many can become meaningless and boring for your audience. It is also useful to explain what the statistics mean—what their implications are. As Messmer (2003) writes, "Instead of reading a series of numbers or calculations, try to focus instead on your interpretation of the data. This will make for a more interesting speech."

## Citing Sources

When you use other people's material, you must cite your sources; otherwise, you are plagiarizing, a dishonest practice that is grounds for dismissal from colleges and universities. The final two boxes in the chapter offer examples of ways you can cite your sources both during your speech and in any written documents you might have to provide.

## Testimonies

Testimonies refer to people or institutions that are known experts in a particular area, and their inclusion can enhance credibility by mere association. For example, you might say, "According to Mr. Bill MacDonald, president of Westmount Investors, in a presentation to the university investment club, you could easily retire with over $1 million if you begin to invest right now."

## HOW TO CITE SOURCES DURING YOUR SPEECH

### MAGAZINE ARTICLE

Provide the author, article title publication, and date.

*John Intini, in his article titled "The Resourceful Generation," published in* Maclean's, *January 17, 2005, argues that many under-thirties read literary essays from Web sites such as. . . .*

### INTERNET SOURCE

When citing information from the Internet, do not give the site address, unless it's simple like niki.com. Rather, cite the Web page or organization and the date the information was retrieved.

*According to "The Online Communicator: It's Hard to Say," retrieved from the Internet July 8, 2005, a good way to improve one's delivery of normal phrases is to practise on difficult ones.*

### JOURNAL ARTICLE

When citing a journal article, include the author(s), the journal title, and the publication date.

*According to Halbesleben and Buckley, in a research article published in the* Journal of Management, *2004, burnout in organizational life can be explained by . . .*

### NEWSPAPER ARTICLE

Make sure to include the author, the newspaper name, and the date.

*Kathy Banks Hoffman, in an article titled "Canada Making Inroads" published by the Associated Press in* The Chronicle Herald, *July 18, 2005, describes how less expensive health care and changing tastes have Canada challenging U.S. auto production and . . .*

### BOOK

Include the author, book title, publisher, and date.

*Laura Penny, in her bestselling 2005 book* Your Call is Important to Us: The Truth About Bullshit *published by McClelland & Stewart Ltd., describes how pharmaceutical companies promote . . .*

**INTERVIEW**

Include that individual's names and the interaction date.

*In a telephone interview with Sam "The Record Man" Sniderman on April 18, 2005, regarding his take on public speaking, he said that he only speaks on topics that he's completely sold on.*

## HOW TO CITE SOURES IN WRITTEN DOCUMENTS (APA STYLE)

Many instructors expect students to submit speech outlines and a review of the sources used as support material in the speech. References typically contain the author or authors; the title, where the piece came from (such as a book, periodical, magazine, etc.), the publisher, and the place of publication. While there are several referencing styles, the most commonly used in the social sciences, and the one that I think is the easiest, is the American Psychological Association (APA) style. Many of the sources you might site can be found at OWL Online Writing Lab. The site at *http://owl.english.purdue.edu/workshops/hypertext/apa/sources/reference.html* offers a simple guide to citing a variety of sources. Below are real and fictitious reference examples not from the site above.

### BOOK, ONE AUTHOR

Penny, L. (2005). *Your call is important to us: The truth about bullshit*. Toronto: McClelland & Stewart Ltd.

### BOOK, TWO OR MORE AUTHORS

Littlejohn, S.W., & Foss, K.A. (2005). *Theories of human communication* (8th ed.). United States: Thomson Wadsworth.

### JOURNAL ARTICLE, ONE AUTHOR

Burk, J. (2001). Communication apprehension among Master's of Business Administration students: Investigating a gap in communication education. *Communication Education, 50,* 51–58.

### JOURNAL ARTICLE, TWO TO SIX AUTHORS

Aly, I., & Islam, M. (2005). Factors affecting oral communication apprehension among business students: An Empirical study. *The Journal of American Academy of Business, 2,* 98–102.

## MAGAZINE ARTICLE, ONE AUTHOR

Intini, J. (2005, January 17). The resourceful generation. *Maclean's*, *118* (3), 54.

## NEWSPAPER ARTICLE

Hoffman, K.B. (2005, July 18). Canada making inroads. *The Chronicle Herald* (Halifax), p. C2.

## BROCHURE

*Studying Communication at Cape Breton University. (2004.)* Guidelines for degree requirements. [Brochure]. Sydney, NS: Author.

## MUSIC RECORDING

Crowe, S. (2003). Fell back up. Recorded by Susan Crowe. On *Book of Days* [CD]. Toronto: Corvus Music.

## PERSONAL OR TELEPHONE INTERVIEW

S. Sniderman (personal communication, April 18, 2005).

## ONLINE ARTICLE, NO DATE OR AUTHOR

The online communicator: It's hard to say. (n.d.). Retrieved July 8, 2005, from http://www.online_communicator.com/hard2say.html.

## ONLINE PERIODICAL ARTICLE WHEN YOU HAVE NOT LOOKED AT THE PRINTED VERSION

Halbesleben, J.R.B., & Buckley, M. R. (2004). Burnout in organizational life [Electronic version]. *Journal of Management*, *30* (6), 859–79.

## MULTIPAGE DOCUMENT CREATED BY PRIVATE ORGANIZATION

Own Online Writing Lab, American Psychological Association (APA) Style Workshop. (n.d.). Reference List Examples. Retrieved July 23, 2005, from http://owl.english.purdue.edu/workshops/hypertext/apa/sources/references.html.

## DAILY NEWSPAPER ARTICLE, ELECTRONIC VERSION AVAILABLE BY SEARCH

Faster, B. (2005, February 14). What love and chocolate have in common. *The New York Times*. Retrieved April 1, 2005, from http://www.nytimes.com.

# CHAPTER AT A GLANCE

- Learning about your audience is called an audience analysis.
- The more you know about your audience, the better you can adapt your material to your listeners.
- Select topics based on your experience and interests.
- Do not give written papers as speeches without first adapting them for the spoken word.
- Speeches can be researched using print, CD-ROM, and online or Web sources, as well as through interviews and surveys.
- Support material can be adapted as definitions, examples, statistics, narratives, and testimonies.

# APPLICATION AND DISCUSSION QUESTIONS

1. Answer the following questions in your communication journal:
   a. *Cognitive dimension:* If you were going to research the history of your town or city, how would you go about doing it?
   b. *Affective dimension:* If you had to give a 10-minute speech next week, would the topic you select affect how you feel about yourself? What types of topics would make you feel good about yourself as a speaker? Which ones would make you feel less confident? What types of positive and negative feelings do you experience as you begin to research a topic?
   c. *Behavioural dimension:* Do an audience analysis on the members of your speech class.
2. The following questions are designed to help you with topic selection. Note that they cover only a few topic areas—the possibilities are limitless.
   - *Sports:* What sports do you play? What sports have you coached or assisted in? Are you an avid sports fan? Are you interested in the financial implications of sports? How do you feel about violence in sports? What about sport promotion?
   - *Clubs and organizations:* What clubs or organizations did/do you belong to? What offices did/do you hold? What contributions did/do they make to a particular or a general community?
     Have you participated in any special events the organization has sponsored? Do you feel strongly about some organizations and the work they do? Do you have a disease or disability that you could explain?

- *Volunteer positions:* What volunteer positions or jobs have you held? For instance, have you been a Sunday school teacher? A leader or assistant with the Canadian Girl Guides or Scout Movement? A candy striper? A food bank or soup kitchen worker? A volunteer with a political party?
- *Hobbies and interests:* What hobbies and interests do you have? Gardening? Woodworking? Astrology? Feng shui? Card playing? Crafts? Remodelling antique cars? Genealogy? Reading? Chess? Fishing? Racing cars? Making beer or wine? Sewing? Computer games?
- *Pets:* Do you own a pet? How do you train and care for your pet? Can you tell us about a particular breed of pet?
- *Music:* Do you make music either professionally or for fun? Do you play a musical instrument? Have you been involved in recording, crewing, performing, or touring? Do you listen to a particular type of music?
- *Travel:* Have you done much travelling? What unique customs and experiences may be of interest to your audience? Have you encountered intercultural or language differences, and if so, what impact did they have on you or your opinions and assumptions about a group of people? How would you characterize pre- and post-9/11 (U.S. terrorist attacks) travel?

3. Choose a topic and research it with a partner.
4. Working with a partner, come up with five broad topics, and then narrow down each one into three possible themes for presentation.
5. Refer back to Chapter 1. Into which experiential learning dimension would you put researching your topic: cognitive, affective, or behavioural? Why?
6. Practise interviewing a friend, and try to use as many open-ended questions as possible. Then have your friend interview you, and have him or her concentrate on probing questions. To check your results, videotape the interviews.

## REFERENCES AND FURTHER READINGS

Babbie, E. (1998). *The practice of social research* (8th ed.). New York: Wadsworth Publishing Company.

Barone, J.T., & Switzer, J.Y. (1995). *Interviewing: Art and skill.* Boston: Allyn and Bacon.

Bender, P.U. (2001). Stand, deliver and lead. *The Canadian Manager, 26*(2), 14–17. Retrieved on April 10, 2005, from http://uccb-elearning.uccb.ca:2058/pqdweb?index=1&sid=4&srchmode=1&vinst=PROD&...

Bernard, S. (1996). *Speaking our minds: A guide to public speaking for Canadians.* Scarborough, ON: Prentice Hall.

Commissioner of Official Languages. (1999). *Annual Report 1998.* Cat. no. SF1-1998. Ottawa: Minister of Public Works and Government Services Canada.

Conway, M. (2004, April). Web survey guidelines. *Learning Circuits.* Retrieved July 20, 2005 from http://www.learningcircuits.org/2004/apr2004/conway.htm.

DeVito, J. (1997). *The elements of public speaking* (6th ed.). New York: Longman.

Eisenberg, A.M., & Gamble, T.K. (1991). *Painless public speaking: A work/text approach.* New York: University Press of America.

Halbesleben, J.R.B., & Buckley, M. R. (2004). Burnout in organizational life [Electronic version]. *Journal of Management, 30*(6), 859–879.

Harris, R. (1997). Evaluating internet research sources. *Media Awareness Network.* Retrieved July 26, 2005 from http://www.media-awareness.ca/english/resources/special_initiatives/wa_resources/wa_tea...

Hanna, M.S., & Gibson, J.W. (1995). *Public speaking for personal success* (4th ed.). Dubuque, IA: Brown & Benchmark.

Hoffman, K.B. (2005, July 18). Canada making inroads. *The Chronicle Herald* (Halifax), C2.

Huber, N. (2005). Most senior managers fear public speaking. *Computer Weekly, 2*(18), 20.

Intini, J. (2005, January 17). The resourceful generation. *Maclean's, 118*(3), 54.

Ivy, D.K., & Backlund, P. (2004). *Exploring gender speak: Personal effectiveness in gender communication* (3rd ed.). Boston: McGraw-Hill Ryerson.

Johnston, D.D. (1994). *The art and science of persuasion.* Madison, WI: WCB Brown & Benchmark.

Messmer, M. (2003, November). Public speaking success strategies. *National Public Accountant,* 26–27. Retrieved April 7, 2005, from http://uccbelearning.uccb.ca:2237/citation.asp?tb+1&_ug=sid+FC3A4341%2D6782%2D4...

Osborn, M., & Osborn, S. (1994). *Public speaking* (3rd ed.). Toronto: Houghton Mifflin.

Passmore, C., Dobbie, A.E., Parchman, M., & Tysinger, J. (2002). Guidelines for constructing a survey. *Family Medicine, 34*(4), 281–286.

Pearson, J.C., Turner, L.H., & Todd-Mancillas, W. (1991). *Gender and communication.* Dubuque, IA: Wm. C. Brown.

Penny, L. (2005). *Your call is important to us: The truth about bullshit.* Toronto: McClelland & Stewart Ltd.

Publication Manual of the American Psychological Association (5th ed.). (2001). Washington, DC: American Psychological Association.

Rolls, J.A. (2000). *Introduction to public communication.* Sydney, NS: Performance Enhancement Communication Consultants.

Stack, L. (2004). Ten time-management tips to aid presenters. *Presentations, 18*(11), 50. The online communicator: It's hard to say. (n.d.). Retrieved July 8, 2005, from http://www.online_communicator.com/hard2say.html.

University of Calgary Library. *Search the internet: Evaluating internet sources.* (n.d.). Retrieved July 26, 2005, from http://www.ucalgary.ca/library/netsearch/evaluation.html.

Zarefsky, D., & MacLennan, J. (1997). *Public speaking: Strategies for success* (Canadian ed.). Scarborough, ON: Allyn and Bacon.

# Chapter 5
## Organizing the Speech

## CHAPTER GOALS

In this chapter, you will learn
- how to develop a speech
- how to select a speech goal
- how to organize your speech
- how to open a speech so that you grab the audience's attention
- how to end a speech with a bang
- how to outline a speech

# ▊ INTRODUCTION

I attended a conference a while back and was particularly excited about the prospect of hearing one of the speakers. I had read her work and liked what she had to say. I actually met her at the opening gala the night before her presentation and found her personable and quick-witted. Her funky clothes and jewellery led me to believe that she was smart, but also cool.

I don't know what happened between then and the next day but her presentation was terrible. She was all over the place, and it looked as if she was working from three manuscripts at once and couldn't get it together. At times she would just zing along, only to switch gears, and have everything come out jumbled. She would say the same sentence three or four different ways as she attempted to clarify her thoughts. At those points, she appeared to be very unsure of herself.

What made it even worse was that the speaker before her was superb. He had a clearly stated goal and he kept us in tune with the speech structure by saying things like: "And this brings me to the third reason why . . . " In contrast, the disappointing speaker looked pretty bad.

As I write this, it occurs to me that perhaps speaker number one covered topics she had planned to present—stole her thunder, so to speak. Or, maybe she suffered from high communication apprehension and had not learned how to handle it. Whatever it was, I was surprised that such an esteemed academic would give such a poorly organized presentation.

This story underscores the importance of speech organization and this is the goal of Chapter 5—to teach you how to develop a presentation. When you *give* a speech, you

---

### SPEECH TOPICS SHOULD BE LEGAL

Whatever topic you select for your presentation, it should be legal. I say this not only because instructors do not wish to promote illegal activities in their classrooms, but because of an experience I had when I taught public speaking at Indiana University. Students were required to incorporate a visual aid into their speeches, and one young man actually pulled from a brown paper bag a real handgun! Although he innocently used it to convey just how accessible firearms were, his decision to point a gun at the class during what seemed like an interminable opening, was a poor one. It did catch our attention, though. So, no speeches on how to *commit fraud and get away with it*, how to *make false documents,* or how *to engage in money laundering.*

essentially present an opening, a body, and a conclusion. When you develop a speech, you work in a different order. You begin by finding a topic (in general), then narrow it down to a more specific one, and finally, you develop the topic in conjunction with the speech goal. Then you put it together; you select an organizational pattern, fill in the content, develop the opening, then formulate the ending. The suggestions introduced in this chapter should enable you to shape well-organized, thoughtful speeches that will move you into the realm of the professional speaker.

# DEVELOPING THE SPEECH

## About the Speech Goal

Having a specific goal makes it easier for you to develop your speech and for listeners to follow what you are saying. The speech goal is also referred to as the *speech purpose* or the *thesis statement*. When presentations lack a clear purpose, they can sound jumbled and disconnected, as did the speech that was described earlier. Speakers move back and forth between topics rather than progress in a steady, forward fashion. This can confuse and irritate listeners as they struggle to follow along. In the worst case scenarios, they give up and stop listening.

## Selecting a Speech Goal

To help you narrow your topic to a particular goal, you can follow a three-step process. Students find it helpful when they are overwhelmed and/or confused by the breadth of possibilities. This technique helps them to see the big picture first (the overall topic) and then to zero in on just one specific aspect of the topic, and that leads them to a specific goal.

### Step 1: Choose a Topic

As noted in Chapter 4, the first step in developing a speech goal is to select a general subject that interests you. At this stage, you do not have to worry about what you will say, how the presentation will be organized, or what you would do for the opening. You just need to come up with something that you find interesting. For the sake of example, take the topic *firefighting*.

### Step 2: Select One Specific Aspect of the Topic

Continuing with the firefighting theme, a thorough search (also called a *literature review*) of your library and the Internet would uncover a huge amount of material on this topic. You would likely find information on general firefighting strategies, heroic firefighting incidents, extinguishing different types of fires (such as forest fires, high-rise fires, chemical fires, etc.), post-fire investigations and forensic work, training firefighters, or fire physiology, to name just a few. Any of the listed topics could be developed into a speech. Your mission in step 2 would be to select one. For example, if fire physiology intrigued you, then your specific topic would be *fire physiology*. If you were more interested in how forest fires are fought, then that would be the specific topic. It is that simple—you choose one aspect of the general topic to speak about.

### Step 3: Nail Down a Goal

The final decision in this process is to decide how you will treat the topic for your audience. When we do speeches, it is not enough to say I'm going *to talk about fire physiology* or *talk about forest firefighting*. Instead, a speech is generally set up in one of three ways: to demonstrate, to inform, or to persuade. So, a speech goal would be *to inform the audience about techniques used in fighting forest fires*. Or, you could *inform the audience about fire physiology*. You could decide to persuade your audience to volunteer to help extinguish the next forest fire that occurs in their area. Then the goal would be *to persuade audience members to become volunteer forest firefighters*. More about the types of speech goals is presented in the next segment.

In all, these three steps take a funnel approach to selecting a goal. You begin with your general, broad topic, then you select some aspect of the topic, and finally, you decide if your goal will be to demonstrate, inform, or persuade. You work from the broad to the specific to turn a jumble of information into something you can work with.

## Types of Speech Goals

While the specific requirements associated with each type of speech goal are discussed later in the text, it is worthwhile knowing a little about these different goals.

### To Demonstrate

In a demonstrative speech, you demonstrate either how something is done or how something works. "How to Improve Your Golf Swing," "How to Manipulate Your Digital Photos," and "How to Feng Shui Your Office" are all examples of demonstrative speeches.

### To Inform

In the informative speech, you advise, familiarize, or teach your audience about something. The spousal abuse presentation referred to in Chapter 4 exemplifies an informative speech. The speaker described the physical and emotional abuse to which she was subjected in an attempt to arouse in us a feeling of just what she survived.

---

## A SPEECH GOAL DIALOGUE

Matthew: Hey Bryan, what's up?
Bryan: Not much, just tryin' to work on my speech.

Matthew: Yeah? What are you doing it on?
Bryan: Something about firefighting. (broad topic)

Matthew: Cool. What aspect are you going to cover?
Bryan: I don't know yet. I'm interested in highrise fires and chemical fires, but I think I'm going to go with forest fires. (specific topic) I was in Kelowna, B.C., a few years back when they were having those huge fires. Oh man, that was something else.

Matthew: I'll bet.
Bryan: Yeah, I was thinking that I could inform the audience about the various forest firefighting techniques they used. (goal) How about you? What are you doing yours on?

Matthew: Not sure yet—something to do with music. (general topic).
Bryan: Yeah, like what?

Matthew: Well, I'm a big Hip fan. (specific topic)
Bryan: Oh yeah—me too. I've got all their CDs. They're great, and they opened for the Stones. Me and a bunch of guys from work went. It was like the most amazing experience of my life.

Matthew: Yeah; I was hoping to go but I had to work.
Bryan: Oh, that sucks. But, you could do your speech on why the Hip is Canada's top band, although you might get some flack from the Billy Talent fans.

Matthew: Ah, they'll get over it. That's just what I'll do. I'll inform the class why the Hip are tops! (speech goal)
Bryan: Sounds great. That's one speech I know I'll enjoy.

## To Persuade

In a persuasive speech, you coax your listeners to change their opinion about something. For instance, one persuasive goal might be to convince the audience that the campus radio station performs a valuable service for the college community.

### *To Persuade to Actuate*

A second type of persuasive speech is persuasion to actuate. In this style, you attempt to induce audience members to take some form of action. For example, you could convince listeners to contact the student union and request an increase in the campus radio station's operating budget. Or, you could recruit the audience to sign a petition that calls for an increased operating budget for the station.

## Refining Your Main Points

Once the speech goal is clear, your next task is to determine the main points of the speech. I'll refer again to the topics of *fire physiology* and *extinguishing fires*. At this point, you gather the information you have collected, and decide just what you could tell an audience about *fire physiology* or *extinguishing fires*. For *extinguishing fires*, for example, you may have uncovered a lot of research on chemical fires or highrise fires but very little on burning rates. It would be wise, then, to exclude the latter and include segments on chemical fires and highrises in the speech.

Remember that you also choose information on the basis of your audience characteristics (audience analysis) and in relation to the time limit for the speech. In this case, you may think your listeners know little about fire physiology, and given that you have about six minutes for your presentation, you determine that your goal (*to inform the audience about fire physiology*) could be attained by covering three main points: backdrafts, smoke inhalation, and how fire works on various materials. Bingo—not only do you have a specific goal, but you also have the content of the

---

### DEVELOP YOUR SPEECH IN JUST NINE STEPS

1. Select a general topic that interests you.
2. Research that topic.
3. Narrow down the topic to a specific speech goal.
4. Decide whether your speech will demonstrate, inform, or persuade.
5. Think of three main points that support that goal.
6. Find interesting material that explains, supports, or exemplifies the three main points.
7. Organize the body of the speech so that it flows smoothly.
8. Develop the speech opening.
9. Develop the speech closing.

speech. You are now ready to further refine these three sub-topics and decide what you will say about each.

Working through this process goes a long way toward developing the speech you will present. However, now your task is to decide specifically how you are going to organize the speech. Public speaking does not just happen—addresses are arranged in specific ways. In fact, several conventional methods can be used to outline a speech (or even an essay or academic paper, for that matter). You could think of these as blueprints. You certainly would not build a house without a blueprint, and nor would a top speaker give a presentation without a plan for what would be said, how it would be said, and when it would be said.

# STRUCTURING THE SPEECH

Some people are natural organizers in that they know intuitively how to structure their main points so that they flow logically and make sense to an audience. Others, however, are not so lucky. Regardless of your organizational abilities, the following organizational patterns can be used to help you arrange your speech. While not every schema is discussed in this section, those most often used by students and professional speakers are profiled. These include *chronological, topical, causal, spatial,* and *problem-solving* structures.

## Chronological Structure

When you think *chronological*, think words like *successive, sequential,* or *the order of events*. A chronological pattern takes a time line or historical approach, setting up the topics in their order of occurrence. The chronological pattern is also referred to as a *temporal* (relating to time) one. If you were going to present a speech to inform visitors to Toronto about how they could spend a three-day vacation, a chronological approach might work well. The three segments in the body of the speech could be set up as day one, day two, and day three.

### Past Events

Speeches with goals to describe a series of past events work well with a chronological organizational schema. For instance, to inform the audience about the construction of the Trans Canada Trail, Canada's success rate at the Olympics, or the increase in vending machine sales could each be well executed with this type of approach.

### Demonstrative Speeches

If your speech goal is to show the audience how something is done, then a chronological approach is almost a must. When we explain how to do something, it usually makes the most sense to listeners if the steps are described in the order that they occur. Demonstrative speeches with goals such as "how to streak your own hair," "how to start a one-match campfire," or "how to sign up for courses online" could be very confusing if another approach was used.

I just hated the thought of having to do a speech and dreaded it throughout the semester. But then, as I learned how to select a topic and then organize it, it wasn't that bad. It was as if I could see the whole speech in my mind— the outline was clear. That took off a lot of pressure.

*Colin, Former Speech Student*

## Topical Structure

The *topical* approach, sometimes known as a *categorical* pattern (Zarefsky & MacLennan, 1997) is probably one of the most commonly used designs among student public speakers. You simply organize the speech around three (sometimes two and occasionally more than three) main points that ultimately meet your goal. The goal referred to in the last section, "informing the audience about how visitors to Toronto could spend a three-day vacation," could also be set up topically. The three main points could be (1) cultural attractions (museums, plays, art galleries), (2) music venues (opera, stage musicals, pop music), and (3) general tourist attractions (CN Tower, Canadian National Exhibition, Canada's Wonderland).

Refer back to the firefighting example—more specifically, the goal *to inform the audience about firefighting techniques.* If you were to use a topical pattern to organize your speech, then there could be three logical segments: fighting forest fires, fighting highrise fires, and fighting chemical fires. If, however, you wanted to inform the audience about the phases that fires typically follow, then a chronological pattern would probably be a better choice than a topical one.

# Causal Structure

This pattern is often explained as cause–effect or effect–cause in that you can set up causal arguments in either way. Zarefsky and MacLennan (1997, p. 220) put it very simply when they write, "You can focus on causes and then identify their effects, or you can begin by identifying the effects and then try to determine their underlying causes" (p. 220).

This first example is a cause-to-effect argument.

*Claim:* An increase in tuition will leave students with less spending money.

*Supporting evidence:*

a.  Students will still have to pay high rents and residence fees.

b.  They will still have to buy groceries and supplies.

c.  They will still have transportation costs.

*Conclusion:* A tuition increase will cause a reduction in students' standard of living.

---

 **EXPERT ADVICE**

How would I do a speech? I'd pick a general topic—say, eating disorders, for example—and the first thing I'd do is narrow it down. I could inform the audience about three types of disorders—anorexia, bulimia, and binge eating. To determine what I'd say about each one, I have three rules for myself: the information I include must be interesting for the audience, be something I know about, and be easy to research. Because classroom speeches are short, I'd select just the most stimulating information that I uncover in my literature search. Further, if I knew someone with an eating disorder, I would include their personal experiences with the problem.

The last thing I would do is figure out the intro and conclusion. I could possibly start with some statistics, like how even toddlers are aware of their body images. Or I'd describe how, in my experience as a Brownie leader, that little girls, ages seven to nine years, are already sensitive to the flaws in both their own and others' bodies. That's how I'd go about organizing a speech.

*Ann Cordeau, Teacher*
*Former Communication Lab Peer Facilitator*

---

The next example is an effect-to-cause argument.

*Claim:* Jim failed his course because of neglect.

*Supporting evidence:*

a.  He skipped half of his classes.

b.  He did not hand in the required assignments.

c.  He did not study for the exam.

*Conclusion:* Jim needs to pay more attention to his work if he wants to pass.

## Spatial Structure

In a spatial structure, you discuss or set up your topic in terms of where it is located in space. For example, if your speech goal was *to characterize employment opportunities in Canada,* you might begin on the West Coast with British Columbia and work your way across the country. You would end by describing the situation in the East and cite examples from Newfoundland and Labrador.

Speeches that have as their goal to describe equal parts of a whole work well with a spatial pattern. Topics such as "Product Arrangement in Super Market Chains," "My Trip Across Europe," or "How to Plant a Vegetable Garden" would work well with a spatial arrangement.

---

##  EXPERT ADVICE

I like to encourage my students to find creative (but informed) solutions or approaches to the presentations they will be doing in their business classes. They may have the best idea or the best "answer" for the situation at hand, but if they are unable to support that idea with solid evidence (do your homework!) and unable to get that idea across in a logical, well-thought-out, organized manner, they will be 'shouted' down in the boardroom.

*Kendra Carmichael, Lecturer*
*F.C. Manning School of Business, Acadia University, N.S.*

---

## Problem-Solving Structure

According to DeVito (1997, p. 218), "The problem-solving pattern is especially useful in persuasive speeches where you want to convince the audience that a problem exists and your solution would solve or lessen it." The body of the speeches organized in this manner has only two main parts: the first part focuses on the problem, and the second part presents the solution. This strategy is particularly good for showing people what is wrong with something and how it can be fixed. It is very straightforward.

I think a lot of politicians use the problem-solving structure. For instance, to convince an audience to vote for them, politicians point out the economic and social problems that exist in their riding. If the politician is not the incumbent, then the problems are blamed on the opposition's policies. Once the problems are outlined, the politician entertains the listeners with how her or his party will solve them.

Once you have outlined your speech and determined what content you will include, your next step is to work on the opening.

---

 **EXPERT ADVICE**

Sometimes speakers have a very catchy verbal opening, but look down at their notes (and even read their names) at the onset of the speech. I realize that some people are just so high-strung and nervous that they look aside as a form of escape. However, even if their departure lasts only a split second, such a nonverbal message reduces a speaker's credibility. I think it is exceedingly important to supplement a great verbal attention getter with an equally great nonverbal display of confidence.

*Bob, Member of Toastmasters International*

---

## ◼ OPENING THE SPEECH

Having a well-thought-out speech opening is vital for success because this is when you create your first impression, and you want it to be a good one. It is the time to appear confident, trustworthy, and honest—all the characteristics associated with credible speakers. As well, it is during the opening that you set the tone for your presentation. This helps the audience understand how they are to interpret your message. Some speakers like to begin with an incentive. They reason that if you tell the audience what's in it for them, they are more likely to listen to you.

You can achieve all of this by organizing your introduction in a way that allows you to make and maintain a connection with the audience. Below is the magic recipe— the outline, blueprint, or key—to a successful opening. Your job is to fill it in so that your introduction is unique and engaging. Each of these steps is discussed in this section of the chapter.

1. Provide a good, strong attention getter.
2. State the goal of the speech (your thesis statement) and present an overview of what you are going to speak about (your enumerated preview).
3. Provide a smooth transition into your first major topic.

## Attention Getters

Once the audience is settled and you are ready (the clean beginning), start your presentation with something that will grab the listeners' attention. Do this by using anecdotes or narratives, questions, visual aids, songs, pertinent quotations, innovative uses of your body or the space around you, or whatever is relevant to your topic. I have often had students whose speech goal was to inform the class about tae kwon do begin by breaking a block of wood in half with their bare feet. Clearly, the audience pays attention to such students. Compare that type of opening with a more staid question, such as, "How many of you exercise regularly?" Surely, most listeners would be more attracted by an initial kick-start demonstration.

Below is an overview of typical attention getters that can be used to get your audience to tune in to you and your presentation.

---

 **EXPERT ADVICE**

If possible, I like to start my conversation with my audience after I introduce myself by promising them a reward for their attention. I might say that in this group, there are five of you who will become rich. Or, in my particular role, I offer them a discount on purchases or support for their organizations.

*Sam "The Record Man" Sniderman*
*Toronto, Ontario*

---

### *Anecdotes and Narratives*

Anecdotes and narratives are short stories that are particularly useful for attracting attention. And, because most people enjoy a good story, especially a personal one about the speaker, using one lures the audience into listening to you. Further, listeners tend to remember anecdotes; I know my students always recall the stories I share in class far better than the theoretical perspectives these stories support.

However, a few cautions regarding the use of narratives are in order:

- They should be relevant to your topic.
- You should point out to the audience "the connection between your story and the point you are making" (DeVito, 1997, p. 153). While the correlation between the two may be obvious to you, it may not be so clear to some listeners.
- Watch that your stories are not too personal, because you do not want to disclose something you may later regret.
- Narratives should not be too long. Even though they may be interesting and provocative, keep them in proportion to your speaking time. A narrative that takes up half of your time is definitely too long.
- Finally, because narratives work so well in the opening, some students insert several throughout the presentation and thus overdo it. Keep in mind that stories should supplement the main points, not become them.

## Questions

Posing questions is another possible way to get the audience's attention. Questions can be rhetorical (where you do not expect a response) or not. For example, you might ask for a show of hands on some topic or issue. Questions work because they engage the audience. Listeners respond either out loud or in their heads. Either way, you have gotten into their heads and pulled their minds toward you.

However, the questions also have to be thoughtful. What do you think of the following as an attention getter? "How many of you went to the women's basketball game last night? (Pause for a show of hands.) That's just what I expected. Today I am going to encourage you to support our women's team. I will discuss . . . " As a listener, I just do not find the one-question opener is much of an attention getter because there is not enough time to become engaged. However, for some subjects the right question—one that has some emotional impact and that relates precisely to that particular audience—just might do the trick.

The more developed and descriptive the questions are, the more listeners are forced to psychologically and cognitively identify with the process and, hence, to provide a thoughtful response. For instance, "How many of you have experienced feelings of nervousness or insecurity before you had to make a major presentation. How about physiological symptoms of nervousness? How many of you have experienced butter-flies, fears of forgetting, irrational thoughts like, 'Everyone knows exactly how I feel?' " Compare this with the lone, naked question, "How many of you feel nervous before you do a speech?" I personally think the first, longer opening with multiple questions garners more interest on the listeners' part.

## WHAT MAKES YOU PAY ATTENTION?

It is the perception process that accounts for our ability to take in, process, and give meaning to the wide array of stimuli to which we are exposed. According to psychologists and communication scholars, we have to select information from our surroundings before we can attach significance to it. What is it that makes you pay attention to certain messages and yet be oblivious to others?

Well, it is really quite simple: people are likely to pay attention to messages that are more intense than others, that are repetitive, or that contrast sharply with the environment. Developing attention getters that include these elements is very effective.

Another major factor in determining what information we pay attention to has to do with our own motives. If you are late, you see the clock; if you're after a bargain, you spot the sale sign; if you are listening to a speech, you zero in on what relates to you. This suggests that your material must be relevant to the audience.

## *Quotations*

Quotations make good attention getters because you can use the words of talented individuals to more eloquently voice what you wish to express. When you quote a famous, respected person, you are also psychologically associated with that person, which in turn can actually elevate your status in the eyes of the audience. When you begin with a quotation, try to provide a clear segue, or transition, from the quotation into your opening remarks. This will ensure that the relationship between them is apparent to all listeners.

## *Statistics*

Statistics are most effective as attention getters when they are extreme or staggering, when they are unknown to the audience members, and when they relate specifically to the listeners. Just starting your presentation with one line that includes a statistic will not be enough to engage your audience. Nor will bombarding the audience with so many facts that they cannot possibly process that amount of information. When you use statistics, you must include your source; for instance: "According to Statistics Canada's 1996 Census Nation tables, there were about five times more single female than single male parent families." Notice that this sentence simplifies the data for the listeners, helping them to see the message contained in the precise statistics: 945 230 single female parent families and 192 275 single male parent families.

### Visual Aids

Visual aids that are professionally prepared and used well can be very effective. They give the audience something to focus on. In a discussion among communication scholars about whether PowerPoint or other computer-mediated devices should be used in introductory speech courses, one professor argued strongly that the visual presence of key words or an outline reinforced the speaker's message. This, in turn, enabled listeners to follow more easily the arguments being presented. I agree. Visual aids can support and enhance your verbal message . . . and make fitting attention getters.

## How *Not* to Open a Speech

### What's Wrong with a Little Humour?

There is a common misconception that starting with a little humour or a joke is a good way to begin a speech. In some cases this may be so, such as in contexts where you are familiar with the audience. Perhaps you have worked with them before and know

"If I can put everyone to sleep within the first five minutes, the rest of my presentation should go pretty well."

Randy Glasbergen

them well. If I am doing several consecutive communication consulting sessions, humour can make a compelling opening, especially if I refer to past events we have all experienced.

Humour, however, should definitely be avoided if you do not know your audience. What is funny to you and your friends may not be relevant to the particular group. Even worse, you could end up insulting audience members. One former politician in my area started a presentation with a joke that most people thought was better suited for the locker room. On top of that, it was sexist and alienated more than half of the audience.

Another problem with using humour is that some people just lack the timing required to present a joke in a way that makes it funny, so the joke falls flat. If you are such a person, avoid using jokes. Imagine that you were very nervous about a particular presentation, you decided to open with a joke—and it bombed. What would that do for your confidence?

### Why Shouldn't I Apologize?

Never open a speech with an apology because it will be interpreted as a lack of preparation on your part and can actually leave the audience seeking out your weaknesses and slight imperfections. For example, "I'm afraid I was asked to do this speech only yesterday so I haven't really had time to prepare . . ." is not a good opening—in fact, it almost tells the audience to prepare for an inadequate presentation. If you act in a confident manner, the audience will think that you are confident.

Many professionals end up doing unprepared presentations because they are asked to do so at the last minute. They may feel nervous, but they do the speech anyway, and often no one is aware of their apprehensiveness or lack of preparation. Recall from Chapter 2 that regardless of how you may feel on the inside, listeners cannot perceive this unless you communicate it to them.

## Miscellaneous Openings

Other considerations for the speech opening include naming specific audience members, complimenting the audience, and introducing yourself and establishing your credibility.

### Refer to Audience Members

Referring to audience members by name can be an impressive way to open your presentation. This strategy sets a personal, interactive tone and it definitely attracts attention, particularly from those to whom you have referred. Others in the audience may choose to listen because of the possibility that you may mention them as well. With this technique, everyone's ears perk up.

## Compliment the Audience

Finally, the openings I have discussed so far relate mostly to classroom speeches. When you speak to professional or community audiences, thank the organizers for inviting you to speak. You might also refer to the specific occasion, and in some instances, compliment the audience: "It is always a pleasure to speak to the Canadian Paraplegic Association."

## Introduce Yourself and Establish Your Credibility

Introducing yourself and establishing your credibility is not required if someone introduces you at length, noting your accomplishments and experience. To further increase your credibility in such a situation would be overkill and could actually reduce your credibility. If you are not formally introduced, you might mention experiences related specifically to your topic or purpose.

Now you have several ideas for opening your speech and getting the audience's attention. In some instances, you might choose a combination of the strategies outlined in this section. Choose the ones best suited to the particular occasion.

There are still two important details that you need to provide before you move on to the first main point of your speech—your introduction/goal statement, and an enumerated preview.

---

### OPENING YOUR SPEECH

Below are two openings for the same speech. Read them and consider their strengths and weaknesses. Which one do you think is better? Why? What would you do to improve these attention getters?

#### ATTENTION GETTER 1

Have you ever considered how forest fires operate? Or, perhaps you have noticed on television newscasts how forest fires leap from one area to another? Or, have you ever thought about the influence that wind and air pressure might have on forest fires? Today I am going to inform you about forest fire physiology. In this presentation, I will provide facts and information about forest fire conditions, backdrafts, and wind changes.

#### ATTENTION GETTER 2

It was unusually warm that summer evening as Justin, Caleigh, and I sat on our summer cottage deck that overlooked the oddly quiet lake. Justin was fooling around, trying to get an ant to crawl up his finger; Caleigh was writing

---

in her journal; and I was just staring at nothing. But something wasn't right, although I couldn't put my finger on it. Then, out of the silence, the phone rang. It almost gave me a heart attack as shots of adrenaline swept through my body. Even on this very calm, beautiful evening, it seemed like we were courting disaster.

I jumped out of my chair and, almost in one movement, landed in the cottage at the telephone. It turned out to be nothing, just my mom wondering if everything was OK. I thought it odd that she should call. We were in our late teens, and had second-degree black belts in tae kwon do.

We decided to play Monopoly, and just as we finished organizing everything, this gust of wind came out of nowhere. Everything went flying, and it took three of us to hold down the big green market umbrella. But, strangely enough, as quickly as that rogue wind blew up, it became still again. As we tidied up, I could smell whiffs of wood smoke, probably coming from a cookout farther down the beach.

We started up the game again, but it didn't last. That wind–smoke incident was just the beginning. You see, we were about to face the most challenging ordeal of our lives. We were about to be engulfed in a forest fire.

In this presentation I will inform you about forest fire physiology and review three major aspects of forest fire physiology: forest conditions, backdrafts, and wind changes. Hopefully, after hearing this speech, you will be more attentive to the telltale forerunners that we sensed, but did not understand.

## Introduction and Goal Statement

After you do your attention getter, you should introduce yourself, particularly in classroom speeches where students often do not know one another's names. Of course, in contexts where you have already been introduced, there is no need to do so.

Once you have completed your introduction, it is crucial to state the specific goal of your speech. This is called the *goal statement* or the *thesis statement*. Recall from earlier in the chapter that the goal statement must be expressed in the following terms: to inform, to persuade, or to demonstrate. To say you will "talk about" such and such is not specific enough.

Failing to include such a statement in your opening is a serious public speaking error. As discussed earlier, it is imperative for listeners to understand the purpose of your presentation so they will know where you are going. They learn this through your goal statement, and knowing it in advance keeps listeners on track.

## Enumerated Preview

Because listening is difficult, it is up to the speaker to provide as many markers as possible for the audience. The first one is the goal statement. That should be followed by an *enumerated preview*, which refers to the overview of the topics you will cover in your speech. For example, if you are going to inform the audience about sexually transmitted diseases (STDs), the goal statement and enumerated preview might go something like "Today I will inform you about the prevalence of STDs by explaining their symptoms and complications, how they are transmitted, and how they can be prevented." This enumerated preview tells the listeners just what you will be speaking about. (By the way, can you identify the type of organizational pattern this example is following?)

## Transitions

After you have gained the audience's attention, introduced yourself and the topic, and presented the enumerated preview, the last step in the introduction is to provide a smooth transition into your first main point. Transitions serve as markers that will further help to keep the listeners on course. They are employed throughout the speech each time you segue into a new topic or subtopic. In particular, they are required between the opening and the body, between the topics within the body, and between the body and the conclusion.

Using the STDs example, here are two sample transitions from the "symptoms" topic to the "transmittal" topic:

- Now that you are aware of just some of the symptoms of STDs and the problems they cause, you might be more interested in learning how they are contracted, and that is what I will speak about next. STDs . . .
- STDs are much more prevalent and more easily transmitted than most people believe. You probably do not want to get them or pass them on to others. There are several ways you can prevent the acquisition and the spread of STDs. First, you can . . .

## HOW TO USE TRANSITIONS

Gregory (2005) describes four types of transitions that will enable you to link your thoughts and ideas. They are: bridges, internal summaries, signposts, and spotlights. Examples of how to use these are included below.

**Bridges:** With bridges, you tell the audience you're moving from one thought to another. For example, say you were giving a speech titled *Managing through Communication* and you had just completed your first major point—that managers need to be sensitive to the nonverbal messages they are both sending and receiving. Your next main point would be focused on verbal communication, saying what you mean. Your bridge transition would go something like the following: "So while being more aware of what your body is saying to others is one way to improve your management skills, being able to say what you mean is another."

Here are more examples of bridges.

"Although crime rates in Canada are going down each year, we still need to protect our homes against invasion."

"Undercoating your car each year is a good way to maintain the body. Regular oil changes also increase the car's lifespan."

"These are some of the ways you can motivate potential clients to use your firm. But once you have them, you need to provide quality service. Here are some ways to do that."

"So you can see that Canadians pay pretty much the same for their hardware goods at Canadian Tire, Home Hardware, and Home Depot. Let's compare this to our American cousins."

**Internal Summaries:** Internal summaries provide a "concise review of material covered during the body of the speech" (Gregory, 2005, p. 244). This type of transition is particularly useful when your speech contains complex issues and ideas. See the following:

"I've explained the classifications of nonverbal communication and offered some strategies to help you avoid language pitfalls that prevent you from saying what you mean. But now, for all that to work, you have to be willing to change your communication style."

"I hope I've convinced you why it is so important to protect yourself against West Nile virus. My next job is to inform you how to do this."

"I've tried to show you how the boomer generation influenced changes in the way society viewed a lot of things. But this new generation is going a long way to fight racism, sexism, ageism, homophobia, and the like."

"So far, I've discussed what goes into the speech opening, how to organize the body, and how to use transitions. You aren't finished, however, until you have a zinger of an ending."

"So far, the steps in running a training session are—complete a needs assessment, design the training, and develop visual aids and materials. Next I'll discuss some delivery strategies."

**Signposts:** The third type of transition that Gregory (2005) talks about is the signpost. Just like most road signs indicate where you're going, so too do oral signposts. These transitions generally involve numbers.

"The third way to make your storefront more appealing is . . ."

"If you want to invest in penny stocks, the first thing you must do is . . ."

"The first available option is . . .. The second is . . ."

"Once you decide how much you want to pay for your entertainment centre, there are two more major decisions you need to make."

"In addition to the financial remuneration, there are the personal benefits."

**Spotlights:** The last type of transition is the spotlight and this informs the audience that what you are going to say next is very important.

"If you know the answer to the following trivia question, you could win a laptop computer."

"But wait! That's not all. If you . . ."

"Here is probably the most important thing you can do to get the staff on board."

"You will be amazed how this next technique will improve your game."

"Once you've dispensed with these preliminaries, you can get down to business."

# ENDING THE SPEECH

Although the ending is short, it deserves attention because it serves several functions: to summarize, to motivate, and to provide closure (DeVito, 1997). Some students let their speeches just fizzle, or they say something like, "Well, that's all I have to say." Other students do the opposite: they introduce new material, or they drag out the ending. Neither approach makes for a professional conclusion. A clear, distinct closing allows you to finish on a positive, confident note.

You can do several things to end your speech in a professional manner: summarize and restate your major points, make a plea, use a quotation, or present a poignant anecdote. You may also do a combination of these, choosing the ones most relevant to your goal.

Finally, you may wish to thank the audience members for their attention.

## SNAPSHOT OF A TOPIC OUTLINE

### INTRODUCTION
- attention getter
- introduction and goal statement
- enumerated preview
- transition into first major point

### BODY

### MAIN POINT ONE
- supporting point one
- supporting point two
- supporting point three
- transition into second major point

MAIN POINT TWO
- supporting point one
- supporting point two
- supporting point three
- transition into third major point

MAIN POINT THREE
- supporting point one
- supporting point two
- supporting point three
- transition into conclusion

**CONCLUSION**
- summarization/main points
- possible plea, quotation, anecdote
- thanks

## Summarize and Restate Your Major Points

Summarizing and restating your major points reminds the audience about what you have said and provides another opportunity to offer a listening marker. Remember too that audience members have probably not paid total attention throughout the presentation. Thus, the summary and restatement can alert them to some fact they may have missed, or that the speech is coming to a close.

Using the STDs example, you could summarize by saying something like "I have informed you of the symptoms and complications of STDs, how STDs are spread, and what you can do to prevent STDs."

## Make a Plea

Once you have restated your main points, you might like to end by making a plea. You could say, "I have informed you of the symptoms and complications of STDs, how STDs are spread, and what you can do to prevent STDs. So, regardless of how well you think you know your new sexual partner, or how upstanding he or she may be, please use condoms."

## Use Quotations and Anecdotes

Just as quotations and anecdotes work well as attention getters, they also make good concluding remarks. They incite the audience to pay more attention, they offer a unique avenue for you to communicate your thoughts and ideas, and they can bolster your arguments. A compelling quotation or anecdote leaves the audience with a revitalized sense of your energy, conviction, and effectiveness as a speaker.

## Thank the Audience

Whether or not to thank an audience is a matter of preference. Some instructors teach students not to thank the audience and in some contexts, this would be appropriate. Other communication scholars hold that a simple thank you signals the end of the speech, functions as a clean ending, and sends a polite, professional message.

# ▉ OUTLINING THE SPEECH

As you go through the process of deciding your speech goal, the three major points you will make, and how you will open and close the speech, it is a good idea to write out a speech outline. This way, you have a visual representation of the speech.

Another important reason for writing an outline is that speech instructors can review it to determine whether your speech will work. They can do this because they know if your attention getter is a fascinating one or requires further development, whether you have incorporated smooth transitions into the speech, whether your major points support your goal, and whether the speech is organized in a way that will allow it to flow well. It is common practice among public speaking professors to require students to submit a speech outline before the presentation so they can review it and offer suggestions on how the speech could be improved, all before you go in front of an audience. You may also be requested to submit the references you use in your speech. See pages 128 and 129 in Chapter 4 for a review of the APA reference formatting style.

Speeches can be outlined in two ways: a *topic* outline and a *complete-sentence* outline. Gregory (2005) notes that many people use both styles. They use the topic at the beginning of the process to help them sort out their main points and full sentence at the end when they are refining the presentation.

## Topic Outline

In the topic outline, you include the major topics you will discuss. For example, one student's speech purpose was "How to Improve Your Listening Skills" (a topic outline is provided in the accompanying box).

---

| **HOW TO IMPROVE YOUR LISTENING SKILLS** |
| --- |

Opening
1. Things that block listening
   - A. *Faulty hearing*
   - B. *Language barriers*
   - C. *Perception problems*
2. Bad listening habits
   - A. *Pseudolistening*
   - B. *Selective listening*
   - C. *Defensive listening*
3. Steps to improvement
   - A. *Hard work*
   - B. *Problem elimination*
   - C. *Practice*

Conclusion

## Complete-Sentence Outline

The mechanics of the complete-sentence outline are much more specific. First, there is a precise system for numbering and lettering the items that are included in the speech. A combination of Roman and Arabic numerals are used. See the box below for an empty outline that you can use as a template for your speeches. Instructions in each section of the template serve as reminders of what should be included. A sample of a complete-sentence outline submitted by public speaking student Stephanie Wadden is provided in the box on pages 161–164.

### *Notes*

You will find that the complete-sentence outline is almost like writing out a speech and serves to help speakers clarify their thoughts. It should not, however, be used as a practice guide. Once you have written your outline, the next step is to transform that information into notes.

The quality of your notes and how you use your notes during your presentation has a great influence on your credibility. Therefore, they are included in Chapter 6, which looks at how to present a speech in a credible manner.

## TEMPLATE OF A COMPLETE-SENTENCE OUTLINE

INTRODUCTION

### I. Attention Getter
*(Select anecdote/narrative, questions, visual aids, quotations, statistics, and so on.)*

### II. Goal Statement
*(Select from demonstrate, inform, persuade, or persuade to actuate, and state the specific goal of the speech.)*

### III. Enumerated Preview
*(State the three main points you will make in support of your goal.)*

### IV. Transition
*(Include a transition that will take you to your first main point.)*

BODY

### I. Main Point One
*(All points are written in declarative sentences. For example, "STDs are much more prevalent than we tend to believe.")*

A. SUPPORT FOR MAIN POINT ONE
*(All points are written in declarative sentences.)*
1.   example of support for main point one
2.   example of support for main point one
3.   yet another example of support for main point one

B. MORE SUPPORT FOR MAIN POINT ONE
1.   example
2.   another example

TRANSITION INTO MAIN POINT TWO

### II. Main Point Two

A. SUPPORT FOR MAIN POINT TWO
1.   example of support for main point two
2.   another example of support for main point two

B. MORE SUPPORT FOR MAIN POINT TWO
1. example
2. another example

TRANSITION INTO MAIN POINT THREE

### III. Main Point Three

A. SUPPORT FOR MAIN POINT THREE
1. example of support for main point three
2. another example of support for main point three

B. MORE SUPPORT FOR MAIN POINT THREE
1. example
2. another example

TRANSITION INTO THE CONCLUSION

CONCLUSION

### I. Summarize main points.

### II. Include a plea, quotation, or anecdote.

### III. Thank the audience.

REFERENCES

## SAMPLE OF A COMPLETE-SENTENCE SPEECH OUTLINE

by Stephanie Wadden

### TITLE: DIETING—THE GOOD AND THE BAD

INTRODUCTION

### I. Attention Getter
A recent survey showed that 70 percent of Canadian women wanted to reduce their weight, one in four Canadians is currently dieting, and within 1–5 years about 95 percent of people who lose weight will regain it, and often more.

### II. Goal Statement
Today I'll inform you how to diet so that you will be healthy and successful.

### III. Enumerated Preview

I will start off by talking about some of the reasons why we choose to diet. Then I'll discuss fad diets, and explain how to diet in a healthy manner.

### IV. Transition

I'm sure that many of you may have known, or know people, who have tried dieting. I will start by offering some of the reasons why people choose to diet.

BODY

### I. Main Point One

Before we make the decision to go on a diet, there must be a reason or triggering event that provokes us to make the decision. However, the reason for dieting varies among different people.

A. Some people want to change some aspect of their physical appearance.

1. Society itself has a large effect on the way people look at themselves and the pressure from society and the media may cause you to want to go on a diet.
2. Upcoming weddings, reunions, and different social events are other reasons why some people decide to diet. They want to look a certain way, fit into a certain outfit, or impress others.
3. Some people want to change their body image just for themselves. Whether it is for personal satisfaction or to fit into certain trendy clothes, they diet just for themselves. They are not pressured or influenced by anyone else.

B. Many people diet to stay healthy or to stay in shape.

1. Obesity is a growing problem in Canada and many of us are aware of the devastating effect it can have on a person's health.
2. Regardless of age or weight, some people just like to eat nutritious food because it helps them to maintain and repair their body or to keep their body healthy.

**Transition:** However, sometimes people don't choose the healthiest methods of dieting.

### II. Main Point Two

Fad diets are used world wide and there are so many different ones that it is hard to keep up with the latest diet "trends."

A. Some well known fad diets include the Atkins diet, the Cabbage Soup diet, and the Grapefruit/Fruit juice diet.

1.  The Atkins diet is a low carbohydrate plan. Avoiding carbohydrates keeps your body from adding weight. The method includes no more than 20 grams of carbohydrates per day. (Go on to explain the negative effects of the diet.)
2.  The Cabbage Soup diet consists mostly of eating cabbage soup. You can eat it as often as you like and you can eat as much as you would like. This is incorporated into a seven-day plan that only allows you to eat certain fruits and vegetables, and on two of the seven days, meat. (Go on to explain the negative effects of the diet.)
3.  The Grapefruit/Fruit juice diet is based on drinking large amounts of water and grapefruit/fruit juice. You can also consume large amounts of meat, fatty foods, and condiments. However, you are not allowed to eat any carbs or fruit. (Go on to explain the negative effects of the diet.)

B. Other fad diets are designed within specific time frames, such as the 3 Day diet or the 7 Day All You Can Eat diet.

1.  The 3 Day diet runs over 3 days and allows you to drink coffee and eat a lot of protein foods such as eggs and peanut butter. There are specific instructions to drink four glasses of water or diet soda per day. (Explain further.)
2.  The 7 Day All You Can Eat diet allows you to eat large amounts of specific foods on certain days of the week. This includes fruit (except for bananas) on Monday; vegetables (using only soy sauce, vinegar or mustard) on Tuesday; fruits and vegetables on Wednesday, etc. (Explain further.)

**Transition:** Although these diet plans seem to be a quick way to lose weight, you can see that they really are not good for your health in the long run. So now that I've talked about the bad dieting plans, I will speak to you a bit about how to lose weight in a healthy and effective way.

### III. Main Point Three

Most dieters want to see fast results. However, faster isn't always better, as you can see by the negative effects many of the fad diets can have on your body. If you can be patient and diet the correct way, then you will see results. Sometimes it just takes a bit of time and adjusting to get used to it. Effective dieting plans are easier than you think.

A. The biggest issue with dieting is proportion size.

1. Many people eat the proper foods but their proportions are too large. Cutting back on proportion size could work wonders for people. (Explain and compare proportion sizes using objects.)*

2. Another place where we see large portions is in the junk food industry. You do not have to cut junk food out of your life totally as long as you use it in moderation and are aware of proportion sizes. Also, don't eliminate all fatty foods because you do need some fats in order to stay healthy. Fats found in nuts, avocados, olives and fish may protect against heart disease. (Explain more about moderation of junk food and fats.)

B. Here are some tips and ways that you can eat and diet properly without going out of your way to buy fancy diet food.

1. Eat high fibre, whole grain foods instead of white bread, potatoes, sugar, or pasta. Also, if you eat foods that are high in protein, you will feel less hungry.

2. Eat water-filled fruits and vegetables such as watermelon and tomatoes to make you feel full. (Further explain.)

**Transition:** Combining these diet tips with an exercise routine, as well as drinking six to eight glasses of water a day, is a healthier and more successful way to diet.

CONCLUSION
**I. Summarize and restate main points.**
Today I have talked to you about dieting. I've provided information on why people diet, explained some of the popular fad diets, and suggested a more healthy way of dieting.
**II. Include a plea, quotation, or anecdote.**
Should you decide to diet, I hope you will remember my speech and say no to fad diets.
Remember, as Hal Johnson and Joanne MacLeod would say, "Keep fit and have fun!"
**III. Thank the audience.**
Thank you.
* Show a deck of cards to illustrate a serving size of meat and a light bulb to indicate a portion of potatoes.

# CHAPTER AT A GLANCE

- When you organize a speech, you develop the body first.
- Choose a specific goal before you begin to structure your speech.
- Speech goals are generally to demonstrate, to inform, or to persuade.
- Several organizational patterns can be used to outline a speech: chronological, spatial, topical, causal, and problem solving.
- The speech opening and closing are constructed *after* the body of the speech is developed.
- The speech opening contains an attention getter, an introduction and goal statement, an enumerated preview, and a transition into the first main topic.
- Anecdotes and narratives, questions, quotations, statistics, and visual aids all make good attention getters.
- Speeches generally have three main points and support for each of those main points.
- Transitions are used throughout the speech to link ideas and to help listeners follow along with ease.
- In the speech conclusion, you summarize and restate your main points, make a plea or offer a quotation or anecdote, and thank the audience.
- A speech outline provides a visual representation of your speech.

# APPLICATION AND DISCUSSION QUESTIONS

1. Answer the following questions in your communication journal:
   a. *Cognitive dimension:* Which of the issues covered in this chapter will have the most impact on how you will develop and organize your future speeches? Why?
   b. *Affective dimension:* Think back to a time when you were developing a speech. What emotions did you experience? Did you feel excitement, frustration, nervousness, pressure, apathy, insecurity, confusion, optimism, panic, calm, boredom, bewilderment, cockiness, laziness, exhaustion, strength, fury, happiness, hope, or other emotions? How can the knowledge you gained from this chapter alter any of these emotions? Explain.
   c. *Behavioural dimension:* Think about some of the speeches or presentations you have given. Do you typically open or end them in the same way? Do you often use the same organizational schema?

2. Think back to the last speech you heard. How well was it organized? Was a specific organizational pattern used? If so, which one? How would the speech have been different if it had been arranged, say, with a spatial or chronological approach?

3. Design a speech goal that would work well with each of the common organizational patterns discussed in the chapter: chronological, topical, causal, spatial, and problem solving.

4. Which organizational patterns would be best for the following informative speeches? Once you have selected the best pattern, make up three main topics that would satisfy the goal, and then organize the topics in an appropriate order.
   a. "How to Paint a Room"
   b. "The Harm Caused by Smoking"
   c. "Unemployment Rates in Canada"
   d. "Three Ways to Safely Invest $1000"
   e. "How to Make Spaghetti and Meatballs"

5. With a partner, develop a topic speech outline for three speeches: one to demonstrate, one to inform, and one to persuade. After you have finished, trade your work with that of another pair. Review their outlines and offer suggestions as to how they may be improved.

6. Ask your instructor to play videotaped speeches presented by former students. As a class, evaluate the openings, bodies, and endings. Are any common mistakes made?

## REFERENCES AND FURTHER READINGS

Adler, R.B., Towne, N., and Rolls, J.A. (2004). *Looking Out/Looking In* (2nd Canadian ed.). Toronto: Thomson Nelson.

DeVito, J.A. (1997). *The elements of public speaking* (6th ed.). New York: Longman.

Gregory, H. (2005). Public speaking for college and career (7th ed.). Boston: McGraw Hill.

Rolls, J.A. (2000). *Introduction to public communication.* Sydney, NS: Performance Enhancement Communication Consultants.

Zarefsky, D., & MacLennan, J. (1997). *Public speaking: Strategies for success* (Canadian ed.). Scarborough, ON: Allyn and Bacon.

# Chapter 6
## Credibility

## CHAPTER GOALS

In this chapter, you will learn
- how to make audiences believe in you
- how to develop notes
- how to use a language style that adds to your credibility
- how to adapt your language style to the setting
- how to avoid common grammatical errors
- how and why to use inclusive language

# INTRODUCTION

Have you ever noticed that some speakers just seem gifted? They grab your attention the minute they walk to the podium. While it may be difficult to pinpoint exactly what it is about them—maybe their mannerisms, clothing, or the way they take command— one thing is certain, they garner credibility. For example, I once attended an annual businesswomen's dinner, and of course there was the proverbial guest speaker. While I have long since forgotten her name, I well remember her dynamism. She was young, bright, interesting, and funny. She knew what she was talking about, she connected with the audience, and she delivered her speech in a professional and personable manner. She kept the audience on its toes and the women loved her. In other words, she was a hit!

On the other hand, we have all been subjected to speakers who lacked appeal. As a result, we tended not to trust or believe them, and sometimes, we may have even labelled them as shifty or sleazy. Again, credibility—actually, a lack of it—contributes to such a response.

The goal of this chapter is to explain how to deliver a presentation so that your expertise, trustworthiness, and competence are highlighted. The chapter focuses on message delivery. *Message delivery* in this chapter refers to the use of notes and the seemingly subtle and inconspicuous language strategies that contribute to, rather than detract from, credibility. While the previous chapter zeroed in on how to select and organize a topic—what to say—this chapter looks at how to say it.

# SPEAKER CREDIBILITY

## What Is Credibility?

Credibility has been recognized as an important ingredient in the success of speakers since the days of the ancient Greeks and Romans. Johnston (1994) notes, "According to Aristotle, a speaker is evaluated according to his or her knowledge on a topic—the extent to which the speaker is believable (expertise) and the extent to which the audience feels the speaker has its best interest at heart (trustworthiness)" (p. 151).

These factors—expertise and trustworthiness—still hold true today. For example, who would you accept advice from: people who do not know what they are talking about, or those who have a handle on the situation? Similarly, who is more likely to persuade you to do something: someone you trust, or someone you do not? To have a positive impact on an audience, you must be credible.

## Charisma

Related to credibility is the notion of charisma. Johnston (1994) writes that "Charisma is often equated with personality and dynamism but is perhaps best described as a diffuse, magical, mesmerizing quality that draws people to attend to, enjoy, and genuinely like a speaker" (p. 153). The speaker I referred to at the beginning of this chapter was charismatic—at least on that occasion. Johnston suggests that charisma is a combination of modesty, wit, and rapport, and listeners may feel that such speakers are directing their remarks to them personally.

In general, charismatic speakers are rare, and it is a joy to listen to one. Former Prime Minister Pierre Elliott Trudeau was described by many as charismatic. Although later in his term of office he was perceived by detractors as arrogant, the eruption of Trudeaumania during his election campaign in 1968 attests to his exceptional appeal. Clearly, charismatic speakers are credible speakers. When Trudeau's son Justin delivered the eulogy at his father's funeral, people across Canada commented on the father and son's likeness and allure. Perhaps one day the nation will see Justin follow his father's example.

One caution, though: coupled with the notion of charisma is ethics. Hitler was also a charismatic speaker, but clearly not an ethical one. Some speakers use their talent for evil rather than for good, which is why it is important for audience members to be critical listeners.

## Establishing Credibility

Establishing credibility is an interesting phenomenon. First, speakers should engage in such commonsense behaviours as informing listeners of their competence and expertise in the area, citing sources and statistics, speaking in a confident tone, and limiting the use of distracting adaptors or vocal fillers (*ums, ahs, and-as*). They should know their material, connect with the audience, and be animated. That is to say, they must have a good delivery.

One part of a good delivery involves the speaker's use of notes. The next section offers suggestions for developing and using notes.

# ■ NOTES

As you may recall, Chapter 5 ended with a discussion and an example of how to outline a speech. Sometimes, that outline could be quite long, which leaves the problem of making the transition from the speech outline to the notes that are used during the actual speech. This segment describes how to do this.

**EXPERT ADVICE**

I don't like using prepared texts but prefer to speak from brief notes that basically consist of bullets of the subjects I'd like to cover in the order that I would like to get to them. This allows me to speak as if I'm speaking one on one.

*Brian Rogers, CA*
*KPMG, Calgary, Alberta*

## What Are Good Notes?

Good notes are clear and they can be seen with the naked eye. Speakers do not have to squint or hold them up to their face to decipher them. Good, serviceable notes consist of key words that outline the speech and they may house statistics, specific names, dates, or direct quotations that will be used in the presentation. Messages regarding delivery might also be inserted—things like "slow down" for the fast talkers, "use gestures" for the less animated speakers—you get the picture.

Referring back to Stephanie Wadden's sample complete-sentence outline in Chapter 5, the accompanying box shows how her first main point and the supporting statements can be transformed into notes merely by using key words (see text in square brackets). It is easy to see, based on this one section, how an entire speech can be reduced to a few trigger words.

---

**OUTLINE**

**I. Main Point One**
Before we make the decision to go on a diet, there must be a reason or triggering event that provokes us to make the decision. However, the reason for dieting varies among different people. [**REASONS FOR DIETING**]

A. Some people want to change some aspect of their physical appearance.
   1.  Society itself has a large effect on the way people look at themselves and the pressure from society and the media may cause you to want to go on a diet.

---

2. Upcoming weddings, reunions, and different social events are other reasons why some people decide to diet. They want to look a certain way, fit into a certain outfit, or impress others. [**PHYSICAL APPEARANCE— SOCIETY/EVENTS/THEMSELVES**]

3. Some people want to change their body image just for themselves. Whether it is for personal satisfaction or to fit into certain trendy clothes, they diet just for themselves. They are not pressured or influenced by anyone else.

B. Many people diet to stay healthy or to stay in shape.

1. Obesity is a growing problem in Canada and many of us are aware of the devastating effect it can have on a person's health.

2. Regardless of age or weight, some people just like to eat nutritious food because it helps them to maintain and repair their body or to keep their body healthy. [**HEALTH—OBESITY/NUTRITION**]

**Transition:** However, sometimes people don't choose the healthiest methods of dieting [**UNHEALTHY DIETING METHODS**].

Refer to the accompanying box entitled "From Speech Outline to Speech Notes" and follow the basic steps that will allow you to convert your outline into good, workable notes. It is also a good idea to make up your notes before you begin to practise your speech and use those same notes during the actual presentation. In that way, you become accustomed to looking at particular areas of the card for specific information. Many speakers also colour-code their notes. This creates a connection in their mind between the colour and the content. During the speech, a glance at a particular colour will conjure up the accompanying part of the presentation without even having to read the keywords.

## FROM SPEECH OUTLINE TO SPEECH NOTES

1. Read over your speech outline and determine if there are direct quotations, stats, sources, or names that you think you may have trouble recalling and mark them.

2. Look over each main point and write a keyword or phrase to signify that point.

3. Look over the supporting statements and designate keywords for each one.
4. Check transitions and see if they need to be included in the notes. If so, determine keywords to help you remember them.
5. Review the introduction and conclusion. Find prompt words for these.
6. Transfer all the keywords and any stats, quotes, etc. to a note card. You might put main points in capital letters and supporting points in lowercase letters.
7. Develop a colour-code system and highlight your points. For example, you could have each main point be one colour and the supporting points a different one. Or, have each main point and its supporting points be the same colour. Maybe you only want to highlight stats. Create a system that works for you.
8. Practise using the notes and make any adjustments. If there are a lot of changes, write a new card.
9. Practise with the same notes that will be used during the presentation.

### Sample Note Cards

Figure 6.1 reproduces the actual note cards of two students. The first belonged to Kimberley Fraser, a Cape Breton fiddler. The goal of her speech was to inform the audience about the resurgence of Scottish fiddle music. The darker print indicates where she tinted the notes with a yellow highlighter. Take a look and see if you can infer the organizational scheme Kimberley used. Her three main points were (1) to describe the fiddle scene prior to 1970, (2) to explain the influence of the 1971 Glendale Fiddle Festival, and (3) to depict the present-day scene.

The second note card belonged to Heather MacLellan and the goal of her speech was to inform the audience about child poverty. Heather used coloured markers to create her card: brown for the introduction and conclusion, green for her first major point, red for her second, and purple for her third. You may wish to do the same.

## The One-Card Approach

Readers may be surprised to see that each speaker had only one note card. Some public speaking teachers and texts recommend using several, and transferring parts of the speech outline onto note cards. This can help students become more comfortable as they deliver their speeches. Those who teach *extemporaneous speaking*, however, often prefer

**Figure 6.1—Sample Note Cards**

**THE RESURGENCE OF SCOTTISH FIDDLE MUSIC by Kimberley Fraser**

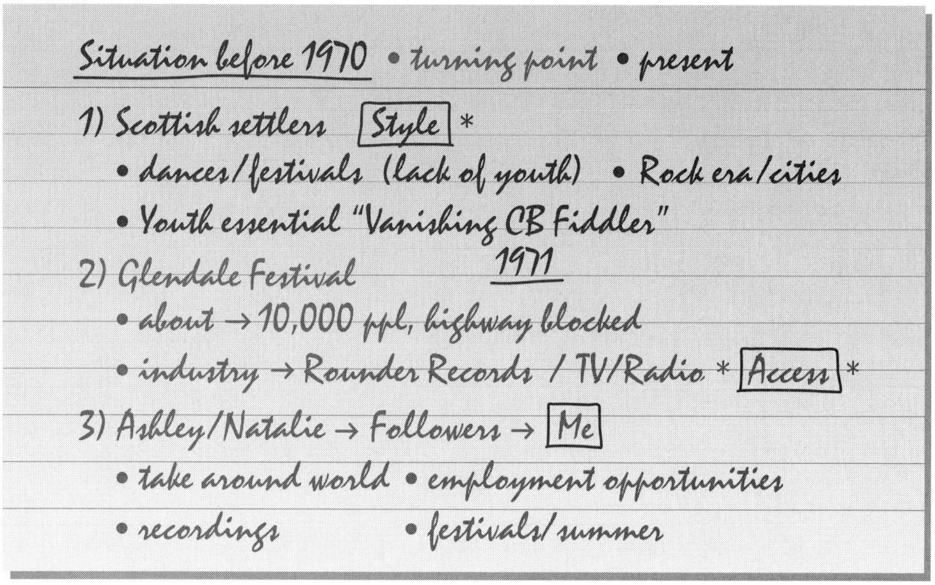

Situation before 1970  • turning point  • present

1) Scottish settlers  [Style] *
   • dances/festivals  (lack of youth)  • Rock era/cities
   • Youth essential "Vanishing CB Fiddler"
2) Glendale Festival  ___1971___
   • about → 10,000 ppl, highway blocked
   • industry → Rounder Records / TV/Radio * [Access] *
3) Ashley/Natalie → Followers → [Me]
   • take around world  • employment opportunities
   • recordings       • festivals/summer

**CHILDHOOD POVERTY by Heather MacLennan**

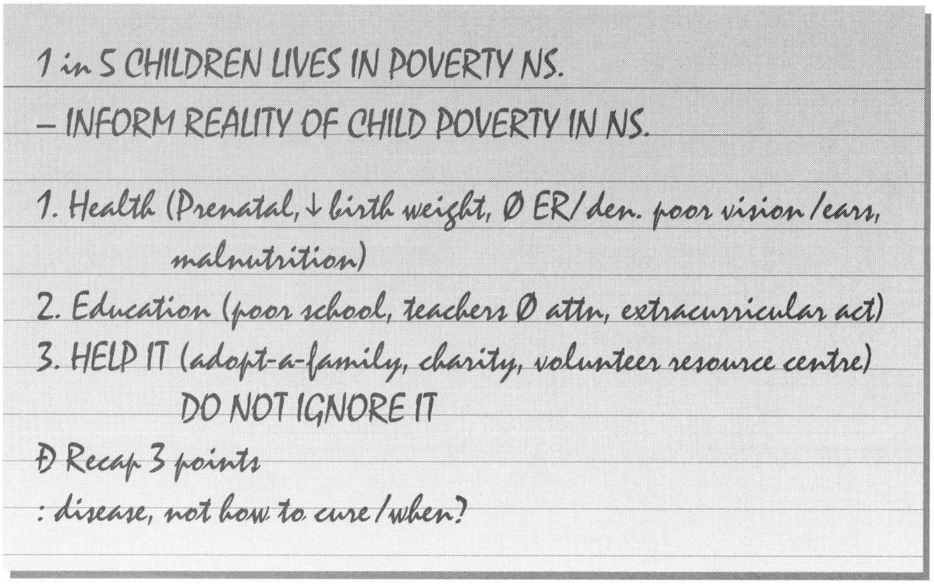

1 in 5 CHILDREN LIVES IN POVERTY NS.
— INFORM REALITY OF CHILD POVERTY IN NS.

1. Health (Prenatal, ↓ birth weight, Ø ER/den. poor vision/ears,
        malnutrition)
2. Education (poor school, teachers Ø attn, extracurricular act)
3. HELP IT (adopt-a-family, charity, volunteer resource centre)
        DO NOT IGNORE IT
Ð Recap 3 points
: disease, not how to cure/when?

that students use just one. Extemporaneous speaking, as noted in Chapter 1, refers to speeches that are well organized and thought out, but not memorized. This is the type of speaking that is encouraged in this text. Extemporaneous speaking can result in exciting presentations that allow speakers to interact with the audience. Such speakers do not use extensive notes because they know their material, which means that they can talk about it in different ways in an interpersonal conversation. Therefore, there is a correlation between the types of notes speakers prepare and how their delivery may be perceived.

The one-card approach can also prevent speakers from continually shuffling and playing with their cards during the speech, a behaviour that can be perceived in business and educational settings as amateurish. It can also leave an impression that speakers are more concerned with getting through the speech than with relating to the audience.

However, it is wise to use whatever method your instructor suggests. Thoroughly researched, well organized, and skillfully delivered speeches are possible with one or many note cards.

 **EXPERT ADVICE**

If you must write it out in full, you are not prepared to speak it. I get totally immersed in selling the audience individually in what I believe. If you should stumble, just stop and take time to compose yourself. I've had it happen. I have seen it happen to the top personalities and that's what they do. Then they continue.

*Sam "The Record Man" Sniderman*
*Toronto, Ontario*

## What Are Bad Notes?

Bad notes contain the entire speech, use complete sentences, and are often written or printed in letters so small that the speaker practically needs a magnifying glass to see them. Such notes do not use point form, and give the impression that speakers are ready to read at any given moment. They also suggest that the speaker has memorized the presentation.

Because such references lack visual clarity, they provide little help when it is needed most. For example, students often report that when they lose their place or forget something during a speech, there are so many things going on in their heads that there is virtually no way that their eyes can focus on and distinguish sections of a presentation when it is written out in full on one small note card. They are trying to remember what comes next, processing the nonverbal feedback they are receiving from the audience, and worrying how they look. They are also concerned how the pause will affect their assignment grade, their course grade, their overall GPA, and maybe even their program. It is little wonder that such notes appear jumbled and meaningless.

Bad notes may also come in the form of several sheets of tattered paper, each containing handwritten material. In addition to looking unprofessional, they suggest little or no preparation or effort.

When I was practising my speech at home, I used this messy, but useful, one-card outline. However, when I got to class, something came over me, and, like a fool, I wrote out the entire speech in tiny print while waiting for my turn to speak. I know I should never have done this. To this day I don't know what got into me.

Anyway, when I was making the speech, I couldn't for the life of me recall a particular person's name. But do you think I could find it on that sheet of notes? No way. Everything became a big blurry mess of words without any meaning whatsoever. All of this was going on as I tried to spit out my speech. Not good, not good at all.

Thank God it was only worth five points, and I was able to redeem myself in my next presentation. But let me tell you, I took just one, colour-coded card that time . . . and you might know, I didn't need it. I remembered everything. Go figure.

*Danielle, Former Communication Student*

## Using Notes

To use notes in a professional manner, lay them on the podium or table. Although you can keep them in your hand, be aware that this limits your use of gestures. Also, jittery speakers have a tendency to manipulate or play with their notes, almost creating origami designs during the presentation.

As you make your speech, glance down at your notes to keep you on track. Should you need to refer to something, such as a statistic or quotation, take the note card into your hand. While it is bad form to read an entire classroom speech, it is perfectly acceptable to read a quotation. When you are finished, simply put the card back. Using notes in this manner may require a little practice.

## HOW TO PRACTISE A SPEECH—A REVIEW

Practice is the only way to ensure a smooth delivery. Even in those instances where you may be required to read, practice is still a must. It allows you to become familiar with the text, to uncover words or names you cannot pronounce, and to decide how you will use your vocal variety to emphasize parts of the script. Whether reading or speaking extemporaneously, check out the following practice tips.

- Develop notes that work for you.
- Use the same notes throughout the rehearsal sessions that will be used during the actual delivery.
- Find a private room with a mirror in which to practise.
- Take some time to say the speech in your head or out loud. Get familiar with the content.
- When you feel comfortable with, but have not memorized, the speech, stand and say it in front of a mirror.
- Say the speech from beginning to end and envision the audience in front of you.
- If you make a mistake, fix it immediately and continue, just as you would during the presentation.
- Keep practising until you feel satisfied. You may say things differently each time, but that is to be expected.
- You may wish to say the speech in front of a person who will critique you. Afterward, continue practising and incorporate any suggestions into the delivery.
- You may wish to record your presentation on video. Review the playback at least five times to ensure an objective assessment or have someone offer recommendations for improvement. Continue practising and incorporate any improvements.
- Go on with your rehearsals until you feel confident and enthusiastic . . . but not memorized.

## Should You Go "Noteless"?

Sometimes speakers feel so confident and excited about their speeches that they opt to go "noteless." While in some cases this works, in others the speakers lose their place or omit key points of their presentation. Regardless of how poised and positive you may feel, take along your notes just as a safeguard. If you do not refer to them, all the better. However, should you lose your place or forget a relevant fact, having that outline will prevent a potentially embarrassing pause.

As you develop and practise with your notes, think about how you will word your main points. Again, the concern of this chapter is presenting your message in a credible manner. The next section describes several language dimensions for you to consider.

# LANGUAGE FORMALITY AND CREDIBILITY

In the last decade or so, there has been a move toward using more relaxed and unceremonious language styles. The amount of profanity in everyday encounters, the use of off-colour humour, and the lack of censorship in the media suggest that the world has loosened up considerably. But has it? While it is admissible to hear words and phrases such as *pissed off, butt, smart-ass,* the "F word," and the like on the Internet and on television, such language is still not appropriate in formal, business, or educational contexts. In fact, speakers who use this ribald "bathrobe" style of language are thought to lack a sense of propriety, and their credibility can plummet.

To help you distinguish the various levels of language formality, think of four dress styles—*tuxedo, casual/dress code, blue jeans,* and *bathrobe.* Just as the type of apparel suggests a level of formality, so too does the speech that accompanies the dress style. For example, on formal occasions such as proms, weddings, black tie dinners where tuxedos and gowns are the norm, there also exists a communication protocol. People act and speak in a more reserved, polite, or ceremonial manner and the communication style could be labelled *tuxedo.* Now consider the opposite end of the spectrum and how differently we communicate when we are in pyjamas or bathrobes. For the most part, we are likely to be with people with whom we have intimate relationships—lovers, family, or good friends. In such contexts, communication is open and unguarded (unless children are present) and can be referred to as *bathrobe communication.*

Most of our communication, though, falls somewhere in between, in more of a blue jeans or casual/dress code. For example, at work, in the classroom, in meetings or interviews, or speaking with superiors, there is a tendency to be somewhat guarded in how we speak. In these situations, such behaviour is sensible. Just as we are expected to dress in a certain mode in these contexts, so too does the outfit complement the communication style and this can be referred to as casual/dress code. But, when we are in these same contexts, communicating with colleagues we have known for many years, or with people whom we have become good friends, then the communication gets pretty relaxed. If we know the person really well, the communication might be so relaxed that it could be considered bathrobe. Typically, the interactional style would more likely resemble blue jeans communication where we are unpretentious, candid, earthy, obscene, or even lewd. See the accompanying box entitled "Language Style and Formality" for further clarification of this theory.

To ensure credibility, it is wise for speakers to adjust the degree of conversational formality in accordance with the audience. This concept of equating clothing style with language style was originally designed to help customer service representatives monitor their use of overly familiar language with clients (Rolls, 2001), but the model can be applied to public speaking contexts as well.

## EXPERT ADVICE

Language! That really says it all. My mother used to call me "potty" mouth because I had a bad habit of using vulgar language. I even had a slip in class once. Now that was embarrassing and my pride was really hurt. It especially hit home after I read the chapter on delivering the speech in a credible manner and learned just how important the use of proper language was. I am a professional and I want to be seen and heard as one. I want to come across to people as a credible and charismatic speaker. As an organizational trainer, I don't want my bad habits to ruin my chances of becoming a great speaker. I found this information useful, easy to read, and it helped put language appropriateness into perspective.

*Arlene Michelin, Former Communication Student*
*Labrador-Grenfell Regional Integrated Health Authority*
*Happy Valley-Goose Bay, Labrador*

Most public speaking situations are somewhat conventional in nature, so tuxedo or casual/dress code language styles work well. When students in a "pet peeve" classroom presentation use a blue jean phrase such as *pisses me off*, it sounds vulgar, even though the same phrase might be perfectly legitimate and acceptable in conversations with their friends. Keep in mind that the type of spontaneous, relaxed, or playful language that works so well with friends is not fitting in the majority of public speaking contexts. Instead, a more refined, traditional approach is appropriate, and works to enhance your credibility. However, when it comes to stand-up or satiric comedy, these guidelines do not apply.

---

### LANGUAGE STYLE AND FORMALITY

#### TUXEDO
This type of communication is used in public forums and various cultural and religious rites. The language is conventional, prim, reserved, formal, stately, proper, and even decorous.

#### CASUAL/DRESS CODE
Relationships in this category centre on acquaintances or individuals we do not know. Casual/dress code style is used in professional contexts. The talk is polite, tasteful, appropriate, and correct.

#### BLUE JEANS
Blue jeans communication occurs with our good friends and family—people we know well and with whom we are very comfortable. The talk is unceremonious, unpretentious, candid, straightforward, earthy, and sometimes obscene, ribald, or lewd.

#### BATHROBE
This style of talk is reserved for people with whom we have very private, close relationships, such as lovers and life partners. Bathrobe talk is intimate, private, exclusive, personal, and sometimes vulgar or suggestive.

---

## ▪ GRAMMAR AND CREDIBILITY

*Often people thinks that grammar don't matter, but it do. I seen it over and over again in my classes—some students what write good don't necessarily talk good. Youse can't expect to get in front of them people and speak bad, and then expect them to listen to what you're talking about. Add in ta dat some poor articulations, an youse got yourself a speaker wit no credibility.*

If you think there are only one or two problems with the paragraph above, you have your work cut out for you. In fact, there are 16 grammatical and articulation errors. Reread the paragraph and see how many you can find.

It is vital to have good grammar if you want to be considered a credible speaker. Poor grammar reduces speaker integrity because listeners automatically equate it with a lack of intelligence or a lack of education. In most cases, however, bad grammar is simply a matter of habit. If you grew up in a home where everyone said, *I seen it*, rather than *I saw it*, then it is likely that you too will speak that way.

What is interesting about poor grammar is that those who use it think that it does not matter. Such individuals are completely oblivious to how they and other language abusers sound and are thus perceived by listeners. Standard speakers who use proper grammar, however, immediately recognize when someone makes a grammatical faux pas. Fortunately, poor grammar can be corrected with a little thought and attention.

I'd say it took me about a year to clean up my grammar. I'm a first-generation university student and my parents, aunts, and uncles, who all spoke grammatically poor English, were no role models for me. But because I was an English major, I knew the difference. I wrote correctly, but I didn't speak properly—that is, until recently. However, so that I don't sound too uppity when I'm around my family, I'll actually say things like "I seen," or "It don't" in order to fit in. Then when I'm at the university, I alter my style and speak right good . . . just kidding.

*Don, Former Communication Student*

## Improving Grammar

Sloppy grammar can be improved in just two steps.

### Step 1: Identify Your Particular Grammatical Problems

The first step is to recognize whether you indeed have poor grammar. To help you, refer to the box titled "Top 11 List of Common Grammatical Errors." Read over the sentences and determine whether you usually say them the right way or the wrong way.

If this proves to be of little use to you, ask your public speaking teacher or another professor, or someone you know who has good grammar to help you assess your command of the English language.

## Step 2: Eliminate Your Problem Areas

Once you have identified any specific problems, it is then a matter of practice to fix them. Work on one error at a time until the correct usage becomes a habit. This may take some time. After you have conquered one grammatical problem, move on to the next.

---

### TOP 11 LIST OF COMMON GRAMMATICAL ERRORS

11. *Wrong:* <u>Me and Kim</u> are going to the mall.
    *Right:* <u>Kim and I</u> are going to the mall.
10. *Wrong:* Many people <u>that</u> exercise are also slim.
    *Right:* Many people <u>who</u> exercise are also slim.
9. *Wrong:* I could <u>of</u> done that.
   *Right:* I could <u>have</u> done that.
8. *Wrong:* She <u>shoulda went</u> home for the weekend.
   *Right:* She <u>should have gone</u> home for the weekend.
7. *Wrong:* <u>Youse</u> are going to be sorry if you don't have a good attention getter.
   *Right:* <u>You</u> are going to be sorry if you don't have a good attention getter.
6. *Wrong:* I'm not partial to <u>them</u> kinds of organizational schemes.
   *Right:* I'm not partial to <u>those</u> kinds of organizational schemes.
5. *Wrong:* I <u>don't got none</u> of those.
   *Right:* I <u>don't have any</u> of those.
4. *Wrong:* Things are going <u>good</u>.
   *Right:* Things are going <u>well</u>.
3. *Wrong:* I <u>done</u> it.
   *Right:* I <u>did</u> it. *or* I <u>had/have done</u> it.
2. *Wrong:* Where's it <u>at</u>? Where's she going <u>to</u>?
   *Right:* Where is it? Where is she <u>going</u>?
1. *Wrong:* I <u>seen</u> her last night at the movie.
   *Right:* I <u>saw</u> her last night at the movie.

---

Regardless of whether you use poor grammar due to habit or apathy, there is one sure method for improving. When you have isolated a particular problem you wish to address, correct yourself whenever it comes out of your mouth, regardless of when or where you are speaking. Just repeat the sentence saying it correctly. People do this all the time and it is hardly even noticed. You could also ask a friend to help you by pointing out when you have had a grammatical slip. Start now to develop your new habits.

As you continue to monitor and modify your grammar, there is something else you can do. Shertzer (1986), the author of a well-known grammar book, offers the following valuable advice: "In order to use English correctly and gracefully, it is necessary to recognize and to practice using good grammar. Listening to speakers who are accustomed to speaking grammatically helps train the ear to recognize correct usage" (p. 1). Therefore, listen more attentively to your professors and others to help you develop your style.

# ■ LANGUAGE STYLE AND CREDIBILITY

## Deferential versus Nondeferential Language Style

Regardless of the message you intend to present or how your speech is organized, the presentation can be given in what is called a deferential or a nondeferential language style.

A *deferential language style* is one in which the speaker defers to the listener. Some people refer to it as a powerless language style (Erickson et al., 1978). You probably speak like this when you are unsure of yourself. This style is characterized by the use of tag questions, disclaimers, polite forms, few or no expletives, more discriminations in naming colours, intonational patterns that essentially make declarative sentences sound like questions, and so on. Further, deferential language users give way to interruptions. See the accompanying box for an overview of deferential language markers.

A *nondeferential language style*, on the other hand, is the absence of such markers. As a result, it is considered a more powerful language style. Interestingly, the research overwhelmingly shows that women use a deferential language style (the powerless type) more often than do men.

## Why Language Style Is So Important

Language style is important for public speakers simply because listener perceptions of the speaker vary dramatically according to the style that is used. For example, deferential speakers are generally thought of in less favourable terms than nondeferential speakers.

That is, researchers have actually found that listeners regard deferential speakers as less intelligent, less willing to take a stand, and less assertive, although they are thought to be warm, polite, friendly, and submissive. You can see that such perceptions have implications for whether a speaker will be viewed as credible.

Nondeferential speakers, on the other hand, are rated much more positively. In fact, the results of one study showed that stronger speakers were judged as more organized, competent, systematic, decisive, intelligent, confident, logical, serious, and stronger than deferential speakers (Quina, Wingard, & Bates, 1987). Liska, Mechling, and Stathas (1981) reported that nondeferential speakers were perceived as assertive, dominant, believable, and willing to take a stand, although less friendly and warm.

## DEFERENTIAL LANGUAGE MARKERS AND NONDEFERENTIAL ALTERNATIVES

The following markers are indicators of a deferential language style. Compare the deferential with the nondeferential examples. Which markers do you regularly use?

### VOCAL FILLERS

*Examples:* uh, and uh, um, like uh, you know, well uh

*Deferential speaker:* "The goal of, uh, my speech is to, uh, like inform you of the kinds of, well uh the factors that, um, will make you, uh, a better public speaker."

*Nondeferential speaker:* "The goal of my speech is to inform you of the factors that can make you a better public speaker."

### DISCLAIMERS

*Examples:* I could be all wrong, I may be off the mark, maybe it's just me, in my opinion, at least I think, I think that's right, as far as I know

*Deferential speaker:* "I could be all wrong, but in my opinion one of the more influential factors is speaking style. You know, whether you use, at least I think, a deferential or nondeferential language, style can maybe affect speaker credibility."

*Nondeferential speaker:* "One influential factor is speaking style, and both deferential and nondeferential styles can have an influence on speaker credibility."

## HEDGES

*Examples:* I think, perhaps, it seems, maybe, I guess, kind of, probably, may
*Deferential speaker:* "Perhaps, I think, it seems to me that it probably depends on, I guess, the type of audience you are addressing."
*Nondeferential speaker:* "It depends on the type of audience you are addressing."

## TAG QUESTIONS

*Examples:* Right? Isn't that correct? What do you think? Isn't it?
*Deferential speaker:* "Don't you think that maybe you could, at least in my opinion, use both styles, right?"
*Nondeferential speaker:* "You could use both styles."

## INTENSIFIERS

*Examples:* really, awfully, very, so
*Deferential speaker:* "Language style, has, I'm pretty sure, a very big effect on listener perceptions."
*Nondeferential speaker:* "Language style affects listener perceptions."

## ALLOWING INTERRUPTIONS

*Examples:* And then I was . . ., Then I was going to . . ., If it . . .
*Deferential speaker:* "Speakers who take . . . what's that? . . . Yes, speakers who take control of the situation appear confident."
*Nondeferential speaker:* "Speakers who take control of the situation appear confident."

## POSING QUESTIONS RATHER THAN MAKING STATEMENTS

*Deferential speaker:* "I wonder, ah, if maybe you should integrate both types?"
*Nondeferential speaker:* "You should integrate both types."

## MAKING STATEMENTS THAT SOUND LIKE QUESTIONS

This marker involves voice pitch or tone—usually raising the pitch at the end of the sentence so it comes out sounding like a question.
*Deferential speaker:* "My first main (raise voice pitch) point (lower voice pitch) is organizing the (raise voice pitch) speech?"
*Nondeferential speaker:* "My first main point is organizing the speech."

In all, speakers who use the stronger, nondeferential language style have more credibility when speaking in public. They are also thought to possess more leadership potential than deferential speakers (Rolls, 1991). Therefore, if you wish to be regarded in a positive manner, be sure to use a strong, nondeferential language style for your speeches. This will give you a more self-assured, confident air. You can do this by assessing your style, and then eliminating those deferential markers that you use regularly.

However, while a nondeferential language style adds to your credibility in public speaking contexts, a deferential style works better in interpersonal, one-on-one contexts. It is not a matter of one style being superior to the other—they just work better in different contexts and when the speaker has different goals in mind. As a skilled speaker, it is advantageous to be aware of the different language styles, when to use each style, and how to use each style.

### ))) SPOTLIGHT ON SPEAKERS

Nondeferential language need not sound overpowering. For example, Adrienne Clarkson, Canada's former governor general, exemplified this style in a speech "on the occasion of a luncheon hosted by the Regina Public Library" on May 16, 2005. Below is a short segment of that speech.

*Without our library's deep roots in the public good, without that belief that they should be freely accessible to everyone, we do not have the basis for a democratic society. Canada takes in, each year, around 200 000 immigrants from dozens of different countries, and invites them to enrich and to weave themselves into the fabric of our communities. We cannot properly fulfill this mission—the building of a diverse and free society—without public libraries.*

## LANGUAGE BIAS AND CREDIBILITY

So far, credibility and delivery have been discussed in terms of language formality, grammar, and language style. It is evident that presenters must choose their words carefully if they want to be accepted as knowledgeable, trustworthy speakers. Language bias is another dimension of language that affects credibility. This goal of using unbiased language is not to appear politically correct, but rather to "avoid perpetuating demeaning attitudes and biased assumptions about people" (Publication Manual of the American Psychological Association, 2001, p. 61). Obsolete and demeaning terminology can insult audience members and make speakers come off as uninformed yokels.

Keeping up with language change is not easy and using inclusive language can seem cumbersome and awkward. Some people resist change because they think it sounds weird (or that the political correctness police are working overtime). But, with a little effort, a more informed way of speaking can become a habit. To be a credible speaker, this is a must.

Ivy and Backlund (2004, pp. 158–189) list several advantages to using nonsexist language, some of which relate to public speaking: it reflects nonsexist attitudes, it is contemporary, it is unambiguous, and it demonstrates sensitivity. All of these contribute to public speaking attractiveness and credibility. To understand and eliminate sexist language, four language problems are outlined in this section: the generic pronoun problem, man-linked terminology, outdated associations, and the ordering of terms.

About to graduate with our B.Sc. in nursing, we looked forward to a presentation by the renowned oncologist Dr. Owen Jones (fictitious name). But it turned out to be very disappointing. While he may have meant well, Dr. Jones began by saying, "I'm happy you girls are so interested in this area of medicine." And it just went downhill from there. Throughout his talk, he referred to doctors as males and nurses as females, and even made a sexist joke. My respect for Dr. Jones dropped a few notches that day. He had no idea that his outdated use of the language was condescending and passé. It made him seem old and out of touch.

*Jane, Former Nursing Student*

## Generic Pronoun Problem

The generic pronoun refers to the use of *he, him, himself,* and *his* to refer to both women and men. The problem is that this can cause confusion, and it demeans women. For example, I might say something like "Don't worry. If Hunter said he would pick you up at the university, then he will show up on time." In this instance, *he* clearly refers to Hunter—just one specific man. How about the next example? "A public speaker who has style and charisma will be welcomed wherever he goes." In this case, the *he* is intended to refer to both men and women, but listeners are inclined to presume it refers only to men. What gender came to your mind when you read this example?

## *The Solution*

There are two ways to eliminate the generic pronoun problem, and thus make the message less ambiguous and more inclusive. The first is to say *he or she, his or her, him or her,* or *himself or herself.* This is common practice now. The second less cumbersome approach is to speak "in the plural." Instead of saying, "A good speaker practises his or her speech," say, "Good speakers practise their speeches." This style of expression is easy, contemporary, and inclusive.

---

### PLURALS ELIMINATE THE GENERIC PRONOUN PROBLEM

Below are examples of how to use the plural to eliminate the generic pronoun problem.

*Awkward:* A speaker will be better received if *he or she* makes eye contact with the audience.
*Better:* Speakers will be better received if *they* make eye contact with the audience.

*Awkward:* Because a speaker sometimes needs a little encouragement, give *him or her* positive nonverbal feedback by nodding your head and looking interested in what *he or she* is saying.
*Better:* Because speakers sometimes need a little encouragement, give *them* positive nonverbal feedback by nodding your head and looking interested in what *they* are saying.

*Awkward:* One way for a speaker to establish *his or her* credibility is to have a good delivery.
*Better:* One way for speakers to establish *their* credibility is to have a good delivery.

---

# Man-Linked Terminology

Before reading on, stop and quickly sketch a picture of cavemen. What did you draw? Women, children, and men, or just some cavemen, as the man-linked word suggests? When a class of 30 to 40 students is asked to draw cavemen, they do just that. Only one or two will draw women, boys, girls, or infants and toddlers. This is because man-linked language, like the pronoun problem, is supposed to refer to everyone, but most often people think of men when those terms are used. Ivy and Backlund (2004) hold that such

**❝ ❞**

I hated politically correct language. My attitude was, "Give me a break and don't be so picky." It was all so stupid and ridiculous. After taking a couple of communication courses, however, I came to realize that there are all kinds of changes in language, especially with recent advances in technology. I have no problem keeping up with that and I'd be embarrassed if I spoke like my grand-mother. In fact, I get a kick out of ribbing her about using old terms like *record* instead of *CD*, *Walkman* instead of *iPod*, or *quarter to nine* instead of *8:45*. Gosh, I can't even get the temperature out of her—she still talks in Fahrenheit—"It's going to be in the 80s today," she'll say. That means nothing to me and so I say, "Come on, Gran, get with it; start using Celsius." And this brings me to the point I'm trying to make. To me, she sounds kind of backward when she uses the old language, and then it occurred to me; perhaps I might sound that way too if I don't keep up. It was that simple. So, I'm much more willing now to get with the language times. It's all part of being cool.

*Gilles, Former Communication Student*

thinking maintains sex-biased perceptions of the roles of women and men, and shapes attitudes that careers are sex-"appropriate," that more careers are available to men, and that men deserve more status in our society. This is why terms like *mailman, mankind, handyman, doorman, chairman,* and others are being replaced with inclusive language such as *letter carrier, humanity, handyperson, doorkeeper* or *porter,* and *chairperson* or *chair.*

## The Solution

To embrace all audience members, use nonsexist alternatives. And, like other forms of language discussed in this chapter, do not wait until your presentation day—start using inclusive language now in your everyday talk. A number of nonsexist alternatives are listed in the accompanying box.

---

### ALTERNATIVES TO MAN-LINKED TERMS

| Man-Linked | Inclusive |
|---|---|
| anchorman | anchor, newscaster |
| businessman | businessperson |
| chairman | chair, chairperson |
| doorman | porter, doorkeeper |
| fisherman | fisher |
| foreman | supervisor |
| garbageman | garbage collector |
| layman | layperson |
| manhole | sewer, utility hole |
| mankind | humanity, humankind |
| manmade | synthetic, artificial |
| ombudsman | ombudsperson |
| policeman | police officer |
| repairman | repair technician |
| salesman | salesclerk, clerk |
| spaceman | astronaut |
| spokesman | spokesperson, speaker |
| stuntman | stuntperson |
| watchman | security guard |

**Source:** Most of these were selected from a list entitled "Man-Linked Terminology and Alternatives," in Ivy & Backlund (2004, p. 161).

---

## Outdated Associations

I once saw a television promotion for a show called *Women Explorers*. The title implied that the production would feature women, not men. However, if male explorers were to be highlighted, the title would likely be just *Explorers*, not *Men Explorers*. This is because the English language is devised so that maleness is the standard.

Although changes are definitely coming about, words such as *actor, doctor, major, lawyer, minister, professor,* and *chief executive officer* have traditionally denoted men—probably because males most often held these positions. The female version of the role has tended to be signified through suffixes (*actress, hostess, majorette, poetess,* and *waitress*) or by pointing out that the position is held by a woman, as in *lady doctor, woman minister,* or *lady lawyer*. Of course, the opposite is also true: some positions are stereotypically associated with women, as in *nurse*. When the position refers to a man, then the male adjective is added, as in *male nurse*.

### The Solution

The passage of time is a solution, in that more women and men are opting to work in positions that were once associated with the other sex. In the meantime, help the process along by eliminating the adjective—instead of saying, "Jack is a male nurse," just say, "Jack is a nurse" or "Mary is a lawyer," as opposed to "Mary is a female lawyer." These changes may seem small and inconsequential, but they can add to your credibility.

## Ordering of Terms

The last way in which language can be sexist has to do with the ordering of terms. With the exception of phrases such as *ladies and gentlemen*, most often the male term is placed first (Mr. and Mrs., boys and girls, his and hers, Jack and Jill, king and queen, men and women). The problem is that just as you subconsciously associate only men with the word *caveman*, people tend to consider men first because the language is framed that way.

### The Solution

Try on occasion to put the female form first. See what kind of a reaction you get. For instance, use *women and men* and *men and women* interchangeably when speaking and writing. This may feel awkward and conspicuous at first, but it will soon become a part of your everyday language.

**PUBLIC SPEAKING IN THE 21ST CENTURY**

You might find the following Web sites interesting. Should you come across helpful links or sites, consider recommending them to your classmates or to me at *judy_rolls@capebretonu.ca*.

**For the Sports Fan**—Language and metaphors have a powerful influence on audience perceptions. Are you familiar with a Dennis Rodman–fan–coach incident? This interactive site demonstrates how language affects how an audience who did not witness the event can perceive what happened.
*http://www.americanrhetoric.com/rodmanphase1.htm*

**Gifts of Speech: Women's Speeches from Around the World**—This site provides hundreds of speeches and speech excerpts from women. Use them as models or select a couple for analysis.
*http://gos.sbc.edu*

**Pope John Paul II Speeches**—Some readers might be interested in the speeches of Pope John Paul II. They are available in five languages!
*http://www.vatican.va/holy_father/john_paul_ii/speeches*

**Southwest Missouri State University**—Relevant to instructors and students, this site offers a large number of public speaking exercises, as well as famous/historical American speeches.
*http://www.missouristate.edu/com/com115/staff.htm*

**Speech from the Throne**—This site offers every Canadian Speech from the Throne since Confederation in 1867 up to the present.
*http://www.parl.gc.ca/information/about/process/info/throne/index.asp?lang=E*

## Other Areas of Inclusiveness

Thus far, inclusion has only been discussed in terms of gender. However, we also live in a multicultural country, which is particularly evident in urban centres. Individuals from diverse cultures and religious backgrounds deserve to be respected by public speakers. Although it should go without saying, all racial, ethnic, or religious slurs and jokes are to be avoided. They are not appreciated by most audiences, and speakers who use them are considered racist. Here are some other ways to show respect for diversity in all its forms:

- Rather than say *homosexual,* use *lesbian, gay,* or *bisexual* as in, "He is a gay man."
- Rather than say *church* or *synagogue,* use *place of worship* when making a generic reference.
- Rather than say *the elderly,* use the term as an adjective to say, "He is an elderly man," or "He is a senior citizen."
- Do not label people by their disability as it has negative overtones and suggests helplessness. For example, rather than say, *a cripple,* or *confined to a wheelchair,* say, "A person who uses a wheelchair." The latter statement suggests that the wheelchair is just one aspect of the person's life while *cripple* suggests that that is the major factor about the individual. *Confined* suggests helplessness.
- Rather than say, *He is retarded or mentally handicapped,* say "He is mentally challenged," Do not say, *She's an epileptic* or *diabetic* but rather say, "She has epilepsy," or "She has been diagnosed with diabetes."
- When referring to individuals from various races, make sure you are using an updated term. Terms change over the years due to preference and preferred designations. For instance, do not say *Oriental,* which is an outdated and often derogatory term—say *Asian. Indian* is no longer appropriate, but *First Nations people* is. While the term *black* was once appropriate, the more contemporary term is *person of African descent.* The best way to learn how an individual would like to be referred to is to ask.

## ■ OTHER LANGUAGE FACTORS AND CREDIBILITY

### Evidence

You would think that using evidence would automatically make a person more credible. Well, with some people it does, and with others it does not. Johnston (1994) reviewed the research in this area and writes that the use of evidence by individuals who are already credible adds little to their believability. However, for speakers who lack credibility, evidence can contribute to their effectiveness, but only if their delivery is good. Further, for evidence to be convincing, it must be new or unfamiliar.

Johnston (1994) sums up her investigation of credibility and evidence like this: "Thus, we can conclude that the use of evidence increases perceptions of credibility under the following conditions: (1) the persuader has low to moderate credibility; (2) the evidence is unfamiliar to the receivers; and (3) the message delivery is of high quality" (p. 152). The last point underscores the notion that you must attend to those delivery skills discussed in Chapter 3: how you convey your message through your voice and body.

---

### ⏵)) SPOTLIGHT ON SPEAKERS

For excellent use of evidence, read this excerpt from a speech by Matthew Coon Come, the former National Chief of the Assembly of First Nations. A portion of the speech was read on *Cross Country Checkup* on CBC Radio, April 8, 2001. The title of the program was "Is Canada Making Enough Progress with Aboriginal Issues?" and Chief Coon Come responded to questions after the host, Rex Murphy, read a segment of the presentation.

*The death of our Aboriginal People from injury, poisoning, and violence is five times higher than the national Canadian average. A very disturbing number of our children suffer from fetal alcohol syndrome—about 25 times greater than the world average.*

*Our people smoke too much and drink too much. HIV from intravenous drug use and casual and careless sexual contact threatens the future of our nations—our women and youth.*

*TB in our communities is still 10 times higher than in the rest of Canada. Our people are twice as likely to suffer from cancer, and three times more likely to be afflicted with heart disease.*

---

## Language Intensity

Johnston also discusses how credibility affects language intensity. *Language intensity* refers to descriptive language or a presentational style that involves lots of metaphors, adjectives, or modifiers (Johnston, 1994, p. 153). Like the use of evidence, whether such a style helps or hinders speakers depends again on their credibility. An intense language style works when speakers already have high credibility and the audience favours their position; otherwise, it can have the opposite effect.

## Opinionated Language

Johnston further notes the impact that using opinionated language has on listeners, and again its appeal depends largely on the speaker's credibility level: "*Opinionated language* cuts down people who do not believe in the advocated position or people who adhere to the counter position" (1994, p. 153). What do you think happens when high- or low-credibility speakers use such language? You can probably recognize the pattern that the high "creds" can get away with using it, while the low creds cannot.

When listeners hear high-credibility speakers using opinionated language, they think that these people must really believe in what they are saying. This can have a persuasive impact on the audience. On the other hand, when low-credibility speakers use opinionated language, there is a tendency for listeners to question their believability, which further diminishes their credibility, and hence their ability to persuade listeners.

---

### ◀)) SPOTLIGHT ON SPEAKERS

When it comes to environmental issues, no one is more credible than David Suzuki, scientist and broadcaster. The excerpt below is from a speech entitled "The Threat of Technology," presented at the Executive Forum on the Management of Change in Toronto on December 4, 1986. It is a good example of how both language intensity and opinionated language can work.

*Science and technology are accompanied by costs. If these are not considered equally with the benefits, then I believe we are simply indulging ourselves. In the 20th century, the list of scientific and technological achievements has been absolutely dazzling. The entire history of human flight, the automobile, telecommunications, nuclear power, antibiotics, oral contraception, computers and much more, have occurred within the span of a single human life. This is really an astounding achievement.*

*But lurking behind the glittery illusion of achievements is another reality—vanishing species. This is a ticking time bomb that is only now beginning to achieve prominence among the scientific community. We are now approaching a rate of extension that occurred in the last great extinction when the dinosaurs disappeared. By 1990, one species of plant and animal will be going extinct every hour. . . .*

---

# Level of Abstraction

*Level of abstraction* refers to how specific or vague and ambiguous the terms you use are. High-level-abstraction language is characterized by words that are unclear and equivocal, and generally allow listeners to interpret words according to their connotative meanings. Politicians use high-level abstraction, as in the following statement:

> If we upgrade the program, it will have a lot of implication for the systematicized decision making. This will give us a balanced and innovative programming approach. For total diffusion, we can take an active role. We can formalize a policy for a better image and ongoing educational research.

This passage may sound good in some vague way, but it says absolutely nothing. It was actually created from a list of empty words from the Gobbledygook Exercise (Goldhaber, 1993) that is provided in the "Application and Discussion Questions" section at the end of the chapter. To communicate effectively with an audience, speak in specifics or listeners will not understand you. Frankly, there will be nothing for them to understand.

To say what you mean, and with maximum clarity, start with a general statement and then follow it with something more precise. This is exactly what you do when you introduce your speech topic and provide an enumerated preview. It also occurs when you make a major point and then support it with illustrations and examples. Adhering to this well-known technique, as outlined in Chapter 5, helps you to be understood more clearly by your audience. You will be misquoted less often, audience members will be more apt to grasp what you are expressing, and you will be credible.

Morgan (2004) recommends that public speakers eliminate extraneous details and cut to the quick. Otherwise, you risk losing listeners' attention and reducing your credibility. He suggests practising until you get everything down to the bare minimum. As he explains it, "In conversation with a friend a sentence like 'As I entered that interview room, I reflected that I really, really wanted the job' is fine, but in a speech it's baggy and distracting. Instead, say, 'I entered the interview room desperately wanting the job' or 'I went into the interview wanting the job'" (p. 4).

## *Vocabulary*

Using low-level abstraction language does not suggest that vocabularies should be limited. In interpersonal communication contexts, speaking is spontaneous and the same words are used repeatedly. In public speaking contexts, however, speakers have an

## 🔊 SPOTLIGHT ON SPEAKERS

When it comes to Canadian orators, Rex Murphy is one of the nation's finest. His extensive vocabulary and skill at turning a phrase delights and entertains CBC audiences. Through his analytical prowess, he provides insight into situations beyond what the average person might see and finds the most interesting language to articulate it for us. Murphy's expertise as a wordsmith is exemplified in the excerpt below that was delivered on CBC's *The National*, September 8, 2000, in honour of Pierre Trudeau.

*He bore a symbolic relationship with his time. This angular, complex, multi-faceted personality seemed to say things to this country outside the words of his speeches or his policies. There was some element within him, or of him, that acted like a summons to the Canadian imagination; to live a little larger, think a little more carefully, or bring more courage or daring to our dreams.*

opportunity to contemplate in advance what words will best suit the context and the message content. Rex Murphy, mentioned in the accompanying spotlight, is noted for his extensive vocabulary. Inclusion of fitting, poignant, and descriptive language in a speech creates a strong audience impact. More information on language and rhetorical techniques is provided in Chapter 8.

---

### THE CANDIDATES

Language intensity and the use of opinionated language can be illustrated by two opposing political candidates: Mr. Whipsnaithe and Mr. Gotittogether.

Mr. Whipsnaithe was a large, gruff, middle-aged man, dressed in a white shirt and dress pants, with the shirt bulging out on one side. He spoke in a loud voice, pounded his fist a lot, and seemed to be concerned more with what he had to say than with connecting with the audience. I'd rate his credibility as low.

The second candidate, Mr. Gotittogether, was older, white-templed, and dressed in a suit, and his warm smile exposed straight, white teeth. He had a calm speaking style and a good delivery, and he made lots of audience contact. He possessed credibility.

Both speakers used language intensity and both integrated opinionated language into their speeches. At the end of the presentations, Mr. Gotittogether had the audience in the palm of his hand, while Mr. Whipsnaithe came off as untrustworthy. It was not surprising that Mr. Gotittogether was elected shortly after. In my personal estimation and knowledge of the candidates, Mr. Whipsnaithe more accurately represented the needs and desires of the populace. However, because of the impact of his delivery and the use of language intensity and opinionated language, this low-credibility speaker's true intentions were not evident.

This example demonstrates just how powerful speech delivery can be. Further, while you may want to use your knowledge of the public speaking process to enhance your delivery, you may also want to become a more critical consumer of the messages to which you are exposed. Do not take speakers at face value—use your knowledge and other research to get a clearer picture of the true meaning behind their words.

# CHAPTER AT A GLANCE

- Effective public speakers are credible speakers.
- Good notes are brief, clear, and often colour-coded.
- The level of language formality must suit the context.
- Credible speakers have a good delivery and use proper grammar.
- Use a nondeferential (powerful) language style in public speaking contexts.
- Use inclusive language by using plural pronouns, eliminating man-linked language, and altering the ordering of terms.
- Include all members of the audience in your presentations.
- Strive for a good delivery so you can use opinionated language and alter your level of intensity.
- Say what you mean by avoiding ambiguous and abstract language.

# APPLICATION AND DISCUSSION QUESTIONS

1. Answer the following questions in your communication journal:
   a. *Cognitive dimension:* Language was discussed in this chapter in terms of deferential versus nondeferential language styles, level of formality, grammar, inclusiveness, use of evidence and opinionated language, and

level of abstraction. Which of these did you find the most enlightening? Describe why.

    b.   *Affective dimension:* This chapter points out that speakers must be extremely aware of not only what they say but also how they say it. How does this affect your feelings about yourself before you make a speech, during the speech, and after the speech?

    c.   *Behavioural dimension:* Assess your strengths and weaknesses in each of the language topics discussed in the chapter. Where would you say you need the most work? Devise an improvement plan.

2.  Below is the paragraph that opened the section on common grammatical errors. Check how many of the grammar and articulation problems you identified. The corrections are in brackets.

*Often people thinks (think) that grammar don't (doesn't) matter, but it do (does). I seen (I have seen) it over and over again in my classes—some students what (who) write good (well) don't necessarily talk good (well). Youse (you) can't expect to get in front of them (eliminate the word or use* these *or* those*) people and speak bad (poorly), and then expect them to listen to what you're talking about. Add in ta (to) dat (that) some poor articulations (articulation), an (and) youse (you have) got yourself a speaker wit (with) no credibility.*

3.  Play the Gobbledygook Exercise (from Goldhaber, 1993). It shows how speakers can say absolutely nothing but sound good to the less discriminating ear.

    a.   Write 10 three-digit numbers in the following spaces:

_____ _____ _____ _____ _____

_____ _____ _____ _____ _____

    b.   Find a partner.

    c.   Starting with your first three-digit number (363, for example), develop a sentence using the corresponding words listed below. The first digit refers to the word number in Group 1, the second digit to the word number in Group 2, and the third digit to the word number in Group 3. Your sentence might go something like, "We have to (3) formalize the (6) differential dimensions before we can continue with the (3) planning stage."

    d.   Develop a conversation with your partner, moving from your three-digit number to your partner's and back and forth so that it sounds like an important discussion.

| Group 1 | Group 2 | Group 3 |
|---|---|---|
| 0. evaluate | 0. educational | 0. competencies |
| 1. coordinate | 1. diffusion | 1. research |
| 2. upgrade | 2. program | 2. implications |
| 3. formalize | 3. professional | 3. planning |
| 4. total | 4. leadership | 4. subject matter |
| 5. balanced | 5. clientele | 5. role |
| 6. finalize | 6. differential | 6. image |
| 7. systematized | 7. decision making | 7. focal point |
| 8. ongoing | 8. innovative | 8. flexibility |
| 9. responsive | 9. policy | 9. programming |

4. List a few speakers you enjoy and analyze their style in terms of the language factors discussed in this chapter. Do they use a deferential or nondeferential language style? Do they use inclusive language? Is their formality level appropriate for the setting or location? How about their grammar? What would it take for them to lose or gain credibility in your eyes?

5. How would you assess the grammar used by your family and friends: excellent, good, fair, or needs work? What are the most common grammatical errors you hear?

6. Develop notes for Stephanie Wadden's speech outline and try to limit them to one note card.

7. Visit the CBC Radio-Canada site for scripts of speeches and interviews that have aired since 1998. Select a couple and analyze them according to language formality, language style (deferential vs. nondeferential), inclusive language, grammar, language intensity, level of abstraction, and vocabulary. You can reach the site at *http://cbc.radio-canada.ca/speeches/index.asp*.

## REFERENCES AND FURTHER READINGS

Bohra, K.A., & Pandy, J. (1984). Ingratiation toward strangers, friends, and bosses. *The Journal of Social Psychology, 122,* 217–222.

Campbell, K.K. (2000). Man cannot speak for her. In B. Brummett, (Ed.), *Reading rhetorical theory* (895–903). Fort Worth, TX: Harcourt College.

Clarkson, A. (2005, May 16). Speech on the occasion of a luncheon by the Regina Public Library. Retrieved August 12, 2005, from http://www.gg.ca/media/doc.asp?lang=e&DocID=4443.

Coon Come, M. (2001, April 8). Is Canada making enough progress with aboriginal issues? *Cross Country Checkup*, Canadian Broadcasting Corporation. Retrieved August 12, 2005, from http://www.cbc.ca/checkup/archive/2001/intro010408.html.

Erickson, B., Lind, E.A., Johnson, B.C., & O'Barr, W.M. (1978). Speech style and impression formation in a court setting: The effects of "powerful" and "powerless" speech. *Journal of Experimental Social Psychology, 14*, 266–279.

Goldhaber, G.M. (1993). *Organizational communication* (6th ed.). Dubuque, IA: Wm. C. Brown.

Ivy, D.K., & Backlund, P. (2004). *Exploring gender speak: Personal effectiveness in gender communication* (3rd ed.). Boston: McGraw-Hill Ryerson.

Johnston, D.D. (1994). *The art and science of persuasion.* Madison, WI: WCB Brown & Benchmark.

Lakoff, R. (1973). Language and a women's place. *Language in Society, 2*, 45–80.

Liska, J., Mechling, E.W., & Stathas, S. (1981). Differences in subjects' perceptions of gender and believability between users of deferential and nondeferential language. *Communication Quarterly, 19*, 40–48.

Morgan, N. (2004). Preparing to be real. *Harvard Management Communication Letter, 1*, 3–5.

Murphy, R. (2000). Pierre Trudeau: He has gone to his grace, and that leaves so much less of ours. *The National,* Canadian Broadcasting Corporation. Retrieved September 2, 2001, from http://www.cbc.ca/news/national/rex/rex20000928.html.

O'Donnell, W.J., & O'Donnell, K.J. (1978). Update: Sex-role messages in TV commercials. *Journal of Communication, 28*, 156–158.

Pearson, J.C., Turner, L.H., & Todd-Mancillas, W. (1991). *Gender and communication* (2nd ed.). Dubuque, IA: Wm. C. Brown.

*Publication manual of the American Psychological Association* (5th ed.). (2001). Washington, DC: American Psychological Association.

Quina, K., Wingard, J.A., & Bates, H.G. (1987). Language style and gender stereotypes in person perception. *Psychology of Women Quarterly, 11*, 11–22.

Rolls, J.A. (1993, November). *The influence of language style and gender on perceptions of leadership potential: A review of relevant research.* Paper presented at the 79th annual meeting of the Speech Communication Association, Miami Beach, Florida.

Rolls, J.A. (2001, November). *Personal, professional, and public communication: A competency based training model.* Unpublished paper.

Shertzer, M.D. (1986). *The elements of grammar.* New York: Collier Books.

Suzuki, D.T. (1987). The threat of technology. *Canadian Speeches,* 01, 01. Retrieved August 2, 2001, from http://www.canadianspeeches.ca/search_results_detailsasp?Speech_Id=11&member=0.

# Chapter 7
## Visual Aids

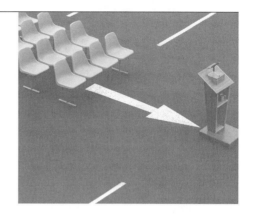

## CHAPTER GOALS

In this chapter, you will learn
- what constitutes a visual aid
- why to use visual aids
- some general tips for using visual aids
- how to design impressive-looking visual aids

## ▨ INTRODUCTION

Five professionally dressed students (two women, three men) were huddled around the photocopier making overheads—lots of them. I knew this because I had been waiting a long time to use the machine. Finally, as the minutes ticked closer to class time, I asked whether I could interrupt their work for just a few moments to run off my copies, and they agreed. They were business students, about to make their final marketing presentation. Given what I do, I could not help asking how they were getting along. Their enthusiastic response was amazing—almost in unison, they exclaimed, "Great! We've got 47 overheads!" "Hmmm," I said, in that Marge Simpson kind of way after Homer makes a questionable decision. But my tone did not dampen their spirits. I asked when their class was scheduled to meet, and one group member responded excitedly, "In 15 minutes." Just then, my copies were ready, so I thanked them and wished them well.

Using visual aids in a professional manner demands some finesse. All I could envision with this presentation was an audience sitting bleary-eyed through bursts of intermittent light and darkness as one overhead after another was slapped onto the machine. When the overheads were finished, the presentation would be finished. Unfortunately, I have come to think of an excessive number of transparencies not as tokens of ardent and eager preparation but rather as crutches to aid inept or debilitatingly nervous speakers.

In this chapter, you will learn how to use visual aids well. Specifically, you will learn what constitutes a visual aid and why they should be incorporated into your presentations. You will also review some guiding principles of visual aid usage. Then you will learn how to design and construct visuals that are both impressive to behold and useful to the listener. The skills you hone by reading this chapter can make a major difference in how your presentations are received.

## ▨ ABOUT VISUAL AIDS

A *visual aid* is something that contributes to, clarifies, or enhances your presentation so that it is better with the visual aid than without it. Visual aids generally fall into several common categories: objects, marker aids (blackboards, whiteboards, and flipcharts), prepared printed materials (charts, graphs, posters, and flipchart presentations), and audiovisual aids (audiotapes, overheads, slides, videotapes, and computer-generated/multimedia displays such as Microsoft PowerPoint presentations). Sometimes even people and animals serve as visual aids.

# Why Use Visual Aids?

Well-developed, well-executed visual aids can add to the overall effectiveness of your presentation. In fact, visual aids can enhance your credibility and heighten the dramatic effect. DeVito (1997, p. 164) suggests that they can also help speakers to gain and maintain audience attention and to reinforce and clarify their message. These factors are explained below.

## *Add to Credibility*

Speakers who develop interesting and appropriate visuals are considered more professional, and hence more credible, than those who do not. If you are making a formal business presentation and the norm is to use slides, overheads, or computer-generated visual aids, then your credibility is increased when you also meet that standard.

## *Contribute to Dramatic Effect*

Visual aids can also be used for dramatic effect, as the following example demonstrates. Zena, a former student, started her speech by taking a can of beer out of her sack. It was so cold you could see the beads of sweat wend their way into little trails down the side of the can. As she snapped the can open, that distinct popping and sizzling sound permeated the quiet classroom. Only then did Zena begin to speak: "For many of you, this sound may conjure up visions of drinking a chilled beer on a hot summer's day. To others, however, that same fizzle signifies a danger signal. Those individuals are alcoholics who cannot savour just one cold beer. They cannot stop once they've downed that first compulsive drink. I am going to inform you about what it is like to live with an alcoholic."

## *Gain and Maintain Attention*

Clearly, visual aids help gain and maintain audience attention because they provide something other than the speaker on which to focus. This can be beneficial to nervous speakers because, as one public speaking professor pointed out, as soon as a speaker says, "If you will look here . . .," the audience members immediately take their eyes off the speaker and look toward where they are directed.

Visual aids can also add a good deal of variety and vitality, and in general, enliven a speech. The following example demonstrates what one person did to gain and maintain attention.

I had asked students to do a short presentation on a person, place, thing, or event that had an impact on their lives. They were also required to use a visual aid. Todd, an older, reentry student, began his speech by naming all the members of his immediate family. Then he opened the classroom door, and to our surprise, in marched his three children and pregnant wife. While one might presume that these visual aids would be disruptive, they actually worked out very well. Todd ushered them in, made his point about the importance of his family (which, by the way, was evident by the children's proud, beaming faces), and showed them out without incident. It was all very smooth and effective.

## Reinforce Message

When you offer an audience visual aids, your verbal message is strengthened because information is given through additional types of data and media. As Brody (1998) notes, "Our ability to retain information increases by close to 40 percent when visual aids are used" (p.89). Therefore, when statistics, keywords, or other pertinent information are both verbalized and displayed, listeners are more likely to remember your message.

Keep a simple rule in mind: the more senses (sight, hearing, taste, touch, and smell) you engage in the audience through your presentation, the more likely the audience will remember your message.

## Clarify Message

Because speakers depend on listeners to attach meanings to their words, speakers' intended meaning can be clarified via a visual aid of some sort. The following interpersonal example shows how even simple, everyday language can cause confusion.

I once told an acquaintance that I liked to paint when I spent time at my summer cottage. The individual seemed both surprised and impressed. "Oh, yes," I continued, "I just love it; it is so relaxing and very rewarding. I often play classical music, and so there I am, out in the forest with Beethoven blaring and me painting away." Then she inquired about the kinds of things I painted. I told her, "Oh, you know, the usual. Every year the back steps need to be done. This year I have to do the trim on the front of the house—the salt air fades it so much over the winter months." Her expression changed, and I immediately understood that she thought that I painted artistically!

If you wish to show a video excerpt or information from a computer, you can use an LCD (liquid crystal display) machine to enlarge it. We used one in our persuasion class last year so we could analyze television commercials. With the big screen, everyone could see really well. I highly recommend it.

*Benjamin, Former Communication Student*

If I had been making a presentation, a series of visual aids could have alerted the listener to the interpretation of the simple word *paint*. The message would have been clearer earlier on.

# Guiding Principles

Regardless of the type of visual aid you use, there are several guiding principles to consider.

## Visual Aids Have Three Distinct Dimensions

Visual aids have three distinct dimensions: design, creation, and delivery.

*Design* refers to what the visual aids will embody; that is, what their content will be, and how that information will be arranged or laid out in the visual aids.

*Creation*, or the making of visual aids, means their actual physical construction. This, of course, comes in many forms, depending on the type of visual aid you are making. For example, it could entail printing words in coloured markers on flipchart paper, using PowerPoint's formatting toolbar, or cutting out and pasting together pictures to create a collage.

*Delivery* denotes how visual aids are used during the presentation. When you point to a flipchart, change transparencies on an overhead projector, or hit the remote button during a computer-aided presentation, you are obviously using visual aids.

## Visual Aids Can Never Substitute for Content or Delivery

Visual aids can never take the place of a well-planned, well-researched, and well-delivered speech. They cannot make a bad speech good. Unfortunately, inexperienced speakers think that they can. For instance, such misguided speakers equate a professional presentation with one that uses extensive overheads, and operate under the common misconception that more is better.

---

As listeners, we should not be fooled by the use of fancy visual displays. There is a tendency to assume that such speakers are better prepared, more professional, and more knowledgeable. This is not always the case. The key is to have a good delivery and a good selection of visual aids.

*Clark, Former Communication Student*

---

When speakers choose to hide psychologically behind their visual aids, just the opposite occurs—they are exposed. Listeners soon realize that such speakers will not be addressing them directly, and that in all likelihood, they will be in for a boring presentation.

### Practice Is a Must

Always take time to practise so you can coordinate the visual aid with your verbal message. While visual aids can contribute substantially to your overall presentation, they can also quickly reduce your credibility when you fumble with slides, spend time looking for things on tapes, or tinker with the equipment.

---

 **EXPERT ADVICE**

Sue DeWine, a communication professor and consultant, tells the story of one new manager's speech preparation in her book, *The Consultant's Craft: Improving Organizational Communication* (2001). Apparently, the manager was very nervous about making a presentation in front of his superiors and became even more so when he learned that he was also being considered for an upper management position. Needless to say, he was well prepared and on presentation day, he did two things that averted potential disaster. Prior to the presentation, he checked out the room and found that the overhead projector bulb had burned out. He had it replaced. Then, when he began his practice round, the podium light wasn't bright enough for him to see his notes so he had that replaced. Later, as people came into the room, he greeted them and learned that several were at the wrong session. Taking time to attend to such details paid off. As DeWine says, "A good speech alone will not get a person a promotion, but a bad one can prevent upper management from selecting that person to play a more important role as an official company representative" (p. 245).

*Sue DeWine, Ph.D.*
The Consultant's Craft: Improving Organizational Communication

---

### The Audience Must Not Be Ignored

A general rule in the theatre that also can be applied to public speaking contexts is, *never speak with your back to the audience.* If you do, you lose the listeners' attention. Always try to face the audience members, and try not to get between them and your

"For God's sake, Edwards. Put the laser pointer away."

visual aids. Practise pointing to your visual aid as you face your listeners. If you must write on something, do it, and then turn to your audience and speak.

## Visual Aids Should Suit Your Topic

The type of visual aid you select should complement your speech goal. For example, many years ago, Frances, an avid golfer, presented a speech on the rudiments of the game. Outfitted in dress slacks and a matching blazer, she defined the teeing-off process, and as she did so, she slowly drew a golf tee from her jacket pocket. When she was finished, she slipped it back in. Very smooth. Next, she discussed the importance of selecting the right type of ball for the game. Again, her hand went into her jacket pocket, this time on the other side, and she produced a bumpy, well-used golf ball. As she explained how it was created from wound elastic, Frances raised it up for all to contemplate. After she had made her point, back into the pocket it went.

I was expecting her to haul an iron out of her pant leg at any minute, but she disappointed me there. However, I wonder if I would have remembered that speech so many years later had she not used the discreet, but well-placed, visual aids? The trick is to choose visual aids that are unique and relevant to your presentation. I doubt that Frances's speech would have been so interesting had she presented us with a series of graphs and overheads.

### Visual Aids Need to Be Controlled

Arnold and McClure (1996), two training and development specialists, discuss the notion of *controlling visual aids.* They cite the all-too-common phenomenon where a student, required to use visual aids, circulates a series of pictures around the class during the presentation.

Arnold and McClure would say that when students do this, they have lost control of the visual aids. This is because, at any given time, some audience members will be more concerned about the pictures than about listening to the speaker. Listeners will be conferring with one another, handing the photos in front of and across one another's vision lines, or passing them on to the next individual, whose listening may be interrupted by the intrusion. To maintain control of visual aids, everyone in the class must be able to see them at the very same time—that is, when they are the main point of the presentation.

### Audience Members Need Plenty of Time to See Visual Aids

Make sure everyone can see your visual aid. If, for instance, you are presenting a small object or showing a picture, raise it high enough and direct it toward all parts of the room so that everyone can have a good look at it. Take your time with this. As you speak, move around so that everyone takes notice. In the case of projections, leave images on the screen long enough for listeners to understand their significance.

### Technology Cannot Always be Trusted

While technological aids are stimulating and useful, keep in mind that you can never fully trust them. While the electricity rarely goes off, many other things—with equally horrifying ramifications—go wrong on a regular basis. For example, overhead and slide projector light bulbs burn out at the most inopportune times. People forget cords and cables, or for some reason, nothing happens when you press the correct button. Even multimedia backups can go wrong if the computers on which they will be used do not have the functions that have been programmed into the presentation.

As disconcerting as it may seem, always be prepared to do a "technologically deprived" presentation. Many professional speakers carry backup manual visual aids, such as flipchart presentations. Should some mishap occur, their credibility rises when they present their

## DONNA'S VISUAL AID

Donna's speech goal was to inform the class how rottweilers were not really so deserving of their bad reputation. To augment her argument, she decided to introduce Reggie the rottweiler as a visual aid. She assured me that he was friendly—good with the kids in the neighbourhood, she told me. Although it went against my better judgment I allowed the dog to enter the class, but only if he remained on the leash and if Donna kept the leash secure in her hand throughout the speech.

Things went quite well at first as Reggie sat still, looking around at the class, while his owner spoke. I was even beginning to come around and agree with Donna—did I detect the hint of a dog smile on his face? No, apparently not! Out of the blue, Reggie let out a high-pitched, shrieking yelp and lunged forward at a student in the front row. Wrestling against the taut leash, he bared a set of long fangs that put us on edge while Donna, a petite woman, did all she could do to hold him back. Luckily, as quickly as Reggie shot off, he settled down again, but I was forced to ask that Donna remove her visual aid from the room.

As it turned out, Reggie was not a suitable aid. He neither enhanced nor improved the presentation. If anything, he detracted from it. Clearly, the rottweiler as a family pet did not make a compelling argument. One could say, however, that he added dramatic effect.

backup. Further, these speakers refrain from making comments like, "It would have been much better with my overheads or the PowerPoint presentation." Such assertions do not help people land the contract, get the sale, or clinch their reputation as a public speaker.

 **EXPERT ADVICE**

If you include videotape, audiotape, or CD excerpts in your presentation, they must be cued exactly to what you wish your audience to hear or see. When preparing such audiovisual aids, leave a little lead time both before and after the selections. Make sure you know how to operate the machines and how to use their special features.

*Wanda Harbin, Ombudsperson and Training Officer*
*Marine Atlantic Corporation, North Sydney, Nova Scotia*

## ■ DESIGNING AND USING VISUAL AIDS

It is clear that visual aids can enrich a presentation—that is, when they are done well. If they are not, they can be extremely distracting to the audience. So that your visual aids do not draw negative attention, this section explains how to design visuals that will not upstage you or your message. Some general design rules apply to all visual aids.

## General Design Tips

### *Avoid Clutter*

The most common design error is clutter. Speakers tend to put way too much information on a page—too much text, too much clip art, too much colour, and too many different fonts. Some of the worst overheads contain lines and lines of data and detailed information in such small type that it is impossible for even front-row people to read. I cannot tell you how often I have seen such overheads, many done by professionals who should know better. Further, these third-rate visual aids are often accompanied by announcements such as, "You probably won't be able to make this out!" But the speakers continue anyway.

Clear visual aids keep the amount of information per page to a minimum. (Note that throughout this text, and particularly in this chapter, a page also refers to a slide, an overhead transparency, a flipchart sheet, a poster, an image on a computer-aided presentation, or

any increment in a series of visual aids.) A general rule for page design is to restrict each page to just one primary topic. Also, no more than six bulleted pieces of information should appear on any one page. With the exception, perhaps, of a definition, text should not be worded in sentence form, especially long, run-on ones. Instead, main points should be explained through the use of key expressions.

If you follow these design fundamentals, your spoken message will be clarified and strengthened by your visual one. It will stand out for the audience, especially when words are scripted in large, clear print. See Figure 7.1 on page 214 for an example of a bad visual aid.

## *Use Parallel Language*

Use parallel language in your pages. This means that similar syntax or grammatical forms are used to express different points in a list. For example, the following sentence does not use parallel language:

> Kyle got his favourite magazine, he sat in the overstuffed chair, and opens a can of soda.

Can you see how the parts of the sentence do not all use the same structure or verb tense? Here is the same sentence using parallel language:

> Kyle got his favourite magazine, sat in the overstuffed chair, and opened a can of soda.

Note that each point starts with a verb in the past tense. See the accompanying box for other examples of nonparallel and parallel language forms.

---

### NONPARALLEL AND PARALLEL CONSTRUCTIONS

| NONPARALLEL | PARALLEL |
|---|---|
| 1. the English, the French, and Spaniards | 1. the English, the French, and the Spanish |
| 2. in spring, summer, and in winter | 2. in spring, in summer, and in winter |
| 3. it was both a long ceremony and very tedious | 3. the ceremony was both long and tedious |
| 4. men, girls, and children | 4. men, women, and children |
| 5. up the hill, running down the road, then go over the bridge | 5. up the hill, down the road, and over the bridge |

---

**Figure 7.1—A Bad Visual Aid**

How could this visual aid be improved?

### Stick to a Few Simple Fonts

A *font* refers to a print style (the word *typeface* is also used). Because computer software makes changing fonts so easy, some novice users have a tendency to slip into that "more is better" mentality. Using several distinctive and unconventional fonts in a variety of sizes can distract an audience. Too much font variety also makes for a cluttered-looking page. If you confine your fonts to one or two plain, easy-to-read types, your visuals will look more professional and less distracting.

### Be Consistent

Professional visual aids contain a certain level of consistency. If, for example, you use a double underline or a certain font for main headings, then stick to this style throughout your set of visual aids.

 **EXPERT ADVICE**

When someone has perfect vision, we say their eyesight is 20/20. If a presenter wants the audience to be able to see the PowerPoint slides perfectly, I recommend applying the 20/20 rule. Remember to have no more than 20 words per slide and use a font size no smaller than 20 point.

$$\frac{20}{20} = \frac{20 \text{ words per slide}}{20 + \text{font size}}$$

*Judy Ann Roy, Ph.D., Faculty of Business Administration*
*University of New Brunswick, Fredericton, N.B.*

Also consider whether to use uppercase letters, lowercase letters, or a combination of both. Words that combine upper- and lowercase letters can be baffling, and in some instances, downright difficult to understand. Do you agree that the following consistent examples—*House, house,* or *HOUSE*—are easier to read than these inconsistent ones—*hoUSe, HoUse,* or *hOuSE?*

To increase clarity, adhere to the following rules: (1) use all uppercase, (2) use all lowercase, or (3) capitalize only the first letter of each word. You can emphasize some words by using all uppercase letters.

| WHAT GOOD VISUAL AIDS LOOK LIKE |
| --- |
| **C**lean and uncluttered |
| **L**arge enough for everyone to see |
| **E**asily understood |
| **A**ttractive and colourful |
| **R**elevant to the topic |

## Check Your Spelling

Pay attention to spelling. Have someone look over your work, because the word-processing spell-check feature we have all come to depend on does not detect all errors. As writers and creators, we tend to see what we expect to see. A more objective reader, just like a member of the audience, can spot these errors in a flash.

It's going to be another one of those meetings. As the lights dim and the projection system fires up, you realize that the person running the PowerPoint presentation has just discovered all the bells and whistles that the program has to offer: sounds, animation, flashing text, and a whole host of other special effects. It's too bad, but you're so overwhelmed by the patchwork of effects and features that you've lost track of the presentation's main topic. As you hunker down for a long afternoon, you resolve that you'll never produce a presentation that unsettles an audience as much as this one does.

**Source:** Avoid the Mistakes of PowerPoint Rookies, *Smart Computing*, January 2001.

Thus far, the focus has been on general design tips. The remainder of this chapter focuses on specific visual aids. Think of this section as a reference—it contains useful tips for creating and using a variety of visual aids.

# Computer-Generated Displays

Computer-generated displays, such as those created with PowerPoint, make very popular visual aids. Listeners get a cheap thrill when those little bullets zoom in from the sides or pie charts explode before their very eyes. They also enjoy how media genres can be combined in interesting ways. There is no doubt that these programs can be remarkable tools.

However, some creators overdo it. Rather than become informed by the use of these computer-assisted displays, audiences can become overwhelmed. They may come to view such visual aids as confusing distractions. Jaffa (2004) argues, "You are your own best visual." He suggests that speakers do away entirely with projection aids so that the audience will focus on the speaker and listen, rather than read along with whatever is being projected on a screen.

This section contains pointers that, if implemented properly, should enable you to make presentations that stimulate, captivate, and educate.

## Presentation Tips

If you are going to use computer-generated and -assisted visual aids, familiarize yourself with a good program. A popular one is Microsoft PowerPoint. For a great article that walks you through this program, see "Avoid the Mistakes of PowerPoint Rookies" in the magazine *Smart Computing*, January 2001 (you can find an excerpt of this article at *http://www.smartcomputing.com*). The design principles for creating better slides that are outlined in the box below come from this article. Overall, the

"My PowerPoint presentation went so well, I had it made into a tattoo!"

Randy Glasbergen

article reinforces awareness of general design issues such as clutter, colour confusion, not-so-special effects, conformity, and preparation. The full online version also has "click on" instructions to help you in each of these areas.

### Using Photographs

Many people assume that a computer slide presentation must include text. Steck (2000) points out that this is not true: her students have used PowerPoint presentations merely to display photographs. She writes,

> This semester two students did speeches in PowerPoint that were entirely supported by photographs with no words. The photos came out beautifully, could be seen by all students, and could be clicked through easily without the hassle often associated with using many transparencies. One student gave an informative speech on theatrical aging make-up. She used 16 digitized photos of the stages of make-up and was able to present a speech in

---

## BUILDING BETTER SLIDES FOR YOUR POWERPOINT PRESENTATIONS

As you build your presentation, keep the following design principles in mind:

- Include the body text (bulleted point) information in short, to-the-point phrases, not complete sentences.
- Plan three to five text slides per major concept.
- Use just one main concept per slide.
- Use the minimum number of elements on a slide that will effectively convey your messages.
- Limit each slide to six or fewer bulleted points that support the main idea.
- Use five or fewer data series per chart.
- Avoid too many objects, such as clip art or AutoShapes, on a slide.
- Explode a pie slice or change a data series chart colour to emphasize the most important data.
- Avoid juxtaposing red and green, such as in chart series. Approximately 4 percent of the population is colourblind and will have difficulty viewing the information.

**Source:** Adapted from "Avoid the Mistakes of PowerPoint Rookies" in *Smart Computing* (Jan. 2001, pp. 62–65).

seven minutes. This is much less time than a demonstration would have taken and was extremely effective.

---

 **EXPERT ADVICE**

When it comes to using PowerPoint, all the fireworks in the world won't matter if there's no magic in you.

*Heather Sayeau, Adjunct Professor*
*Nova Scotia College of Art and Design, Halifax, N.S.*

---

## The Controversy over Computer-Generated Programs

There is some controversy as to whether computer-generated programs, such as PowerPoint and others, should even be taught in basic public speaking courses. Some argue that students should be learning speaking skills, not technical ones that serve to promote poor public speaking habits. Others—particularly business communication instructors—hold that computer-generated displays are expected in the real world, so their inclusion in public speaking classes gives students an advantage in the workplace. This makes sense. As Nunberg (1999) points out, being able to use PowerPoint has become a "corporate survival skill." And, it goes without saying that PowerPoint and other similar programs are outstanding in their ability to incorporate a variety of media.

The problem is that slides generally lack creativity and more often than not, serve as detailed outlines of presentations. Some are actually designed to facilitate note taking. In terms of the presentation itself, the worst-case scenarios find speakers reading their prompters word for word as the audience reads along. This is not public speaking. In one case, a senior manager read his entire statistical report to an audience. He made two mistakes: he read every statistic when the audience could already see them and he went overtime, but spent little time interpreting the results or answering questions. His PowerPoint presentation had become, rather than supported, the presentation.

The other potential problem with PowerPoint is that speakers use most of their preparation time gathering data and making slides. Instead, they would be served better by practising their delivery to make the material interesting and informative. See the excerpt on pages 220–221 from Wahl's (2003) article entitled "PowerPoint of No Return" for advice on how to make PowerPoint work for you.

## POWERPOINT OF NO RETURN

**TO MILLIONS OF EXECS, IT'S A HELPER, A SECURITY BLANKET, A TELEPROMPTER. BUT IF POWERPOINT IS SO GREAT, WHY DO SO MANY PRESENTATIONS STINK?**

There's a scourge upon the boardrooms and conference centres of the corporate world. It's sucking the life out of meetings, inflicting boredom and confusion in audiences large and small, and leaving wasted productivity in its wake. The sickness is all too well-known: the dreaded PowerPoint presentation.

We've all been there, sitting in some dark, airless space, straining to keep our eyes open during a presentation that drones on and on. A screen glows with a seemingly endless series of slides and charts, bullet points and words streaking and spinning round. But it's all in vain. Befuddled by the barrage of information, you fail to glean anything of use. The presentation ends, the lights come up, and you stumble away in a haze, thirsty for comprehension.

What's gone wrong? Since Microsoft released its first version of PowerPoint 16 years ago, some 400 million copies have been installed around the world, and experts figure the software is employed in—get this—some 30 million presentations each day. It's the second-most-used corporate communication tool after e-mail. People are so accustomed to working with PowerPoint, in fact, that it's no longer just getting the big-screen treatment—they're using it in ways Microsoft developers never intended. For instance, PowerPoint files are increasingly being distributed as self-published reports to colleagues or via the web to the public.

Want to deliver a stellar presentation? Here are some basic rules from the experts:

**Get comfy with the technology.** Nothing is more irritating than watching a presenter fuss with cables or advancing to the wrong slide. You'll look foolish, and it will suck the wind from your sails.

**Know what you're talking about—cold.** This will help keep you from committing the cardinal PowerPoint sin, which is simply reading bullet points to your audience. "Unfortunately, PowerPoint gets used as a TelePrompTer," complains Paradi. "It was never intended to be that way." Paradi recommends that for every hour of speaking time, you spend between three and six hours preparing.

**Instead of squeezing your speech into bullet points on slides, use the "Notes" view.** It gives you room to write out what you'll say in a space below each slide. Then, says Atkinson, you can figure out what image would be appropriate to accompany that part of the presentation, as a memory tool, but also for the good of your audience. (A plus: it preserves your presentation for another time, or as a more complete package to share with others.) Studies, including one by 3M published in the *Harvard Business Review*, have shown that bullet points merely fragment your message, because they are devoid of context and don't link to anything else. Says Atkinson: "Bullet points were the right answer to the wrong question: How do I squeeze all this information on this limited blank space?"

**Know how to use multimedia.** If you don't, either get help or don't bother. Be careful with getting creative with even the simplest graphics. Most people wouldn't dare publish a brochure without subjecting the material to the deft touch of a design professional, but millions toil late into the night creating hideously ugly PowerPoint presentations. Don't waste your time. If you're an effective speaker, a plain white background won't hurt how you make your case.

**Know what information works on a slide, and what's better presented in another medium.** Be wary of overloading your audience with information that distracts from your key message. If it's complex, give it to them on paper afterward. "If you need to give a detailed handout," says Paradi, "then give a detailed handout—don't just print your slides." Paradi has even started burning CD-ROMs that will self-load a web-based version of his PowerPoint presentations into a browser, including the text of his speech. If he gets really ambitious, he can add an audio file to it, or supporting Adobe Acrobat documents and Internet links. "They can now take you home and refer to it any time they want," he says. "It's a great way to enhance your impact beyond just the 45 or 60 minutes that you spend with the audience." Moreover, it maximizes the time you have with your audience.

**Finally, know the most powerful button on your laptop—the "B" key.** This blacks out the screen during a PowerPoint presentation. Don't be afraid to use it so the slides won't compete with what are ultimately your most effective communication tools: your voice, mannerisms and facial expressions.

Remember, PowerPoint doesn't kill presentations: people kill presentations. Do yourself a favour. From this day forward, vow that you won't make the mistake of subjecting your audiences to any more death by PowerPoint than they've already had to endure.

**Source:** Wahl, A. (2003). PowerPoint of no return. *Canadian Business, 76*(22) 131–133.

## Graphs/Charts, Tables, and Maps

Graphs (or charts), tables, and maps are useful visual aids that enable you to highlight facts, show a lot of information at once, summarize material, or indicate how things change over time. Audience members are able to perceive quickly what might normally take up to 10 minutes to convey verbally. Regardless of whether these visual aids take the form of posters, computer-generated presentations, or handouts, some design suggestions can improve their quality.

**Figure 7.2—Bar Graph**

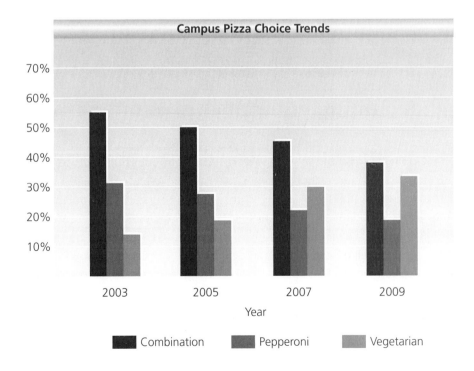

## *Graphs/Charts*

Although software programs enable you to create professional-looking graphs, keep the following design tips in mind:

- All graphs should be simple and easy to read. Make sure labels are written in down-to-earth, understandable language.
- In general, keep text to a minimum and make sure it appears in large print.

Graphs come in three general types: bar, line, and pie. *Bar graphs* are particularly effective for comparing and contrasting two or more elements. Because they are generally pretty simple and straightforward, they are easy to understand (see Figure 7.2).

*Line graphs* are used to demonstrate trends over a period of time. Because you can see increases and decreases, they are suitable for plotting things like growth and decline (see Figure 7.3). To avoid confusion when using more than one line on a graph, use contrasting colours. Also, note that time is always represented on the horizontal axis and it goes from left to right.

*Pie graphs* allow you to see the whole and how it is divided into parts. Most often the percentage of each piece of the pie is also indicated (see Figure 7.4, page 224). When

### Figure 7.3—Line Graph

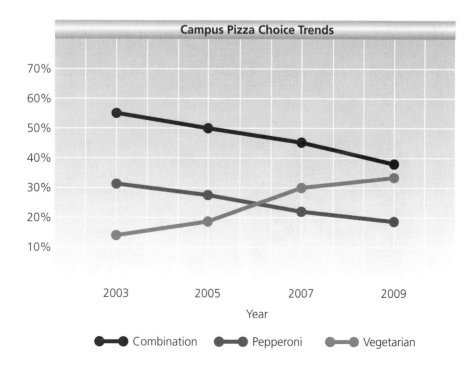

you are creating a pie graph, do not put in too many pieces—five or fewer categories are considered most effective, and each one should be labelled. The piece that you want to accentuate is generally placed at the top of the circle.

## Tables

When you are constructing tables, make sure they are readable. Some speakers take tables directly from written reports or other printed sources. The problem with this practice is that often the tables are too complex and involved for their speech goals (not to mention too small for everyone to see). It is preferable to custom design your own tables so they meet the needs of your particular speech (see Figure 7.5).

## Maps

The most important thing to remember about maps is that they must be big enough for everyone in the audience to see. Preferably, they should contain only the details that relate to your speech. This means that most commercially printed maps will not work because they are too detailed. Think about drawing your own, simpler map instead so your visual aid includes only what you want. (See also the "Posters" section on page 231.)

**Figure 7.4—Pie Graph**

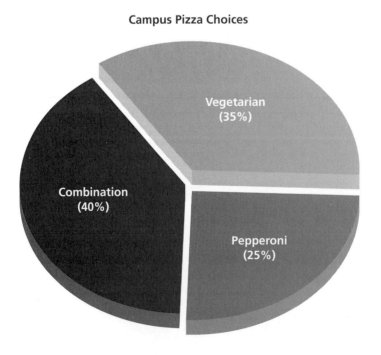

Campus Pizza Choices

Vegetarian (35%)

Combination (40%)

Pepperoni (25%)

## Figure 7.5—A Clear-Looking Table

| SECONDARY SCHOOL[1] GRADUATION RATES | 1997/98 | 2000/01 | 2001/02 | 2002/03 |
|---|---|---|---|---|
| Canada | 76.0 | 76.9 | .. | .. |
| Canada without Ontario | 75.6 | 77.2 | 75.8 | 75.6 |
| Newfoundland and Labrador[2] | 81.5 | 75.2 | 76.0 | 76.6 |
| Prince Edward Island | 86.5 | 83.5 | 82.2 | 82.6 |
| Nova Scotia | 81.7 | 77.9 | 79.4 | 81.1 |
| New Brunswick | 83.1 | 82.6 | 83.2 | 81.5 |
| Quebec[3] | 82.2[r] | 82.9 | 81.6 | 78.6 |
| Ontario | 77.0 | 76.8[E] | .. | .. |
| Manitoba[4] | 75.9 | 77.6 | 69.0 | 71.3 |
| Saskatchewan | 73.0 | 78.7 | 76.5 | 77.0 |
| Alberta | 63.2[r] | 65.7 | 65.9 | 66.5 |
| British Columbia | 71.4 | 76.1 | 74.7 | 77.1 |
| Yukon | 57.9 | 59.8 | 57.2 | 57.2 |
| Northwest Territories[5] | 34.1 | 45.7 | 38.3 | 43.3 |
| Nunavut[5] | ... | 25.4 | 26.5 | 25.6 |

| | |
|---|---|
| .. | Not available. |
| ... | Not applicable. |
| E | Use with caution. |
| r | Revised figure. |
| 1 | Secondary schools include public, private, and federal schools, and schools for the visually and hearing impaired. Equivalencies and "General Education Diplomas" are excluded. |
| 2 | From 1995/96 to 1999/2000, high school graduation was based on school results only; there were no provincial examinations. |
| 3 | Secondary graduations for Quebec include graduates from adult and trade/vocational programs. |
| 4 | Prior to 2001/02 includes Manitoba mature students enrolled in regular high school. |
| 5 | Northwest Territories boundaries included Nunavut prior to April 1, 1999. |

**Source:** Statistics Canada (2005, February 2). Secondary school graduates. *The Daily*. Retrieved August 18, 2005, from http://www.statcan.ca/Daily/English/050202/d050202b.htm.

You wouldn't believe what happened in my speech class. One girl actually presented her entire speech in the dark, with her back to the audience, facing the screen, and reading the presentation word for word from the overhead. I thought the professor was going to go nuts, but he was actually pretty good about it. I could tell that the poor girl was very nervous, I mean really nervous. It was probably the only way she could get through her presentation. What a sin.

*Chelsea, Former Public Speaking Student*

## Overhead Transparencies

Overheads (or transparencies) can be produced in two ways. First, they can be hand printed (or drawn) with markers on transparency film. By using washable markers, overheads can be wiped clean and reused.

Overheads can also be designed with a computer program. If you use such a program, you can print on transparency film specially made for computer printers, or you can print to paper and then copy onto a transparency film using a photocopier. If you use a laser colour copier, be sure to get film that is designed specifically for such machines. Designing and making overheads is the easy part; using them is another story.

So many things can go wrong when using transparencies and overhead projectors. For instance, there is a general inclination to use so many overheads that they end up becoming the presentation rather than a support. Speakers tend not to practise enough: they do things like speak to the screen, show overheads at the wrong times, or mislay them on the projector so that they appear lopsided on the screen. Speakers also show blurry, out-of-focus overheads and confuse their order. This all happens between explosions of blinding light.

To avoid some of these problems, follow these tips:
- Do not use overheads just for the sake of using them.
- To prevent light seepage, put your overheads in cardboard frames (these are reusable and the small investment is well worth it).
- Turn the projector off when you are not showing overheads.
- To prevent the overheads from getting mixed up, number them.
- The most important thing you can do is practise.

**PUBLIC SPEAKING IN THE 21ST CENTURY**

To view professionally developed slides, check out the Canadian Tire Corporation Investor Relations site at *http://investor.relations.canadiantire.ca/ireye/ir_site.zhtml?ticker=ctr.a.to&script=1200.*

It houses multimedia presentations from strategic planning and other meetings. In your estimation, do the slides adhere to the design tips outlined in this chapter? Do you see any room for improvements? Download slides from other sites that you find and bring them to class for discussion.

### Practising with Your Overheads

*Know your equipment!* Practising begins with knowing how the projector works— where to plug it in, whether you will need an extension cord, how to turn it on and off, how to adjust the focus, how to raise and lower the lens, and how to change the light bulb. You also need to know how to operate the screen; some are manual while others are electric.

After you are "one with" the machine, practise your presentation. Focus on three basic moves:

1.  Coordinate your presentation with the transparencies so you know when to put them on.
2.  Rehearse how to get them on and off the machine with as little fuss as possible, including turning the projector on and off.
3.  Practise pointing to things when they are up on the screen, making sure that your pointer, pen, or hand do not obstruct key points. Further, try covering and uncovering parts of transparencies.

While this all sounds so simple in theory, it is much more difficult in practice. Repeat these steps until you can incorporate the overhead into your presentation smoothly and with grace.

## Flipcharts

Flipchart displays are commonly used in real-life presentations when speaking to a small group of 20 people or so. Above that number, they are probably too small for all audience members to see comfortably.

### Preparation

When you use flipcharts, it is best to make them up in advance—when you have plenty of time to give them the attention they require. Many businesspeople and trainers do them the night before, in the comfort of their hotel rooms. Should you find yourself in this or a similar situation, feel free to request that flipchart paper be sent to your room.

For even more professional flipchart sheets, you could use a ProImage XL PosterPrinter, a machine that works like a photocopy enlarger. You can insert your letter-sized pages into the machine, and voilà—out comes a flipchart-sized version. What this means is that you can use a variety of computer programs to help you design and create your pages. Of course, this eliminates the need to use messy markers.

If you use markers, follow the general design principles reviewed earlier in the chapter. Because markers have a tendency to bleed through, slip an extra blotter sheet under the page you are writing on. To help you keep words and figures aligned, draw lines on the blotter page so that it also serves as a guide. The lines should show through and help keep you on the straight and narrow, so to speak. Finally, make sure that flipchart pages are neat, clean, and fresh. It does little for your credibility to show up with tattered, torn, and blotched sheets.

As you create your flipchart pages, keep in mind those instances when you will need blank pages, perhaps when you pose questions and record audience responses. Leaving the required pages eliminates having to flip to the end of your text pages. When you need blank sheets, they will be there. If you plan to make several presentations with the same set of flipchart notes, leave plenty of empties. You may also wish to reserve some

This was to be my first presentation in my new job—sales manager for the western division. My girlfriend gave me a laser pointer as a good luck charm and I felt pretty cool. Remembering my university public speaking course, just for fun, I did a practice run. Well, those little mothers are hard to use! It's hard to stop them from jiggling. Finally I figured out that it's better to keep them moving in a circular motion, around the words or objects I was focusing on. Turned out too that you can shine them in people's eyes really easy. In the end, I didn't feel confident enough to use it for the presentation but I told my girlfriend it had been a good help. Maybe next time.

*Jim, Sales Manager*

blanks for times when you do not want the audience to see anything. Think too about what you want to have on the cover page—for example, your name, the title of your presentation, "good morning," or something entirely different.

### Visibility and Crib Notes

If possible, use wide markers because they attract more attention and are easier to decipher. Of course, use markers that are fresh with lots of ink, and steer clear of lighter colours that are harder to see. And speaking of visibility, a common technique professional speakers use is to place crib notes on their flipcharts. They write prompts—such as examples, statistics, or questions—in pencil. While such cues are not evident to audience members, they are clearly visible to the speaker.

### Using a Flipchart

Place the flipchart where it can be seen by all listeners. When you refer to the pages, stand to one side and point out anything that requires highlighting. Do not stand in front of the flipchart or block the view while you are speaking. Good presenters do not look at their visual aids while they are speaking—they make eye contact with their listeners.

If you plan to be writing on a flipchart, check in advance what type of stand you will have at your disposal. If possible, request an older design because it will have a wooden backing that provides a sturdy support when you are writing. This contrasts with the newer, lighter metal frames that do not sport such a backing. When you write on these stands, the paper tends to dent and sink.

---

 **PUBLIC SPEAKING IN THE 21ST CENTURY**

For practical information and tips on all aspects of presentation making, turn to professional speaker Tom Antion's blogsite. It offers realistic, relevant, and reliable information in short, cut-to-the-quick articles. He knows what he's talking about. Check him out at *http://greatpublicspeaking.blogspot.com.*

---

## Marker Aids

*Marker aids* simply refer to various surfaces that you can mark on. Typically, they consist of blackboards, whiteboards, and of course, flipcharts. They are good if you just want to jot something down for an audience. Perhaps you will take a poll on some controversial topic and display the results as you continue your presentation. You might wish to write out the spelling of a foreign word or an unfamiliar term. Or, you may want to generate some kind of a list with your audience.

In some cases, you may have to use a blackboard or whiteboard to write down a fair amount of information before the presentation. Regardless of what you put on these boards, follow these guidelines:

- It is vital that the audience be able to see anything that you have written. Print size should be large enough for someone in the back row with poor eyesight to see words and figures with ease. The same holds for any drawings you may use.
- Anything you print should be neat. Try to avoid some of the common printing errors: mixing upper- and lowercase letters, or using a style that is half writing and half printing.
- Watch that you do not print on a slant or start out with big letters at the beginning of a word only to end up with tiny letters at the end. If you cannot print neatly, maybe another form of visual aid is more suitable for you.

## Plan Ahead

Never assume that chalk, whiteboard markers, or any other types of marker will automatically be available. Request what you need in advance, or be prepared to supply your own.

I'm a bad speller at the best of times, but when I get in front of an audience I get even worse! This can make me look bad, and what's more, it's embarrassing. Now I have a way to deal with it. Before I do a presentation when I know I will be writing, I review the words that I will be using. If I am creating a list of something with an audience, I sometimes ask someone to help me out. I let them do the writing and the spelling.

*Rob, Trainer in the Insurance Industry*

When buying whiteboard markers, look for the ones with the words *dry erase markers* printed on them. Otherwise, you may end up with nonerasable permanent markers that leave stains. Also use markers with lots of ink in them—markers that are running dry not only make for a less than professional presentation, but also audience members will not be able to read what you have written.

If you find that you like using marker aids, invest in your own set of markers. That way, you will always have good ones on hand. Finally, if you do not want to come away from your speaking engagement with white shadows on your elbows or down your backside, do not lean against blackboards!

# Posters

When I think of posters, I think of a one-page prop, about the size of a flipchart page, that accompanies a speech. Posters can contain text, numbers, charts, drawings, or examples. As with flipcharts, posters should be visually stimulating and neatly constructed. They too must be large enough for easy viewing. My former colleague, Dr. Dejun Lui, had his public speaking students use a poster as a visual aid. In some instances, the poster embodied the structure of the speech in the form of a brief outline. The major points of the student's presentation were highlighted for the audience.

But not all posters need consist of a speech outline. If you are more artistically inclined, you could draw or paint pictures, or create interesting collages. The content and design of the poster depends, of course, on the topic of the speech. If, for instance, a student was giving a speech on the popular Cape Breton Celtic Colours International Festival, the poster might feature a map of Cape Breton and accent the various concert venue destinations.

To ensure a graceful delivery,

- Bring along a strong adhesive so the poster can be hung where it will be visible to all (or make sure a flipchart stand will be available).
- Before the presentation, think about where you will put the poster. It should be in a place where it can be referred to with relative ease.
- While you are presenting your speech, do not spend time looking at the poster. Refer to it, and point to parts of it when appropriate, but otherwise ignore it and get on with the presentation.

# Handouts

Many speakers find it useful to provide handouts. The critical consideration is when and how to distribute them. When I ask students when they think handouts should be given out, some say at the onset of the talk. Others say it is too disruptive to do it then because listeners will be looking at the handouts rather than listening to the speaker. I think both answers are correct.

When to issue handouts depends on the nature of the speech. If you are presenting a complicated topic and your handout consists of a diagram, it could be useful to distribute it right away so listeners can follow along with you. Most often, however, speaker materials provide a follow-up to presentations and are best given out at the conclusion. Always make sure that brochures or pamphlets are high quality and that there are enough for everyone.

# Topic-Specific Objects

*Topic-specific objects* are items that are directly related to what you are speaking about, such as the ones used by Mubanga Siwale (Bangi), a Zambian student who described her country's marriage ritual. She brought in several colourful artifacts and came to class donning a beautiful red and gold silk gown. Another student informed the class about the use of tarot cards and brought in a handpainted set. You get the idea—this category of visual aids consists of objects and, on rare occasions, people or animals. Topic-specific objects are generally interesting and informative, and are often unique.

When considering whether to use this type of visual aid, ask yourself two questions: Will it enhance the presentation? Will the speech be better as a result of including it? If the answer to both questions is yes, then using the visual aid is probably a good idea. Your next consideration is how and when you will introduce it.

## *Displaying Objects*

Timing is an important factor with topic-specific objects. If you do not want your objects to distract the audience while you are speaking, it is best to keep them concealed. Like Frances with the golf paraphernalia, exhibit them in conjunction with your main points. Otherwise, keep them out of sight. It is amateurish to display visual aids when they are not the topic of conversation because they can draw audience members' attention away from you. So, before your presentation, think about a way to introduce and remove the objects with as little fanfare as possible. Try to find a "no-fuss, no-muss" approach like the one Frances used.

However, there will be times when it is fitting to exhibit the objects throughout your speech. Mubanga did just that. But she also had an added feature—she displayed her African artifacts on 30 cm × 30 cm (12" × 12") painted cardboard cartons that were artistically and strategically placed on the table in front of her. It made for a visually stimulating, aesthetically pleasing presentation that was in keeping with her speech theme.

Another student, Jim, did a presentation on the serenity of his family's fishing lodge. Instead of passing around pictures, he brought in framed photographs of the property. He placed some on the wall behind him and others on the table before him where everyone could see them easily. Like Mubanga's exhibit, his looked professional too. As Jim moved along in his speech from one featured area to the next, all he had to do was point to the appropriate photograph for us to understand more fully the peacefulness he experienced in his country hideaway. Jim used good visual aids well.

When you decide to use topic-specific objects, give some thought to how and when you will introduce them, how you will display them, and for how long they will be seen by the audience. While there are no hard-and-fast rules, how you use your visual aids depends greatly on your topic, your goal, and the specific objects you want to display.

# CHAPTER AT A GLANCE

- Visual aids can add to your credibility, contribute to dramatic effect, help gain and maintain audience attention, and reinforce and clarify your message.
- Visual aids can never substitute for speech content or delivery.
- Use visual aids only when they will enhance your presentation—do not use them just for the sake of using them.
- Always practise with your visual aids.
- Never stand between your visual aid and the audience, nor talk to the visual aid rather than to the audience.
- Visual aids need to be controlled.
- Design visual aids that are **CLEAR: c**lean and uncluttered, **l**arge enough to be seen, **e**asily understood, **a**ttractive, and **r**elevant.
- Always be prepared to do your presentation without visual aids.

# APPLICATION AND DISCUSSION QUESTIONS

1. Answer the following questions in your communication journal:
   a. *Cognitive dimension:* Describe what you learned about visual aids from this chapter. Give examples.
   b. *Affective dimension:* Which types of visual aids are you most comfortable using? Which ones make you apprehensive? Explain and give examples.
   c. *Behavioural dimension:* Find three different types of visual aids and practise until you are comfortable using them.
2. In a small group, share stories of some of the best and worst visual aids you have ever seen used in presentations.

3.  Which of the three dimensions of visual aids (design, creation, delivery) is the easiest for you? Which is the most difficult? Once you have identified the most difficult, spend some time working on that dimension until you become more comfortable with it.

4.  Learn how to use a computer presentation program such as PowerPoint.

5.  Develop a poster to be used in one of your presentations.

6.  In what ways do you think visual aids contribute to a speaker's credibility?

7.  Working in pairs, critique the example of a bad visual aid in Figure 7.1 on page 214. What suggestions do you have for improvement? Share your responses with the rest of the classes.

8.  Working in small groups, develop PowerPoint slides that are really bad. Then, switch your work with another group who will redesign them so that they demonstrate all the positive aspects of a good slide. Afterwards, have each group show the sets to the class for critique and discussion. Online students could submit slides to professors to be redistributed.

## REFERENCES AND FURTHER READINGS

Adler, R.B., & Elmhorst, J.M. (1996). *Communicating at work: Principles and practices for business and the professions* (5th ed.). New York: McGraw-Hill.

Arnold, E.A., & McClure, L. (1996). *Communication training and development* (2nd ed.). Prospect Heights, IL: Waveland Press.

Avoid the mistakes of PowerPoint rookies. (2001, January). *Smart Computing, 12*(1), 62–65.

Brody, M. (1998). *Speaking your way to the top: Making powerful business presentations.* Boston: Allyn and Bacon.

Byrns, J.H. (1997). *Speak for yourself: An introduction to public speaking.* New York: McGraw Hill.

Cyphert, D. (2004). The problem of PowerPoint: Visual aid or visual rhetoric? *Business Communication Quarterly, 67*(1), 80–84.

DeVito, J.A. (1997). *The elements of public speaking* (6th ed.). New York: Longman.

DeWine, S. (2001). *The consultant's craft: Improving organizational communication.* Boston: Bedford/St. Martin's.

Jaffa, E. (2004, April). PowerPoint presentations require a challenge to your comfort level. *Presentations, 18*(4), 50.

Metcalfe, S. (1998). *Building a speech* (3rd ed.). Fort Worth, TX: Harcourt College.

Nunberg, G. (1999, December 20). The trouble with PowerPoint. *Fortune*, 330–334.

Rolls, J.A. (1997, November). *Making the teacher/trainer transition: Strategies that enhance facilitator effectiveness.* Paper presented at the 83rd Annual Meeting of the National Communication Association, Chicago, IL.

Steck, L.L. (2000, November 30). PowerPoint can be creative. Message posted to crtnet@natcom.org. Discussion: PowerPoint in the basic course #5579.

Strunk, W., & White, E.B. (1979). *The elements of style* (3rd ed.). New York: MacMillan.

Wahl, A. (2003). PowerPoint of no return. *Canadian Business, 76*(22), 131–133.

Zarefsky, D., & MacLennan, J. (1997). *Public speaking: Strategies for success* (Canadian ed.). Scarborough, ON: Allyn and Bacon.

# Chapter 8
## Demonstrative, Informative, and Persuasive Speeches

## CHAPTER GOALS

In this chapter, you will learn
- how to do a demonstrative speech
- more about informative speeches
- how audience beliefs and attitudes affect persuasive speeches
- how to use the techniques taught by the ancient rhetoricians
- when to present one-sided and two-sided arguments
- where to put your strongest and weakest arguments
- strategies to use when you know audience gender, age, and intelligence levels

# INTRODUCTION

Thus far, the text has covered why it is important to develop public speaking skills, how to deal with nervousness, and how to use your voice and body. It provided information on how to research and organize a speech, how to develop speaker credibility, and how to use visual aids. In fact, it has touched on the basics of just about everything needed to develop and present a speech. However, there are various types of speeches and each of these requires further refinement of the process.

In this chapter, three kinds of speeches are discussed—demonstrative, informative, and persuasive. Except for the occasional social speech, such as introducing a guest speaker, proposing a toast, or giving a eulogy, most of the formal speeches given within work environments fall into these three categories. For instance, someone demonstrates how to use a new piece of equipment or a computer program, briefs and updates are presented to team members, or an upper level management team is persuaded to adopt an idea, approach, or product.

This chapter begins with a description of how to design a demonstrative speech and follows with more information on the informative speeches. Then the persuasive speech is explained. The chapter ends with a description of how rhetorical techniques, stylistic techniques, organizational techniques, and reasoning are used to strengthen a speech so that the desired goal is attained.

---

## EXPERT ADVICE

Public speaking is a gift that leaders use to inspire their audiences, influence opinion, and make change.

*Annette Verschuren, President*
*The Home Depot Canada*

---

# THE DEMONSTRATIVE SPEECH

The goal of the demonstrative speech is to explain, illustrate, or show how to do something. Recall the "How to Make 23 Bacon, Lettuce, and Tomato Sandwiches" in Chapter 4; that was a demonstrative speech. Debbie Travis, Martha Stewart, or any of the guys on the *This Old House* spin-offs essentially do demonstrative speeches when they feature decorating, craft, or repair segments. Instructors have used demonstrative speeches to provide the computer training that has occurred in just about every organization during the last decade. When your chem lab instructor performs an experiment for the class, that is a demonstrative speech. When your stats professor illustrates how to calculate standard deviation, that too is a demonstrative speech.

Demonstrative speeches, in many ways, are the easiest to present because they are straightforward and are often accompanied by visual aids. Hence, they are typically assigned to novice speakers, as in the elementary school "show and tell" presentations. To present a successful demonstrative speech, careful consideration must be given to the following factors: overview, time, expertise level, setting, and topic.

## Overview

Although speeches can be organized in a variety of ways, demonstrative speeches typically begin with an overview of the process or procedure and then follow a step-by-step, chronological pattern. The overview is essentially the enumerated preview, where you inform the audience what will be covered in the body of the speech. For instance, if you were demonstrating how to make a flower box, you might say that you will review the tools and materials required for the job, show how to measure and cut the boards, explain how to put them together, and provide painting and decorating hints. Then you would go on to explain each step in the process.

## Time Factor

The second feature of the demonstrative speech is time. While the flower box example might be well organized, it would probably take too long to do such a demonstration in a classroom speech. Without the magic of television and editing, or the prepared materials available for each step, classroom speeches require shorter demonstrations. Keeping this in mind, try not to overwhelm or confuse the audience by spewing out a lot of minute details and information. It is better to select one smaller goal than to offer too much too fast. In the case of the flower box, it would be better to show how to paint and decorate it, or to demonstrate how to hang it.

## Expertise Level

The third concern is your level of expertise. You have to be adept at the process you are explaining if your description is going to be clear and succinct. Statements like, "Oops, that's not where it goes," or "Geez, I forgot, you have to attach the arm before you plug it in," not only reduce your credibility, but the audience learns little from such a muddled presentation. For the best results, do the demonstration with confidence and finesse which, as you know, come from a lot of practice.

## Setting

Setting is the fourth factor. It is important to select a topic that lends itself to the particular speaking environment. For example, it makes no sense to show people how to do something (such as the different types of knitting stitches) or how something works if what you are doing is too intricate or small to be seen by the audience. It would be almost impossible to demonstrate how to download music to an iPod without the aid of an LCD machine to project the computer screen for all to see. Without such equipment, the demonstration would be very difficult to expedite.

## Topic

As with speeches in general, gear your topic to the academic level of your audience and select one that has some depth. To help listeners understand the process you are demonstrating, relate the material to something they already know. For instance, most people know how to set an alarm clock. Therefore, such a comparison might be made to explain how to set the VCR timer to record a television show. Or, given that most people know how to download and burn music from the Internet onto a disc, that information could be used to explain how to download and burn a movie onto a CD. Always keep your audience in mind, and imagine how people might perceive your directions. Limit the use of jargon and make directions clear and accurate.

---

 **EXPERT ADVICE**

Here are the pointers I give my students before they do their demo speeches.

1. Choose a subject that will allow you to show the end result.
2. Make sure you can obtain and use any necessary equipment.
3. Inform the audience exactly what you will demonstrate and what the end result will be.
4. List the necessary materials before you begin the demonstration.
5. Demonstrate the procedure in the correct order and clarify any technical terms.
6. Emphasize common errors and dangers, and offer advice to offset each one.
7. Show the end result.

*Professor Celeste Sulliman, Department of Communication*
*Cape Breton University, Sydney, Nova Scotia*

---

One caution, though; watch that the demonstration speech does not turn into a performance. One student's goal was to demonstrate how to do an uplift hairdo. Unfortunately, she got carried away, completely forgot the step-by-step approach, and instead flitted about dramatically as if she were in a designer hair show. Although the final product looked great, it was unlikely that anyone in the audience could actually re-create the style.

# ■ THE INFORMATIVE SPEECH

The goal of an *informative speech* is to familiarize the audience with something it does not already know. You, the speaker, are the expert. If you have ever attended an orientation or a debriefing session, you have heard an informative speech. Lectures presented by your professors are informative. Most of the examples used in the previous chapters come from informative speeches. For example, the spousal abuse speech mentioned in Chapter 4, Stephanie Wadden's "Dieting—The Good and the Bad" speech outline, or Kimberly Fraser's "The Resurgence of Scottish Fiddle Music" notes were all informative speeches. In fact, most of the information contained in the text thus far relates directly to informative speeches.

Grice and Skinner (2004) write that informative speeches are about people, objects, places, events, processes, concepts, conditions, and issues (p. 318). Regardless of the topic, it is important to design the speech so that the introduction contains an attention getter and a clear goal, or thesis statement. This enables the audience to know where you are going. The goal statement must be specific and include the word *inform*. It is inappropriate to say, for example, "Today I'm going to talk about global warming." Instead, it is more professional to say, "Today I will inform you about the effects of global warming on Canada's weather patterns." The goal statement is followed by the enumerated preview—the topics that will be covered in the speech.

How an informative speech is organized depends on the topic and specific goal. Common schemes include chronological, topical, causal, and spatial. Some informative speeches take a problem-solving approach, although that style is used more often to organize persuasive speeches.

## Audience Analysis

The audience analysis always plays a major role in the organizational process. That information helps speakers to gauge the level of the audience's knowledge. Sometimes, there is a tendency to overestimate that level but you should not automatically assume that audience members know what you are talking about. If you give an informative speech, you likely will have had some personal experience with the topic and have supplemented that knowledge with further research into the area. This stands you in good stead to offer your insight.

Your audience analysis also helps you to decide what information will be most interesting to listeners. You can include facts, statistics, and stories that relate directly to them and this works to make the presentation come alive.

## Put Yourself in the Speech

Finally, it is one thing to offer an audience interesting and helpful information but what will make your presentation stand out is your willingness to allow a bit of yourself to come through to the listeners. Your enthusiasm, joy, passion, and commitment should be evident because the emotions you bring to the presentation transfer directly to the audience. So, do not be afraid to share your stories and/or express your feelings about the topic. Peter Urs Bender, a motivational speaker, holds that a speech has three objectives: "to inform; to entertain and touch people's emotion; and to move them to action" (Bender, 2001, p. 5). He suggests putting in some humour every three to seven minutes, not in the form of jokes, but by relating stories about your experiences, problems, or even something stupid that you did!

Patricia Fripp (2004) also suggests the use of vivid, descriptive, personal stories to make informative speeches more exciting and advises against the use of "borrowed stories." Use your own, she argues. She holds that you should "organize, wordsmith, and deliver your comments by conversing with the audience" (p. 18) and proposes that speakers increase their "I–You" ratio statements. The example she provides shows how the "I–You" approach can create much more of an emotional connection with the audience than does the lone "I" statement. "I–You" statements oblige listeners to become involved in the process. Fripp (2004) writes that, "An 'I' sentence would be 'When I was growing up, my father gave me this advice.' An 'I–You' sentence would be, 'I don't know what advice your father gave you growing up, but mine always said . . .'" (p. 18). You can see how the "I–You" example better connects the speaker and the audience.

There are two other types of informative speeches: the descriptive speech and the explanatory speech. They require further attention because they are set up just a little differently.

# The Descriptive Speech

## *Details*

The goal of a *descriptive speech* is to create a picture in the audience's mind. This can be achieved by providing so much detail that listeners not only envision what you are describing, but they get a clear feeling for the person, place, or event. This means, then, that the success of a descriptive speech depends largely on the speaker's ability to know what to describe and to use language in a way that captivates listeners' attention.

For instance, saying that, "The palm reader met me at the door, escorted me into a darkened room, and read my hand," sounds sterile and even scientific. The statement includes only the bare facts. In a descriptive speech, however, the speaker needs to embellish the scene. Portraying the palm reader's size, sex, body shape, hairstyle and colour, eye colour, complexion, age, attire, accessories, or voice qualities enables listeners to create a picture in their mind. A description of the room can be shaped by depicting its dimensions; how it was painted, papered, or decorated; what kept it darkened; the type of furniture it contained; its temperature and smell; or any sounds that could be heard. An emotional link can be forged by describing what it felt like to be there. The speaker could explain why he or she was there in and how it felt to be touched by the palm reader. Explain if the manipulations were light and gentle, rough, strong, or intimate and include what the palm reader's hands felt and looked like. Of course, the audience would want to know if the seer read anything outstanding in the palm. Perhaps he or she noted how long the speaker had to live, or made predictions that actually came true. Providing such information, and more, allows listeners to visit the palm reader in their imagination.

## *Organizational Pattern*

The organizational pattern you choose for the descriptive speech depends on what is being described. "A Trip to a Psychic" could be arranged in a topical fashion. "How to Get Around Calgary during the Stampede" would work best with a spatial design. "The Architecture of Rome" might come alive by comparing and contrasting Rome's architecture with that of a Canadian city.

## *Visual Aids*

Visual aids are particularly well suited to descriptive speeches. Whatever aid you select to enhance your presentation, make sure that all audience members can see it and allow them plenty of time for viewing. This is not to be rushed.

## SPOTLIGHT ON SPEAKERS

### WHY DR. DAVID SUZUKI IS SUCH A COMPELLING SPEAKER (TWO REVIEWS BY FORMER STUDENTS)

Dr. David Suzuki spoke at the Membertou Trade and Convention Centre, Sydney, Nova Scotia, on January 22, 2005. Sponsored by the Sierra Club of Canada, the issue that brought him to this part of the country was the clean-up of the local Tar Ponds. Two individuals who attended the presentation offered the following reviews of his speech. Not only is David Suzuki a great Canadian, he is also a great speaker.

*Dr. Suzuki's plane was late because we were having a huge snow storm. Yet, the room was packed and everyone was anxiously awaiting his arrival. Finally, he was there. He used a good icebreaker by informing us that he had given up a chance to meet Fidel Castro in order to present this lecture. Suddenly, that he was 15–20 minutes late starting didn't matter and instead, we were appreciative that he would give up such an opportunity to come here.*

*His speech was eloquent, organized, and well rehearsed and I was fascinated by his structure and style. He had a clean, clear beginning and ending and used a card to keep him on track. His nonverbal communication was in full swing and he used his hands and voice effectively. Dr. Suzuki avoided technical language and the examples he used were easy to understand. For example, he talked about air pollution and the increasing incidence of asthma in a clear language that illustrated his point and reinforced his position against the incineration project. He also used examples from TV shows that the audience had likely seen to further clarify his points. Dr. Suzuki also kept our attention by providing interesting statistics. Overall, he related well to the audience and I enjoyed the presentation.*

*I did have one reservation, though. At one point, Dr. Suzuki said he would talk about sex. Because my eight-year-old daughter was with me, I was uncomfortable with this. I think organizers might have alerted him that there were children in the audience. And, in a packed room, it would be difficult to see small children. This underscores the importance of knowing your audience.*

*As a student of communication, it is a good exercise to dissect a speech (spoken like a true surgeon). Apparently, the principles learned in class are even used by experienced, famous speakers like David Suzuki. In fact, that's probably why he is so successful—he's got content and style.*

*Dr. A. Atiyah*
*B.Sc., M.D., F.R.C.S (C)*

*I heard David Suzuki speak the other evening and he was fantastic. He has a very relaxed and down-to-earth approach and that's why people like him. What I enjoyed was how he related to the audience. For example, he referred to his friend Elizabeth May and to the work of Bruno Marcocchio, both of whom are hard-working, well-known environmentalists. This made him seem that he was in tune with the community and, May and Marcocchio's credibility was further enhanced by his reference.*

*In terms of organization, Dr. Suzuki went from the general to the specific, and I liked that. He asked audience members to think about the environment and what they might do to help preserve it. To get his message across, he used his hands, altered the tone of his voice, and emphasized certain words. He also used humour. For example, he made reference to sex that was both credible and funny. In all, he is an excellent speaker and I was delighted to have the opportunity to hear him.*

*Jo-Anne Rolls, BACS*
*Singer/Songwriter, Community Worker*

## The Explanatory Speech

### Abstraction

The second type of informative speech is the *explanatory speech*. This type is more difficult than a descriptive speech because it is more abstract in nature. In some cases, an explanatory speech explains ideas and concepts that run contrary to accepted popular notions and beliefs. Osborn and Osborn (1994, p. 337) state that "by translating the abstract into the concrete, and by making an audience receptive to new ideas, the speech of explanation can help lift and enrich the lives of listeners." Siva Kodogoda, a former student, presented such a speech as she explained how the political climate and other influences in Sri Lanka induced her family's move to Canada some years ago.

When you present an explanatory speech, you do more than just repeat the facts of the situation or process—you convey a sense of the context or era, and provide insight into what people may have been experiencing or feeling. For instance, if Siva had just explained the political climate in her country, her speech would not have been as interesting or informative. Adding how she and her family felt about leaving their beautiful homeland and describing how they had to adapt to Canadian life (not to mention the weather) created a strong emotional appeal.

## Simplification

Due to the complex nature of explanatory speeches, try to simplify concepts by reducing them to their basic parts. For example, divide an explanation of romantic relationships into three topics: biological attraction, interpersonal interaction, and

---

### SAMPLE SPEECH TOPICS

**DEMONSTRATIVE SPEECH TOPICS**
- How to Change the Ink Cartridge in Your Printer
- How to Administer CPR
- How to Faux-Finish a Painted Surface
- How to Register Online
- How to Crack Open a Lobster

**DESCRIPTIVE SPEECH TOPICS**
- A Day in the Life of Avril Lavigne
- Life in an Inuit Village
- Participating in a Gay Pride March
- The Grandeur of the Canadian Rockies
- Calgary's Transformation during the Stampede

**EXPLANATORY SPEECH TOPICS**
- The Impact of Tourism on Prince Edward Island Residents
- Global Warming and Natural Disasters
- What Went Wrong in Walkerton
- Cultural, Emotional, and Economic Costs of Vying for the Olympic Games
- The Role of Alternative Medicine in Canadian Health Care

long-term sexual satisfaction. Notice that the topics are arranged in a chronological order. However, like all speeches, organize your explanatory speeches according to the topic being explained. Siva's speech followed a topical format.

# THE PERSUASIVE SPEECH

A *persuasive speech* is one in which speakers attempt to change listeners' beliefs, attitudes, or behaviours. They are the most difficult to expedite because they are more complicated. For example, in order to persuade an audience to think differently, speakers must have insight into its beliefs and attitudes. Once again, the importance of the audience analysis cannot be overstated. If speakers know the audience age, sex, or intelligence level, they are better prepared to supply specific strategies and information that appeal to individuals of a certain age, sex, or intelligence level.

Persuasive speakers must also be familiar with rhetorical devices, stylistic techniques, and persuasive techniques such as when to use one-sided or two-sided arguments, when the foot-in-the-door technique works, where to place their strongest and weakest argument, or when to use fear or humour appeals. Adept persuasive speakers must also be able to use reasoning. Finally, some argue that in order to be persuaded, listeners must be exposed to fresh information. Hence, the persuasive speech also includes elements of the informative speech. These factors account for why persuasive speakers must be skilled orators.

Persuasion is a complicated process, and communication scholars and psychologists have dedicated a great deal of study to it. The subject has been examined from the perspective of speaker characteristics, listener characteristics, message content, and a combination of several variables. While it is impossible here to cover the study of persuasion in detail, the remainder of the chapter explains some of the factors that are relevant to putting together a persuasive speech. The segment begins with an explanation of functional attitude theory.

## Functional Attitude Theory

In terms of persuasive speaking, functional attitude theory suggests that speakers must first be aware of the attitudes of their listeners if they intend to persuade them otherwise. This notion is explained in the following example.

To introduce *functional attitude theory* to my persuasion students, I ask how many think that marijuana should be legalized. Inevitably, over half of the students raise their hands. We then generate a list of reasons why they hold such a belief. They conclude that marijuana lessens or eliminates side effects associated with chemotherapy and diminishes some of the pain that cancer patients endure. They offer that legalization would contribute to the country's tax base and simultaneously reduce organized crime. Regulations would ensure that marijuana customers receive pure, uncut cannabis and not be surprised by hallucinogenic, chemically laced marijuana. Other students bluntly assert that marijuana is available as a recreational drug in the Netherlands and they see no reason it should not be legal here in Canada.

It becomes apparent from this exercise that people can hold the same attitude but for substantially different reasons. According to the basis of functional attitude theory, attitudes can serve different functions (Katz, 1960). However, the point of including functional attitude theory in this text is for speakers to be aware that audience members hold multiple beliefs and attitudes. Therefore, to reshape the attitude of students in the class, a speaker has to offer a variety of arguments to offset or alter the range of beliefs represented. Clearly this can be a complicated and difficult undertaking. However, understanding how beliefs, attitudes, and behaviours operate with one another helps to clarify this persuasive process.

## Beliefs, Attitudes, and Behaviours

Although the terms *beliefs* and *attitudes* are often used interchangeably, there are distinct differences between them. Which one do you think would come first in the decision-making process? Where would behaviours fit into all of this? Here is what the relationship among the three terms might look like as a formula:

**BELIEFS**  shape  **ATTITUDES**  and attitudes influence  **BEHAVIOURS**

A *belief* is what individuals hold to be true about something, someone, or some event. That truth then shapes their attitudes toward particular people, things, circumstances, or issues. Peoples' attitudes then determine the kinds of behaviours they engage in.

Take, for example, a woman who has a pro-choice stand on abortion. She does not believe that life begins at conception, and based on that belief, she has an accepting attitude toward abortion. Based on her belief and attitude, she might have or recommend an abortion in the early stage of pregnancy should the circumstances require it. On the other hand, if a woman believes that life does begin at the moment of conception, she might have a negative attitude toward abortion. Because of her beliefs and attitudes, terminating a pregnancy is not an option.

To change either woman's *attitude* toward abortion, you would have to begin by changing what they believe. The same would hold true for those individuals in the class who did not think that marijuana should be legalized. To win them over, the "legalizers" would first have to learn what these students believe about marijuana and its use in order to understand their attitudes. These examples underscore the importance of understanding the differences among beliefs, attitudes, and behaviours if you are going to engage in the persuasion process.

## Changing Behaviours

While changing beliefs is not easy, it is even more difficult to change behaviours. Persuasive speeches to actuate are the most difficult because, before you can alter behaviours, you must first get listeners to modify their beliefs and attitudes.

Even if there is an attitude change, there is no guarantee that a behavioural change will follow. How many times have you made up your mind to change your behaviour—work out more, eat less, have more patience with a family member—and then quit before you really began? It may not take much convincing to get you to believe that giving to the Canadian Cancer Society is a good idea, but coaxing you to fork over a donation might be quite another. In terms of the abortion issue, you might convince the pro-life woman that abortion is warranted in some extenuating circumstances. However, the likelihood of getting her to have an abortion would require a complete reconstruction of her belief system.

## Maslow's Hierarchy of Needs

Related to the notion of beliefs and attitudes is motivation, or why people do what they do. Abraham Maslow (1968) developed a means of categorizing human motivation known as Maslow's Hierarchy of Needs (depicted as a pyramid). Maslow holds that people's needs are divided into five steps and these needs are met one step at a time, starting at the bottom. The specific needs are outlined below:

5. Self-actualization, the highest level, refers to the need for self-development.
4. Self-esteems needs require that a person feels valued by others.
3. Social needs refer to having a sense of belonging.
2. Safety needs refer to a person's need to be physically and emotionally safe.
1. Physiological needs include the need for food, shelter, water, air, and the ability to reproduce.

Maslow's theory has implications for how a persuasive speech is crafted in that awareness of audience needs can help the speaker select arguments that will appeal

---

### EXPERT ADVICE

Your presentation is an act of persuasion. At the very least, you must persuade the audience to listen to you. Beyond that, you also want the audience to accept your ideas rather than to dismiss them or, to take action rather than agree in principle.

Your audience may resist your efforts to persuade because they see the "cost" of agreeing as too high. As the presenter, analyze these costs—are you expecting payment in time? In attentiveness? In money? In mental exertion? In physical effort? Then analyze the benefits you can offer to outweigh these costs—can you offer profit? Knowledge? An entertaining escape? Power? A greater good?

The successful speaker convinces audience members that the benefits they will receive will outweigh the costs they will incur.

*Signe Gurholt, Communication Instructor*
*New Brunswick Community College, Saint John, N.B.*

---

to them. For example, in extreme cases when people encounter natural disasters such as hurricanes, tsunamis, snowstorms, tornados, or ice storms, they are not interested in speeches on politics, the future glory of their towns and cities, or home decorating schemes. At such times, their motivations are directed toward meeting basic needs. They want to hear information about how to attain food, water, and shelter. Therefore, you have to select arguments that satisfy the motivations you identify. As you develop your persuasive speech, keep your audience in mind and try to gauge what their needs are. Then select arguments that satisfy the motivations you identify.

## BORROWING FROM THE ANCIENT RHETORICIANS

Persuasion has been around for a long time. In fact, Aristotle defined *rhetoric* as "finding the available means of persuasion" (Golden, Berquist, & Coleman, 1983). Rhetoric (or persuasion), as a study, began in ancient Greece and Rome with the traditions of such notable rhetoricians as Aristotle, Plato, Isocrates, Cicero, Socrates, Quintillian, and others. It was important to be a good public speaker in ancient Greece because, in those days, there were no lawyers. Ordinary citizens had to defend themselves in the courts. Many of the teachings of those early communication scholars are applied by successful public speakers today.

# Aristotle's Proofs

While a number of ancient Greeks and Romans contributed to our knowledge of persuasion, it was Aristotle, a Greek rhetorician, who was the first to study the process of persuasion in a systematic way. To this day, the influence of his three proofs, or persuasive appeals—ethos, logos, and pathos—still receive scholarly attention and shape how public speaking is taught. Although industrialization and technology have changed tremendously over the time, it appears that the human condition remains stable.

Johnston (1994) writes that, "A persuasive appeal is essentially a method of motivating the receiver. An appeal leads the receiver to evaluate a message with a particular mindset" (pp. 122–123). Speakers who demonstrate ethos, logos, and pathos create more impact with their presentations and are perceived more favourably.

Although Aristotle's proofs are described separately, they would overlap in an actual speech. Rather than offer a step-by-step guide, the proofs create a positive, believable aura or mood through which your presentation is interpreted. From the classical rhetoricians we can also learn some stylistic techniques for public speaking.

## *Ethos (Credibility)*

The first of Aristotle's proofs, *ethos*, refers to a speaker's credibility. As discussed in Chapter 6, speakers must be credible if they are to be persuasive. In fact, Brydon and Scott (2000) write that Aristotle "viewed ethos as the most important aspect of a speaker's persuasiveness" (p. 348). Ethos comes in the forms of character and competence, and speakers must possess both to be considered credible. Listeners have to feel that speakers know what they are talking about and have listeners' best interests in mind in order to be persuaded.

You may recall from Chapter 6 that factors such as speaking in a strong language style, using inclusive language, and using good grammar all contribute to your perceived competence level. So does your expertise. If not mentioned when you are introduced to the audience, establish credibility by informing listeners about your experience with the topic. You might say that you have worked in sales for 10 years. If you have specific training in the area or have worked on a special project that related to it, note that. Another technique is to demonstrate or define any similarities you may have with audience members. For example, if you are making a presentation in a town where you once lived, you can increase audience closeness by sharing that information with them.

Once you are into the speech, include facts, statistics, and quotes that support your arguments or assertions. Studies show that you can be more persuasive if you give a reason for a request, even if that reason is not particularly good or relevant (Langer, Blank, & Chanowitz, 1978; Langer & Piper, 1987). Use language to your advantage, dress appropriately, and give a dynamic presentation. Speakers with poor presentation skills tend to lack credibility no matter how competent or trustworthy they are.

---

 **EXPERT ADVICE**

Corporate speechmaking is most often an exercise in sharing your company's vision and strategy with those who will help you achieve your organizational goals: employees, shareholders, suppliers, regulators, and may others. Your ability to strike the right balance between <u>sharing</u> *information* and <u>providing</u> *inspiration* in how you construct and deliver your message will go a long way to determining how successful you are in gaining their support and commitment.

*Bill McEwan, President and CEO*
*Sobeys, Inc.*

---

## Logos (Logical Arguments)

*Logos* refers to the logic or content that is contained within the message. Larson (2001) states that logos "appeals to the intellect, or to the rational side of humans. It relies on the audience's ability to process statistical data, examples, or testimony in logical ways and to arrive at some conclusion" (p. 55). In Aristotle's time, syllogisms and enthymemes were used to help organize logical arguments.

### The Syllogism

The *syllogism* is a logical format based on the notion that if A is B, and B is C, then A is C. Putting this into words,

All human beings are mortal (A is B).

Petra is a human being (B is C).

Therefore, Petra is mortal (A is C).

This works well, but only if the basic premise is correct. Here is an example where the basic premise is not correct:

> All dogs can do tricks.
>
> Binky is a dog.
>
> Therefore, Binky can do tricks.

Although the example is a simple one, it demonstrates that even though information is offered in a logical format, it may not always be accurate. As a listener, do not be persuaded by something that sounds logical but makes no sense. Give careful consideration to the arguments that are presented to you.

### The Enthymeme

The *enthymeme* is similar to the syllogism in that it works the same way, but listeners are left to fill in or come to their own logical conclusion. Johnston (1994) provides a good example. She writes that, "[I]f the police announce that 90 percent of serial murderers seek young women victims and that they have just received a letter from a person who claims to be a serial murderer living in the city, you are likely to make the conclusion that young women in this particular city are at risk" (pp. 123–124). Enthymemes are particularly persuasive because they involve the listeners. Rather than sit passively, listeners take part in the persuasive process by completing the line of logic.

## Pathos (Emotional Appeals)

Aristotle thought of *pathos* in terms of virtues. Today we generally think of it as an appeal to the emotions. Excellent persuasive presentations generally move the audience in some way by arousing passions or emotions. Aristotle described several deep-seated emotions to which humans respond that are still used in persuasive strategies today: justice, prudence, generosity, courage, temperance, magnanimity, magnificence, and wisdom (Larson, 2001). Others might include pity, humour, empathy, or guilt.

## Classical Stylistic Techniques

As noted earlier, even though the classical era ran from approximately 500 B.C. to A.D. 300, many of the teachings are still applicable some 1700 to 2500 years later! As you develop your next persuasive speech, try to use these three devices to your advantage: repetition, parallel structure, and antithesis. They offer a format in which to present your content so that it has additional significance and impact, making your presentation more persuasive. Also watch for the use of these devices by politicians, preachers, and other presenters—they are used even in television commercials.

When I first learned about the classical stylistic techniques (repetition, parallel structure, and antithesis) I thought of them as just information I needed to know to pass the course. But I started to notice that their use was everywhere—at church, in television commercials (they always say the product name three times), by some of my professors, and get this, even in country music lyrics! Who could believe it? Now when I do presentations in my other classes I try to use these devices whenever I can. People are starting to tell me that I am a very good speaker. I'm going to keep improving until they tell me I'm great.

*Kirk, Former Persuasion Student*

To help you think about these rhetorical techniques in relation to a persuasive speech that you might give, note that persuasive speeches as a whole are set up like other types of speeches: they have a typical opening (attention getter, thesis statement, enumerated preview) and a regular ending (summation, plea, quotation, and so on). It is in how the body of the speech is organized that makes the difference. Persuasive speeches contain material that is set out in a manner that heightens their convincing nature. The three classical stylistic techniques do just that—they enhance the potency of the message. Although it takes additional thought and effort to use these stylistic techniques, their use can make the difference between a presentation that is mediocre and one that is exceptional.

## *Repetition*

Repetition is simply saying the same word or phrase more than once. The strongest number of repetitions is three. For example, one speaker ended a eulogy with "Think about her smile. Think about her energy. Think about how she touched your life." The repetition allows listeners to become part of the presentation because they can anticipate what you will say next. Audience involvement is always a good thing for persuasion. In the excerpt from Martin Luther King Jr.'s "I Have a Dream" speech on the opposite page, King might have told listeners to go back home and know that the situation will change. However, he chose to use repetition and the heavy-duty effect of that decision is evident.

## 🔊 SPOTLIGHT ON SPEAKERS

One of the most famous and highly regarded pieces of public address in the 20th century is Martin Luther King Jr.'s "I Have a Dream" speech. It has been the subject of analysis since it was presented on August 28, 1963, at a peaceful demonstration in Washington, D.C. Its goal was to further the cause of equal rights for African Americans. As Lucas (2004) points out, although the speech took only 16 minutes for King to deliver, it is very well crafted and uses metaphors, repetition, parallelism, and concrete words "to make the abstract principles of liberty and equality clear and compelling" (p. A7). Read the entire speech at *http://douglass archives.org/king_b12.htm*. The following excerpts demonstrate how repetition creates impact.

*Go back to Mississippi, go back to Alabama, go back to South Carolina, go back to Georgia, go back to Louisiana, go back to the slums and ghettos of our northern cities, knowing that somehow this situation can and will be changed. Let us not wallow in the valley of despair.*

*I have a dream that one day this nation will rise up and live out the true meaning of its creed: "We hold these truths to be self-evident, that all men are created equal."*

*I have a dream that one day on the red hills of Georgia the sons of former slaves and the sons of former slave owners will be able to sit down together at the table of brotherhood.*

*I have a dream that one day even the state of Mississippi, a state sweltering with the heat of injustice, sweltering with the heat of oppression, will be transformed into an oasis of freedom and justice.*

*I have a dream that my four little children will one day live in a nation where they will not be judged by the color of their skin but by the content of their character. I have a dream today.*

*I have a dream that one day down in Alabama, with its vicious racists, with its governor having his lips dripping with the words of interposition and nullification, one day right there in Alabama little black boys and black girls will be able to join hands with little white boys and white girls as sisters and brothers. I have a dream today.*

> *I have a dream that one day every valley shall be exalted, every hill and mountain shall be made low, the rough places will be made plain, and the crooked places will be made straight, and the glory of the Lord shall be revealed, and all flesh shall see it together.*

## Parallel Structure

Parallel structure is another stylistic technique that strengthens the persuasiveness of a speech. "Keeping the peace, raising the pay, and making employees happy" exemplify parallel structure in that each unit begins with a verb ending in *–ing*. The repetition examples used by Martin Luther King also adhere to a parallel structure—each sentence begins the same way. Matthew Coon Come, the former National Chief of the Assembly of First Nations, is an accomplished speaker and his use of parallel structure is demonstrated in the excerpts below. Parallel structure not only works to create dynamism, it makes the information easier to process. Use this stylistic technique to create more potent speeches.

### �))) SPOTLIGHT ON SPEAKERS

How parallel structure is used in a speech can be seen in the following excerpts from a presentation made by Matthew Coon Come, the former National Chief of the Assembly of First Nations, at the Council for the Advancement of Native Development Officers (CANDO) Conference in Yellowknife, NT, on September 29, 2000.

*Here is my vision for the future.*

1. *I would like to lobby for a First Ministers Conference on the Redistribution of Resources; so that we can get our fair share.*
2. *I would like to have 1 Billion dollars of the Federal surplus in the hands of First Nations people for Economic Development soon; that surplus is over 12 Billion dollars and our communities still exist in third world conditions.*
3. *I would like to have the recognition of our jurisdiction and control of our community-driven processes aimed at rebuilding our economic structures.*

*I consider myself fortunate to be the National Chief because we are in a time of great change in First Nations' country.*

1.  *We are organizing ourselves for a better life,*
2.  *We are taking our rightful place in the Canadian Polity,*
3.  *We are not taking "no" as an answer any more from government.*

## Antithesis

*Antithesis* is the juxtaposition of two opposing conditions or themes. "Don't take it like a sissy, take it like a man" and "Instead of grieving her death, please join me in celebrating her life" put two opposites side by side. Such arrangements heighten the contrast, and hence the strength of the descriptions. See below how Margaret Atwood used juxtaposition in the excerpt from a presentation made in 1995.

### ))) SPOTLIGHT ON SPEAKERS

Margaret Atwood, renowned Canadian writer, provides many fine examples of language use. The following excerpt from a lecture entitled "On Writing Poetry", presented at Hay on Wye, Wales, in June 1995, describes how she became a poet in 1956 at the age of 16. The contrast between her pre- and post-poet selves is an example of juxtaposition. You can read the entire speech at *http://www.web.net/owtoad/lecture.html*.

*I was once a snub-nosed blonde. My name was Betty. I had a perky personality and was a cheerleader for the college football team. My favourite colour was pink. Then I became a poet. My hair darkened overnight, my nose lengthened, I gave up football for cello, my real name disappeared and was replaced by one that had a chance of being taken seriously by the literati, and my clothes changed colour in the closet, all by themselves, from pink to black. I stopped humming the songs from* Oklahoma *and began quoting Kierkegaard. And not only that—all my high heeled shoes lost their heels, and were magically transformed into sandals. Needless to say, my many boyfriends took one look at this and ran screaming from the scene as if their toenails were on fire. New ones replaced them; they all had beards.*

> ## PERSUASIVE STRATEGIES FROM THE CLASSICAL ERA
>
> Try to incorporate these techniques into your presentations.
>
> | Aristotle's Proofs | Stylistic Techniques |
> | --- | --- |
> | Ethos (appeals based on credibility) | Repetition |
> | Pathos (emotional appeals) | Parallel structure |
> | Logos (logical appeals) | Antithesis |

# REASONING

Although phrases such as *there's reason to believe, that's not reasonable,* and *within reason* are often tossed about in our day-to-day speech, not much attention is actually paid to the reasoning process. Certainly, in a chapter on the persuasive speech, it *stands to reason* that reasoning would be addressed because, in most situations, listeners respond positively to logical, reasonable arguments. *Reasoning* refers to the type of appeal you choose to prove your points to an audience. Five common types of reasoning are explained below.

## Cause–Effect

In *cause–effect* reasoning, you show how a specific event or situation leads to a particular future consequence. In other words, you predict the future, as in the following two examples:

Not buying your textbooks until two weeks before the midterms will result in failing grades.

If you drink too much alcohol you will get drunk and say and do stupid things that will later embarrass you.

To use cause–effect reasoning in your speeches, inform the audience that they can alleviate or reduce the problem or further intensify it by altering the effect. For instance, students will pass their tests if they budget their money to include buying all of their textbooks. Further, they could prevent potentially problematic situations by drinking alcohol in a responsible manner.

## Effect–Cause

With *effect–cause* reasoning, you demonstrate for the audience how an effect was caused by certain events. For example, "Reducing federal education grants to the provinces has caused an increase in university tuition rates across the country."

## Deductive Reasoning (General to Specific)

In reasoning from the general to the specific, or *deductive reasoning*, you apply a general, well-accepted principle to a specific case. For example, "University students are intelligent, career-oriented individuals" (general principle); "Claude is a university student, so he too must be an intelligent, career-oriented kind of guy" (specific case).

One problem with this reasoning style is that it often perpetuates negative stereotypes. However, when the general principle is logical and valid, it can be used effectively to derive a specific case: "Extensive environmental research has proven the connection between acid rain and the destruction of wildlife habitats. The lake our town sits beside has been showing a steadily decreasing fish population, which is likely linked to the increase in air pollution we have seen in the last decade."

## Inductive Reasoning (Specific to General)

Reasoning from the specific to the general, or *inductive reasoning*, works by using examples. You provide the audience with several illustrations, demonstrations, or specific cases so they draw the conclusion you want. For example, if your goal is to

### LEARN INDUCTIVE REASONING FROM A TALKING DUCK

Many students confuse deductive and inductive reasoning. To help sort out the two, think of a lone duck swimming in a pond. Note that this is a very special duck because it can actually talk.

The duck's owners (Mr. and Mrs. Green) have never seen another duck in their entire lives and based on their limited knowledge, they reason that ducks talk. This style of reasoning goes from the specific (their duck) to the general (the rest of the ducks in the world). This is inductive reasoning.

To remember which type of reasoning Mr. and Mrs. Green used, ask yourself where the duck was: the duck was *in* the pond. This is *in*ductive reasoning, going from the specific to the general, or from one to many.

convince the audience that if nervous speakers organize their speeches well and practise them until they feel comfortable, they will make speeches that are as good as or better than those of less nervous speakers. To work from the specific to the general, you could then share several descriptive anecdotes, one after the other, about speakers who started out as nervous wrecks but eventually became top speakers.

## Analogy

In reasoning by analogy, you make a comparison with another person, place, thing, or event. Basically, you take a known situation and apply it to an unknown one. To carry this out successfully, it must be made clear how your situation is similar to the one you are using for comparison.

For example, say you are arguing that renovations to the student union building should include a hair salon. To argue that such a service would generate a substantial profit, you describe the success of a similar operation on another campus. To strengthen the argument, you point out all the characteristics that both campuses share.

# ▒ MESSAGE ORGANIZATION

How do you organize persuasive messages? This section offers several practical arrangements and formats to make your speeches more convincing. When used ethically, these are very practical skills to cultivate.

## Monroe's Motivated Sequence

Monroe's Motivated Sequence (Monroe, 1945) is a well-known organizational format used in persuasive speeches. Although it was developed in the 1930s, like the rhetorical approaches, it still receives positive acclaim and is widely used today as a persuasive rhetorical technique. It is particularly well suited to speeches that attempt to persuade to actuate—that is, in those speeches where you want the audience to take some kind of action.

For instance, say a grocery chain requested to have a section of a residential area rezoned commercial so it could buy an old church and erect a big, new store. A community member opposed to the idea could use Monroe's strategy to persuade other community members to take action against this request. Such a speech could be presented at a town meeting. (This situation actually occurred and the examples that follow are based on real events. The community won its plea.) Monroe's Motivated Sequence consists of five steps.

## Gain Attention

The first important step in any speech is to gain audience attention. As noted in Chapter 5, "Organizing the Speech," you can begin with a startling statement or statistic, a narrative, or a rhetorical question—to name just a few of the possibilities. You need to choose and develop an opening that will undoubtedly have an impact on the audience. For example, do not just state a statistic—describe the repercussions that the statistic actually has in the daily lives of the listeners. That is what the speaker in the following excerpt did.

> It is so good to see 93 percent of the families in this neighbourhood represented here tonight. Further, it is wonderful that we can still hold our community meetings and other events in this old church hall. As you know, if the town accepts the request to rezone this area commercial, we will never be able to meet here like this again. That means no more Sparks, Girl Guides, or Scout meetings; no more wedding and baby showers (Mary, you were feted here just last week); no more AA, Al-Anon, Alateen, or OA; no more teas and fall fairs; no place for the community to come together to celebrate our joys or deal with our tragedies.

## Establish a Need

According to Monroe (1945), you can establish a need by stating the problem as it presently exists or will exist at some future time. You then illustrate with specific examples to develop the problem to its fullest for the audience. Add statistics and other forms of support, and listeners get a clear picture of the problem. Finally, show how this need will affect listeners specifically and individually.

> Instead, we will be greeted with a steady stream of traffic through our quiet, residential streets. Preliminary estimates suggest that the number of cars going up and down Cottage Road and Park Street will increase by 700 percent. This is not acceptable. Our peace will be disrupted as we fear for the safety of our children, and we will be exposed to noise and blaring music at all hours. Our precious starry nights will become polluted by light seepage. In addition to a decline in our overall lifestyle, the value of our Victorian houses—many of which have been recently renovated—will be reduced. And why? Because some big corporation wants to make money. There are plenty of empty buildings downtown that could use new life. We must fight this rezoning bill.

## Satisfy the Need

Once you have established a need, the obvious next step is to satisfy that need. This is achieved by offering your audience a proposal or plan that will do the job. Also include a clear description of how the plan will meet the need. This must be evident, obvious, and apparent in the listeners' minds. Those of you who have participated in formal Oxford-style debates will recognize the similarity of the formats.

> Here is what we need to do. To request a meeting with the mayor and town council, we must have the signatures of all of you here. Those unable to attend will be contacted. Then there will be a meeting with the parties involved, and we will have an opportunity to present to our city council the reasons we do not support the rezoning. The council has the final say, and hopefully they will listen to our concerns and vote against the proposed change.

### Visualize the Need Satisfied

To clarify your proposal and show the audience its relevance, provide a thorough, vivid description and demonstration of what it will be like when the plan is in place. The goal is to make the audience feel and see how good it will be when the problem is solved in the manner you described. Use antithesis to create a visual outline of what will happen if your proposal is not put into action. To ensure the success of this step, provide examples and be generous with descriptive adjectives.

> If we take the appropriate action, we will not have to worry about our quiet, tree lined streets turning into thoroughfares for fast, loud vehicles. We will maintain a neighbourhood where our children play freely, running across the streets to each other's homes and interacting with adult neighbours. If we let this slide, no child or adult will be safe. We do not want to confine ourselves to backyards but rather to communicate with one another in the community spirit that brought many of us here in the first place. We want to keep our wonderful, safe neighbourhood—the neighbourhood we worked so hard to refurbish and beautify.

### Request Action

The final stage in the sequence is to request specific action. Inform the audience about what they must do to ensure that the need will be met. Again, the request must be specific and crystal clear.

> But this will not come without effort. Please sign the forms that are being circulated, and just as we have come together tonight, clear your calendars to attend the future meetings because they will determine our future. We can do this. We can save our wonderful neighbourhood.

---

| **MONROE'S MOTIVATED SEQUENCE AT A GLANCE** |
| --- |
| 1. Gain attention. |
| 2. Establish a need. |
| 3. Satisfy the need. |
| 4. Visualize the need satisfied. |
| 5. Request action. |

# One-Sided and Two-Sided Arguments

Considering whether to use a one-sided or two-sided argument does not occur to most people who are new to public speaking. However, once they understand how and when such an organizational strategy works, they are more likely to exercise this option in their persuasive speeches.

In a *one-sided argument*, you supply the audience with the various reasons that support your position. You do not add anything positive about the opposing side or view. In a *two-sided argument*, you acknowledge the evidence or reasons that support the opposing viewpoint, but you offset them with information that bolsters your take on the issue.

A number of factors determine which type of argument will have a more persuasive effect. Johnston (1994, pp. 141–142) reviewed the literature on this topic and came to the following conclusions:

## Use One-Sided Arguments

- *When the audience favours your position.* When the audience already favours your position, don't waste valuable time that could be spent reinforcing your position, further activating audience emotions, or inciting them to action. For example, speeches at political rallies are always one-sided.
- *When the audience is easily confused about the issue.* If the audience can easily be confused, then adding a second line of arguments that does not even support your position will only cause further confusion. For such an audience, it is better to outline your argument in simple, clear terms. For example, say you chaired a student committee to review potential insurance policies. Of the several that were reviewed, the committee found one to be superior, not in any big way, but in several small ways. If you addressed an audience that knew very little

about insurance policies, then a one-sided argument (why you would propose a particular insurance company) would be best. You would probably lose the audience if you plodded through the intricacies of each policy.

- When your *idea is new.* The one-sided argument is better when you are presenting a new idea. If you provide both sides of an issue, the new idea may become diluted and some audience members may not be able to understand the new idea. Introducing a new idea on its own makes a stronger, more direct appeal. For example, in an era of continuous gas and oil price hikes, a one-sided argument in favour of some alternative energy source would likely meet with success.

I think the notion of using one-sided or two-sided arguments is probably one of the most useful things I learned about public speaking. I'm in sales and am often called upon to present my products (cameras) at industry trade shows. If stores carry another product, I think of them as a hostile audience and use the two-sided argument. For buyers who are new at the game and don't know much about the products, I try not to confuse them. The one-sided approach works best with the novices. This stuff really works—I can see it in improved sales. I'm hoping to win a Caribbean vacation this year . . . and the prospects are looking good.

*Turk, Salesperson*

## *Use Two-Sided Arguments*

- *When you need increased credibility.* Use a two-sided argument in situations where your credibility is not as strong as it could be. People who use two-sided arguments are thought to be more honest, trustworthy, and credible. Imagine a situation where a business owner's daughter or son lacking experience or business training is brought in to head up a division that will introduce a new product line. Such an individual lacks credibility and would be wise to present a two-sided argument in the form of the pros and cons of the change.
- *When the audience faces future resistance.* If you think that your listeners will need to resist future persuasion from some opposition,

presenting a two-sided argument will give them the ammunition to resist the opposing position. However, when you are presenting your two-sided argument, make sure that the argument in favour of the opposing view is relatively weak. Otherwise, you may actually win the audience over to your opponent's position! Sometimes novice persuasive speakers make the mistake of taking more time to support the opponent's claims than trying to refute it with their own arguments.

- *When the audience is intelligent.* Two-sided arguments are more appealing to an intelligent audience. If you know listeners are up on the topic or are well educated, use this tactic.

- When the audience *is aware of contradictory sides of the argument.* Similarly, if your audience is aware that there are contradictory sides to the argument, use a two-sided approach. When an audience hears information that supports both sides of an issue, they believe they are being given more choice in the decision-making process. However, by keeping the opposing arguments light, listeners receive more information that supports your position.

- *When the audience is hostile.* A hostile audience is not necessarily quarrelsome or malicious—it may simply disagree with your position. For example, a Conservative candidate addressing a group of ardent NDP supporters is facing a hostile audience. In such cases, offering some support for the opposing beliefs would help to make the audience more willing to listen to the candidate's opposing perspective.

## Where to Put Your Strongest and Weakest Arguments

Should your strongest argument be placed at the beginning, middle, or end of your speech? Some of you will argue for the beginning, while others will hold that it is even stronger when offered as a final plea at the end of the speech. Well, the answer lies in whether you believe in primacy or recency. If you believe in *primacy*—that listeners remember what they hear at the beginning—then you will probably put your finest argument in the opening. You might just hit them with it. If you believe in *recency*—that listeners remember what they heard last then you will likely save the best for last.

Overall, though, communication scholars agree that the argument of greatest significance should be placed at the beginning of the speech, the second-strongest at the end, and the weakest in the middle, when the listening rate is at its lowest. Taking a moment to apply this to a two-sided argument, where should arguments in favour of your position be placed in the speech? At the very beginning, because if the opposing stance is presented first it could increase the appeal of that position, rather than the one you are proposing.

The most persuasive format for a three-point, two-sided presentation would be

1. best argument
2. data in support of the contender's stance
3. second-best argument

For the one-sided speech, the arrangement would be

1. best argument
2. least-effective argument
3. second-best argument

## The Foot-in-the-Door Technique

Another common persuasive strategy is the *foot-in-the door technique* (Freedman & Fraser, 1966). This approach follows a sequential message organization, meaning that more than one request is made. The foot-in-the-door technique refers to a small request followed by a larger one. However, the first, small request should be a reasonable one if it is going to be accepted by the audience. Otherwise, the second request, which is what you are really after, will not be accepted. Note that the bigger the initial request is, the greater the second request can be.

This strategy works best for prosocial causes. In addition, the second greater request must be related directly to the first. For example, perhaps your initial request is to have audience members sign a petition to organize a chapter of Mothers against Drunk Drivers (MADD), a prosocial cause. Then a second request asking for a loonie from everyone to help send children with burns to summer camp would not make sense. Instead, the second request would get a better response if you asked that everyone contribute a loonie toward opening a local chapter of MADD.

## ▦ MESSAGE CONTENT

Your message content also has an impact on the persuasiveness of your speech. Following are some content suggestions that are effective with specific audience characteristics.

# Fear Appeals

If you wanted to persuade your audience that a local toxic waste site should be cleaned up, there would be a tendency to use high fear appeals in your arguments. In other words, you would probably want to create a very negative, hair-raising depiction of the situation and include the possible horrifying outcome if immediate action is not taken.

Johnston (1994) argues that fear appeals do not work in general. Most of the effect they have on listeners disappears within 24 hours. However, fear appeals can be successful in certain circumstances. A moderate level of fear seems to work best. If you try to create too much fear, listeners just do not believe it. Conversely, if you create too little fear, the issue will be considered trivial and disregarded by the listeners. As well, according to Johnston (1994), there are only three conditions under which even the moderate fear appeal will work.

## *The Speaker Has High Credibility*

First, fear appeals can work when they come from a high-credibility speaker. Whose warnings about the harmful effects of smoking would you heed? Appeals from some unknown actor on a television commercial or appeals from your mother in her final battle with cancer when she asks, "How can you continue to smoke when you see me lying here like this?"

## *A Reasonable Solution Is Offered*

A fear appeal can also work if you offer a reasonable solution. For example, suppose people diagnosed with type 2 diabetes are told at an information session by an endocrinologist that if they do not look after themselves, they will end up with amputations, organ failure, and blindness. While initially overwhelmed by this news, the newly diagnosed diabetics calm down within 24 hours and think that those things cannot happen to them. It is all too much to comprehend—one day they are healthy, the next they are on the brink of serious ill health. The message actually contains too much fear appeal. However, if the endocrinologist offers specific, relatively easy steps that the diabetics can take to prevent such debilitating complications, then the fear appeal, coupled with the reasonable solutions, can be persuasive.

## *The Risk Information Is Specific*

The last condition under which a fear appeal is convincing is when the risk information is specific. For example, because many people with type 2 diabetes have a difficult time accepting their diagnosis, it takes a strong persuasive message to inspire them to participate in their health regime. Telling them that they face amputations, organ failure, or blindness is too scary and general a message. Again, they will likely not believe it can happen to them because they probably do not even feel sick. If, however, they are informed of what specifically will happen to them as the disease progresses, such as what exactly will occur in the next stage, they will be more likely to heed suggestions to maintain their present health level.

Even under these three conditions, fear appeals fade, so you need to reinforce the message with more fear appeals. This suggests that while fear appeals initially seem like strong, workable approaches to persuasion, they are not all that effective. Just think about the fear appeals pitched to you over the years. How influential were they?

"Always start your presentation with a joke, but be careful not to offend anyone! Don't mention religion, politics, race, age, money, technology, men, women, children, plants, animals, food. . . ."

Randy Glasbergen

## Humour Appeals

The use of humour has been mentioned a few times throughout this text. In relation to persuasion, Johnston (1994) states that humour can increase the speaker's attractiveness. That is, people generally like others who are truly humorous. Humour can also be useful for getting the audience's attention.

Johnston (1994), citing Osterhouse and Brock (1970), points out that "Some researchers argue that if you present a humorous message to an audience that is initially opposed to your viewpoint, you may distract the audience from thinking of arguments against your position" (p.132). However, Johnston goes on to state, "On the other hand, if you want to teach an audience new beliefs or attitudes, or if your message is difficult to comprehend, the use of humour can be detrimental to persuasion." Clearly, to present a successful persuasive speech, you must give serious thought to whether, how, and when you should inject humour into your presentation.

## Audience Characteristics

Much of Chapter 4, "Researching the Speech," was devoted to analyzing the audience. At this point, it goes without saying that the better you know your listeners, the better you can adapt your speech to meet their needs. This issue seems even more relevant to the persuasive speech. This section explains Johnston's (1994) review of how certain audience characteristics affect the persuasion process.

### *Sex*

Who do you think are more easily persuaded, women or men? There is a tendency to believe that women are, and indeed, older research would have us believe that. More recent studies, however, suggest that neither sex is more persuadable than the other. However, each sex is persuaded by different types of arguments.

Both women and men are more persuaded by information that is typically within the expertise range of the other sex. A persuasive speech on toilet training by a woman would be more persuasive to men who had never tried to toilet train a child. Some of you probably recognize that this example is based on the stereotypical notion that women are more responsible for child rearing than are men. We know that this is not always true. Men who were involved in toilet training their children would be persuaded less easily than men who were not. Using another stereotypical example, women who have no experience with their car cooling systems might be persuaded more easily by a man whom they think has expertise in this area.

There is one area where different appeals would work with men and women. Johnston (1994) reports that, according to the research, because women generally exhibit more empathy than do men, women would be more persuaded by appeals to sympathy and those based on reciprocity (doing something for someone in exchange for something else).

## *Age*

People assume that young and old people are the easiest to persuade. But when it comes to age, persuasion is related more to cognitive functioning, or the ability to reason, than it is to chronological years.

For instance, it makes sense that children might accept less sensible arguments because of their limited ability to analyze messages critically. They also have very short attention spans, so they miss out on half the messages anyway. To persuade children, Johnston (1994) says that "we must garner the child's attention by using exaggerated or peculiar voices, sound effects, and large, colourful images" (pp. 184–185). For school-age children, simple arguments and associations get the best results.

By the time children are adolescents, they are much more critical. However, because of their high inclusion needs, they respond best to appeals that meet their peer pressure and conformity requirements.

Do you think seniors are an easy group to convince? It depends: if they have diminished cognitive abilities, then they might be pushovers, but if their cognitive functioning is acute, you may have your work cut out for you. Because seniors have been around a long time, their attitudes are based on a lot of experience and wisdom. Some may refuse to change their beliefs and attitudes and to see the world in new ways—even if you present them with lots of evidence.

## *Intelligence*

Earlier in the chapter, audience intelligence was introduced in terms of one- and two-sided arguments. Relevant to intelligence is a person's ability to evaluate persuasive messages critically. It follows that the more intelligent people are, or the more expertise they possess on a topic, the more discerning they can be. But, individuals of varying intelligence levels respond differently to diverse types of arguments. When you design a persuasive speech, be aware of the following (Johnston, 1994):

- Intelligent audience members respond best to logical arguments that are supported by evidence.
- They are also influenced by a logical format. In some instances, that format may have an overriding effect. That is, intelligent listeners may be persuaded more by the persuasive model, or outline, than by the actual content. Perhaps associating intelligence and logic with a coherent, consistent presentational structure, they fail to assess the arguments and the evidence presented.

- Both high- and low-intelligence listeners respond well to emotional appeals (pathos). However, emotional appeals have a greater persuasive effect on low-intelligence listeners, maybe because they are more likely to become caught up in the sentiment and fail to look beyond to the larger picture.

# CHAPTER AT A GLANCE

- Informative speeches can be demonstrative, descriptive, or explanatory.
- You have to change people's beliefs and attitudes before you can alter their behaviours.
- Use Aristotle's proofs (ethos, logos, and pathos) and the stylistic techniques (repetition, parallel structure, and antithesis) to enhance your speech's potency.
- Reasoning (cause to effect, effect to cause, deductive, inductive, and analogy) refers to the type of appeal you use to argue your case.
- Use Monroe's Motivated Sequence, one-sided or two-sided arguments, or the foot-in-the-door technique to organize your persuasive speech.
- Always put your strongest argument first and the second-strongest at the end of your speech.
- Use fear appeals and humour only under certain circumstances.
- Audience characteristics such as sex, age, and intelligence level affect persuasion and thus the type of persuasive strategy you should use.

# APPLICATION AND DISCUSSION QUESTIONS

1. Answer the following questions in your communication journal:
   a. *Cognitive dimension:* What persuasive strategies do you typically rely on in public speaking and interpersonal contexts: rhetorical, organizational, message content, audience characteristics, or others? Explain.
   b. *Affective dimension:* Explain the feelings you experience when you engage in the persuasion process. How do you feel when someone persuades or tries to persuade you to do something?
   c. *Behavioural dimension:* Rate your interpersonal and public speaking persuasion skills. Develop a plan that will help you to improve your abilities.
2. In a small group, share examples of how your beliefs have shaped your attitudes, and then how those attitudes affect your behaviour in various situations.
3. Write down examples of the classical stylistic techniques: repetition, parallel structure, and antithesis. Think of examples that actually exist in your favourite music.

4. Take some time to analyze how your ethos may be perceived by different groups to which you belong—for example, your public speaking class, a club or organization, or your workplace. Develop a personal plan that would help you to enhance your credibility should you be called upon to make a presentation in each of those contexts.

5. In a small group, use Monroe's Motivated Sequence to develop a persuasive argument. Choose a problem related to your school or community. When you have finished, have one person present the mini-speech to the rest of the class.

6. What types of arguments would you use if you had the following information about your audience?
   a. adults in their 60s and 70s, intelligent, female
   b. adults in their 20s, intelligent, mix of both sexes, hostile audience

7. Read Martin Luther King Jr.'s "I Have a Dream" speech in its entirety. It is readily available at various sites on the Web as well as at http://douglassarchives.org/king_b12.htm. Do a rhetorical analysis by answering the following questions: Do you think King would have been nervous when he delivered this speech? What kind of nonverbal communication do you think accompanied the speech? Was there evidence that he knew and understood his audience? How did he organize the speech? How would you assess his opening and closing? What did he do to enhance his credibility, or did he need to? What kind of language style did he use? Did he use inclusive language, language intensity, or abstract language? Did he incorporate the classical stylistic devices? How did he use Aristotle's proofs? What kinds of appeals and arguments did he use? Discuss your answers to each of these questions.

## REFERENCES AND FURTHER READINGS

Atwood, M. (1995, June). *On writing poetry* (Waterstone's Poetry Lecture). Retrieved on August 2, 2001 from http://www.web.net/owtoad/lecture.html.

Bender, P.U. (2001). Stand, deliver and lead. *The Canadian Manager, 26*(2), 14–17. Retrieved April 10, 2005 from http://uccb-elearning.uccb.ca:2058/pqdweb?index=1&sid=4&srchmonde=1&vinst=PROD&...

Brydon, S.R., & Scott, M.D. (2000). *Between one and many: The art and science of public speaking* (3rd ed.). Mountain View, CA: Mayfield Publishing Company.

Coon Come, M. (2000, September). *Presentation at the Council for the Advancement of Native Development Officers.* Retrieved August 2, 2001, from http://www.edo.ca/conference/cooncomespeech.htm.

DeVito, J.A. (1997). *The elements of public speaking* (6th ed.). New York: Longman.

Freedman, J.L., & Fraser, S.C. (1966). Compliance without pressure: The foot-in-the-door technique. *Journal of Personality and Social Psychology, 4,* 195–202.

Fripp, P. (2004). Exciting speeches. *Executive Excellence, 21*(5), 18.

Golden, J.L., Berquist, G.F., & Coleman, W.E. (1983). *The rhetoric of Western thought* (3rd ed.). Dubuque, IA: Kendall/Hunt.

Grice, G.L., & Skinner, J.F. (2004). *Mastering public speaking* (5th ed.). Boston: Pearson.

Johnston, D.D. (1994). *The art and science of persuasion.* Madison, WI: WCB Brown & Benchmark.

Katz, D. (1960). The functional approach to the study of attitudes. *Public Opinion Quarterly, 24,* 163–204.

King, M.L. (1963, August). I have a dream. Archives of American Public Address. Retrieved August 15, 2005, from http://douglassarchives.org/king_b12.htm.

Langer, E., Blank, A., & Chanowitz, B. (1978). The mindlessness of ostensibly thoughtful action: The role of placebic information in interpersonal interaction. *Journal of Personality and Social Psychology, 36,* 635–642.

Langer, E., & Piper, A.I. (1987). The prevention of mindlessness. *Journal of Personality and Social Psychology, 53*(2), 280–287.

Larson, C.U. (2001). Persuasion: *Reception and responsibility* (9th ed.). Belmont, CA: Wadsworth.

Lucas, S.E. (2004). *The art of public speaking* (8th ed.). Boston: McGraw Hill.

Maslow, A.H. (1968). *Toward a psychology of being.* New York: Van Nostrand Reinhold.

Monroe, A. (1945). *Principles and types of speech.* Glenview, IL: Scott, Foresman.

Osborn, M., & Osborn, S. (1994). *Public speaking.* Boston: Houghton Mifflin.

Osterhouse, R., & Brock, T. (1970). Distraction increases yielding to propaganda by inhibiting counterarguing. *Journal of Personality and Social Psychology, 15,* 344–358.

Quina, K., Wingard, J.A., & Bates, H.G. (1987). Language style and gender stereotypes in person perception. *Psychology of Women Quarterly, 11,* 111–22.

Underwood, N. (2001, July 9). Cheating time. *Maclean's, 114*(28), 14–19.

# Chapter 9
## Social Speeches

## CHAPTER GOALS

In this chapter, you will learn
- the characteristics of social speeches
- how to introduce and thank a speaker
- how to propose a toast
- how to give a eulogy
- how to present and accept an award
- how to give an after-dinner speech
- elements of speaking politically
- how to leave voice mail messages

# ▓ INTRODUCTION

When Raymond proposed to Melinda, he just assumed that Theo, his best friend since junior high, would be his best man. In fact, Raymond thought that right until a month before the wedding. One night when he and Theo were shooting the breeze, Theo informed Raymond that he would not be able to accept the role because there was no way he could give the customary speech. Theo said he was too nervous, and on top of that, he did not have a clue what he was supposed to say, let alone how he would go about saying it. This surprised and disappointed Raymond and although his brother stood in, Raymond was still sorry that Theo was not his best man.

*Social speaking* refers to the short speeches that are presented on ceremonial occasions such as the one Theo would have given had he accepted the role. In the speech communication field, social speaking is called *ceremonial speaking*. Aristotle named it *epideictic* (pronounced *ep-uh-DIKE-tick*) speaking, "that which deals with praise and in the case of a ceremonial address" (Golden, Berquist, & Coleman, 1983, p. 60). Proposing a toast at a parents' special anniversary party, introducing a guest speaker at a service club or organization, or accepting an award are all social speeches. In business and organizational settings, giving an after-dinner speech on the company's latest accomplishments, introducing a seminar trainer, or presenting a gift to a retiring colleague are also social speeches.

As noted in Chapter 1, it is not easy to get through your personal and professional life without making a social speech. This fact is recognized by the business community as is evidenced in the number of public speaking courses offered in college and university business programs across Canada. For example, I recently met a young man who gave a wedding toast that was entertaining, poignant, and well delivered—no reading. I spoke with him later to say how much I enjoyed his presentation and he attributed his success to a public speaking course he had taken in his MBA program at McGill University. He said he learned so much that has served him well since then.

The goal of this chapter is to provide guidelines for various social speaking events so that you will be well prepared when called on to give a social speech.

# ▓ CHARACTERISTICS OF EPIDEICTIC (SOCIAL) SPEECHES

Although there are different types of epideictic speeches, they each share several characteristics and these are discussed below.

## They Signify the Reason for the Gathering

The social speech is often what lends pomp, pageantry, focus, and formality to a gathering. People assemble for a particular reason, and that reason needs to be articulated. For instance, consider the following two scenarios.

There was a celebration for a couple in their 70s who had recently married. In honour of their union, the host decorated her beautiful home by placing white flowers and ribbons in each room. The decor was clearly celebratory in nature and a jazz ensemble played in the living room. A traditional wedding cake and a variety of finger foods were housed in the elegant dining room. The affair struck a good balance between the formal and the informal. However, the reason everyone was gathered was not formally acknowledged. The groom later commented that, although he had been somewhat nervous, he was disappointed that the speech he had prepared in dedication to his new bride had gone home in his jacket pocket.

On the other hand, a family held a large beach barbecue to celebrate their parents' 50th anniversary. At the end of the day, everyone gathered at the cottage for cake and a champagne toast to acknowledge the occasion. That brief interaction was very meaningful for both the couple and the attendees.

## They Are Short

Ceremonial speeches are concise and to the point; no one wants an introduction, a gift presentation, or an acceptance speech to go on and on. Ironically, there is a tendency to assume that because a speech is short, it requires little or no preparation. But in some cases, the opposite is more likely to be true: developing, organizing, and practising the social speech may take as long as preparing a regular speech.

However, even though comments should be brief, the work and effort put into the occasional presentation to make it a significant one should be evident to listeners. This is especially important in contexts where a person is being honoured. For example, if a group is gathered to celebrate a friend's accomplishment (getting a coveted job, graduating from a tough course, or having a child), you want to say more than "Ya done good!" or "Way to go." The presentation should offer a moment of reflection on the accomplishment itself. Because social speeches often occur at important, memorable events, the sentiments that are expressed hold great significance.

My mentor taught me a great trick! He said that whenever I have to introduce a head table, a group of dignitaries or visitors, or an organizational team that I should *always* have the individuals' names on a small card, even if I know everyone. As he says, "This is not the time to pull a blank and forget the boss's name."

*Tim, BBA Student*

## They Occur on Happy Occasions

With the exception of funerals and memorial services, most ceremonial occasions are happy ones. The speaker's mood, temperament, and delivery style should reflect that joy. This can be accomplished through enthusiasm, spontaneity, and an animated nonverbal style.

## Speakers Feel Anxious

Even though social speeches are shorter than typical presentations, speakers still feel nervous. Just expect this and work through it. My colleague attended a communication conference where a noted communication specialist presented the welcome remarks. The presentation was superb. In a later conversation with the presenter, my colleague was surprised to learn that the speaker actually felt very anxious, although this certainly was not evident during her welcoming remarks. She disclosed that even after 30 years "in the business," she still practises every time she must make a presentation. Apparently, her apprehension and effort pay off.

Recall the positive side effect of nervousness in that it facilitates energy, which in turn translates into speaker edge and enthusiasm. However, to combat debilitating nervousness, reread Chapter 2, "Dealing with Nervousness," for a review of the techniques to reduce communication apprehension.

## There Is Relatively Little Lead Time

When people give a social speech, they typically comment afterward that it was a last-minute thing. This is often the case—speakers are not asked to present until

> 66 99
>
> I attended an awards banquet and was actually asked during the meal to introduce the after-dinner speaker. The organizer assumed that because I was a communication major, I would have no trouble with it. Because I was aware of the high expectations and I also knew I could not pull it off within the given time frame, I turned down the request. However, as a result of that incident, I developed a generic speech of introduction so that the next time I am asked, I'll feel confident enough to accept and I'll be prepared enough to do a good job.
>
> *Mark, Former Communication Major*

a relatively short time before the presentation. Not having enough time to prepare for a social speech, or any type of speech, can be nerve wracking, to say the least.

Sue DeWine, a communication scholar and organizational consultant, recommends that businesspeople develop some standard, inspirational presentation that they can give on short notice. She writes that she herself has developed and uses one based on the four Cs of life: challenges, commitments, creativity, and choices. As she says, "The message is, accept challenges, do something with your life that you are committed to, allow your creativity to flourish, and remember no one can make you feel a certain way, or behave a certain way" (DeWine, 2001, p. 264). DeWine explains that during the body of the speech she tells a story about each inspirational topic.

You can see how such a presentation could be adapted to a variety of occasional speaking contexts. DeWine also offers readers a template that students might develop: "Success depends on attitude, anticipation, and actions" (DeWine, 2002, p. 264). If you are, or expect to be, in a position where you will be called on to speak, DeWine's strategy could be quite helpful.

To be an accomplished social speaker, it helps to be aware of the unique content that comprises the various types of epideictic speeches. Being aware of what audiences expect in terms of the mood of the speech and the speaker's behaviour can also contribute to a successful presentation. The rest of the chapter explains how to present pertinent and poignant occasional speeches for a variety of situations.

# INTRODUCING AND THANKING A SPEAKER

## Introducing a Speaker

Whenever you go to a big-act concert, a less popular but nonetheless good opening band plays first. Its role is to raise the excitement level and create a sense of anticipation before the name act comes on. This is also the role of the introduction—to get the audience in the right mood and frame of mind to listen. The second goal of the introduction is an informative one: to provide information to raise the speaker's credibility, and to tell the audience why they should pay attention. The final goal is to make the speaker feel welcome. The process of achieving these goals begins well before the actual presentation.

### *Content*

While speakers supply event organizers with a résumé, only the highlights are included in the introduction. It is the introducer's role to select which facts will be shared with the audience. Given that the goal of the introduction is to enhance the speaker's credibility, include an overview of her or his education and credentials. For example, if a speaker possesses four university degrees, rather than report what each degree is or when and where it was earned, condense it into something like "Our guest speaker possesses four university degrees, the top one being a Ph.D. in Folklore from Memorial University of Newfoundland."

#### Major Achievements

Major achievements and accomplishments should also be noted. If the guest speaker started two successful companies that went public, then such a triumph would definitely be included. If your opening remarks demonstrate the speaker's credibility, then you have made the right decisions. Although the introduction should be relatively short, recognize that some speakers might be insulted if all of their accomplishments are not listed. It is appropriate to ask speakers which information they would like included. On the other hand, watch that your introduction is not so grandiose that speakers cannot live up to the image you have created.

#### Link with the Audience

Think of your role as a link between the speaker and the listeners and that you are speaking on behalf of others. To carry this out, include perspectives, thoughts, and feelings that audience members might possess. If you were introducing a noted speaker and you knew the audience was thrilled to have an opportunity to hear in person, then include something to that effect in your introductory remarks. Also, incorporate comments of a welcoming nature.

### Connections with the Audience

Finally, conclude the introduction with factors that are relevant to the audience, or information from the speaker's background that connects him or her to the audience. If, for instance, a speaker graduated from your university, audience members would likely be interested in knowing that. Having something in common with speakers helps the audience to relate more to them. Thus, a speaker–listener bond is established.

### What Not to Include

Certain things should not be included in the introduction. For example, it is bad form to say too much about the speaker's topic. This steals the person's thunder and makes you look bad. Also, do not include long stories about your personal knowledge of the speaker. Details about your relationship should be kept to a minimum, and share only those anecdotes that focus on the speaker.

## Delivery

Regardless of the content in the introduction, you should have a superb delivery. Two factors that result in a poor presentation are reading and mispronouncing the speaker's name.

### Reading

Even though most people know they should not read speeches, it is a common practice among introducers. However, audience members do not listen as well when speakers read, so rather than excite and prepare them for the featured speaker, reading actually does a disservice to the guest. Further, it shows a lack of respect when introducers fumble their way through the introduction and this can insult the speaker. Clearly, it is both important and professional to practise introductions so your delivery equals that of the lecturer.

### Pronouncing Speakers' Names

Do not rely on your assumptions, or how other people pronounce a speaker's name—always check the correct pronunciation either with the speaker or with a reliable source. In addition, it is equally important to use the person's correct title. Again, ask the speaker how he or she wishes to be addressed. Remember that a woman's professional title is ignored more often than a man's. For example, watch that you do not introduce a woman as *Mrs.* when her preferred professional title is *Dr.* Or, for example, if a woman is the mayor, do not refer to her as *Ms. Peterson* from Thunder Bay, but rather as *Mayor Lynn Peterson* from Thunder Bay, Ontario.

---

### HOW TO LOOK AFTER A SPEAKER

Common courtesy suggests that guest speakers should be given special attention. Try the following tips to make speakers feel comfortable and welcome:

**BEFORE THE SPEECH**
- Meet and welcome speakers at the door.
- Take them to a quiet place where they can hang up their coats or place their materials and visual aids. They may also want to see where they will present their speech.
- Act as an escort, especially if there are a lot of people around.
- Make appropriate introductions.
- Give speakers an overview of what will take place.
- Answer any questions, and engage in some small talk.
- If you or someone else needs to know how to pronounce speakers' names, ask.
- Ask speakers whether they need to freshen up, and if so, show them where to go.
- Ask whether they need a few minutes alone to gather their thoughts. If so, provide a quiet place where there will be no interruptions.

**AFTER THE SPEECH**
- Engage in more small talk.
- Introduce speakers to people and allow them to interact with others. Watch to see that they are comfortable with the group.
- When speakers wish to leave, show them back to their things.
- Escort them to the door, thank them again, and send them on their way.

---

## Thanking a Speaker

To thank a speaker in a manner that is both professional and spontaneous, try the following technique. Prepare some general remarks in advance. Then listen tentatively to the speech, take notes, and then integrate the comments into the prepared statements. For instance, you may decide in advance that you will say that the speech was interesting and informative. However, then you add something concrete and specific that you personally found intriguing about the presentation. This approach lends sincerity to your thanks. Your comments could go something like this:

> I know the audience will agree with me that your speech was both interesting and informative. Knowing how to approach my instructors when I feel I need some extra coaching, or when I think I have been graded unfairly, will be a tremendous help in the future.

### Unpopular Speakers

Barnard (1996) raises an issue not typically addressed in public speaking texts—how to thank an unpopular speaker. Speakers are unpopular when they deliver a message that the audience does not agree with. For example, perhaps school board officials are explaining how they are planning to cut five teachers from a 20-teacher school by increasing class size. Most parents would oppose such a measure. Or, maybe a university official is addressing students concerning tuition hikes, another unpopular issue. Bernard (1996) would suggest that in these contexts you thank the speakers for taking the time to come and present their side of the issue.

## ▉ PROPOSING A TOAST

Osborn and Osborn (1994) refer to the toast as a mini-speech of tribute. While toasts are typically thrust on people at the last minute, those planned in advance can be very effective. There are four simple steps in the basic toast: (1) declare the reason for the toast, (2) offer specific examples of the accomplishment or tribute, and (3) wish the individual(s) well, and (4) raise your glass in honour and recognition. A toast need not be any longer than two or three minutes.

## Eloquence

Osborn and Osborn (1994) also suggest that toasts should be elegant, although this is not always easy to achieve. Given that toasts are raised at happy occasions to express appreciation or congratulations, those themes should be the central focus of your remarks.

Dr. Carlotta Parr, a music educator makes the most elegant, poignant toasts I have ever heard. When asked what her secret was, she revealed that she attempts to capture the moment and the people around her in a memorable, metaphorical, and economical way (personal communication, July 26, 2001). By economic, she is referring to economy of words. Parr says not to go on and on because it can make the sentiment seem insincere, and the true essence of the meaning can get lost in too many words.

## Clean Beginnings and Endings

A clean beginning is a particularly salient concern regarding toasts in informal settings. Recall from Chapter 3, "Nonverbal Communication," that a clean beginning occurs when the speaker has everyone's attention, takes a breath, and then begins to speak. In relaxed settings, it can take more time to prepare listeners for the toast. For example, individual conversations, laughter, and general playfulness, while expected in social settings, also mean that someone has to organize the group for the toast. Because the toast may be the only acknowledgement of why the group is gathered, it is important that everyone be a part of this ceremonial rite.

Before the toast is started, make sure that all the guests are gathered, that they have some sort of drink in hand (it need not be alcoholic), and that everyone is close enough to hear the speaker. Finally, ensure that the individual being toasted is located in a position of honour.

A clean ending is much easier to achieve. After making your toast, you simply raise your glass and say, "And here's to . . ." That is the sign for everyone to drink up, which ends the toast.

## Wedding Toasts

One of the most common types of toast is offered at weddings. Because many people neglect to follow any format and assume that you "just get up and say something," these toasts are often very badly presented.

A good wedding toast includes content that honours the bride and groom, provides examples of why they might be a good match and complement each other, and suggests how their lives will be enriched because of their union. Wedding toasts may also include a theme. One enterprising and creative individual I know decided to do his speech in the form of the *Jeopardy!* game. He did a lot of research to find interesting, but not embarrassing, information about the lovebirds.

---

### PROPOSE A TOAST IN FOUR SIMPLE STEPS

Keep these four steps in mind the next time you are called on to propose a toast:

1. Declare the reason for the toast.
2. Offer specific examples of the accomplishment or tribute.
3. Wish the individual(s) well.
4. Raise your glass and say, "Here's to . . ."

---

Equally important when it comes to the wedding toast, is what not to say! Do not include examples or anecdotes that might embarrass and humiliate the couple. For instance, avoid comments like: "It seems like only yesterday that you two started sneaking around with each other. Now that Marcel finally got that divorce, you two are legal." While such a comment may be accurate, it is inappropriate for the setting. Also, avoid sexual innuendoes, racy comments, and naming of former spouses or lovers. Such talk is better left for private celebrations among people who know one another well. Like the attire, wedding toasts should be presented in tuxedo language—not bathrobe.

I don't know why everyone at wedding head tables feel they have to say something. The worst example I ever saw was when each individual got up and made inside jokes that only the bride and groom, and a few others, could understand. In some instances, only one of the spouses knew what the speaker was alluding to. The wedding guests were left out. Finally, the bride's father got up and took some notes from his pocket. There were actually rude comments from some wedding party members like "Oh, here we go. Let's hunker down for a long one." Obviously, the wedding party had had a little too much champagne. Anyway, the father's speech was great. He took the time to consider how marriage would impact the couple's lives. He spoke from the heart, and although he had notes, he seldom referred to them. Both the bride and groom appreciated the thoughtfulness he had given to their meaningful milestone.

*Avtar, Former Communication Student*

| **WEDDING TOAST** |
|---|
| 1. Say why you are there. |
| 2. Give examples of why the bride and groom are a good match. |
| 3. Indicate how their lives will be enriched as a result of the union. |
| 4. Raise your glass in a toast and say, "Here's to . . ." |

Aside from unsuitable content, there can also be problems with the microphone. Speakers who are unaccustomed to using one should try to get in some practice time. While the reception area may not be set up until just prior to the celebration, call the venue to arrange for a short technical rehearsal. Having a sense of how the mike works and sounds will reduce your nervousness and help you to avoid some of those awkward microphone errors such as clunking it on something, blowing into it, or having it in the wrong position so that it does not pick up your voice. If you are the bride or groom, set aside some time for speakers to become comfortable using the microphone.

# THE EULOGY

The eulogy is probably the most difficult type of epideictic speech to present. First, speakers may have a difficult time trying to determine the content and second, if the speaker knows the deceased well, there is the emotional impact to deal with.

### A EULOGY FOR PEARL PEERS—A CASE STUDY

I learned firsthand how difficult it is to write a eulogy when I was asked several years ago to be a eulogist at the memorial service for my long-time colleague and friend, Pearl Peers. It is both an incredible honour and huge responsibility to attempt to sum up a person's life in one short speech. I found myself riffling through public speaking books to locate a specific format; I didn't find one. I spoke with colleagues and former students in an attempt to learn what they would say to capture Pearl's life. I tried to recall absolutely everything I knew about her. What would I say? How could I make my words do justice to the impact she had had on those who worked with and learned from her. Here is what I learned from that process—her final lesson for me.

Based on the elements that comprise a eulogy (the few that I found scattered in various textbooks), I attempted to choose the content for my presentation. At first, I wanted to include a lot of personal feelings such as how I was responding to Pearl's death. Maybe one has to work through this process to arrive at a place where emotional responses are subdued and a more cognitive, logical composure takes over. I began by noting our professional relationship, and then cited the qualities that made Pearl a successful communication lab coordinator. I supplemented that with stories about her interactions with students. Then I highlighted her unique personality characteristics and illustrated those with further anecdotes, some even funny and uplifting. I included the special relationships she had had with others at the university, and I noted that I spoke on behalf of the university community.

Once the content issue was resolved (and that took until shortly before I was to deliver speech), there was still the organization to be worked out. I opted to take a chronological approach, and then turned to the classical stylistic devices to help me present the material. Through the careful use of language, I attempted to paint a picture of Pearl's professional life and the contribution she had made to the communication field, to the department, and to her students. Then I practised, and practised, and cried, and practised some more until I was confident I could deliver a meaningful eulogy in a credible manner. Even though, I was very nervous doing the presentation.

## Content and Organization

A *eulogy* is a speech of testimony in praise of the deceased. When called upon to give a eulogy, begin by explaining how you knew the person. From there, you describe the deceased's virtues, recognize her or his humanity, and depict how the person touched the lives of others. You attempt to arouse the emotions of those attending the service by speaking on their behalf and offering examples of how listeners might be feeling at the moment. Finally, note the pain of the loss, and offer mourners some form of comfort. This needs to be done with little reference to your own personal sense of loss because the goal of the eulogy is to honour the dead, not provide a forum for the eulogist's grief. Giving a eulogy is not easy.

### ))) SPOTLIGHT ON SPEAKERS

In September 2000, Justin Trudeau delivered a eulogy for his father, Pierre Elliott Trudeau, former prime minister of Canada. The excerpt on page 288 contains his opening remarks. Based on those, what insight into his father does he provide? You can find the entire eulogy on the Internet.

*Friends, Romans, countrymen . . .*

*I was six years old when I went on my first official trip. I was going with my father and my grandpa Sinclair up to the North Pole. It was a very glamorous destination. But the best thing about it is that I was going to be spending lots of time with my dad because in Ottawa he just worked so hard.*

*One day, we were in Alert, Canada's northernmost point, a scientific military installation that seemed to consist entirely of low shed-like buildings and warehouses. Let's be honest. I was six. There were no brothers around to play with and I was getting a little bored because dad still somehow had a lot of work to do. I remember a frozen, windswept Arctic afternoon when I was bundled up into a Jeep and hustled out on a special top-secret mission. I figured I was finally going to be let in on the reason of this high-security Arctic base. I was exactly right.*

*We drove slowly through and past the buildings all of them very grey and windy. We rounded a corner and came upon a red one. We stopped. I got out of the Jeep and started to crunch across towards the front door. I was told, no, to the window. So I clamboured over the snow bank, was boosted up to the window, rubbed my sleeve against the frosty glass to see inside and as my eyes adjusted to the gloom, I saw a figure, hunched over one of many worktables that seemed very cluttered. He was wearing a red suit with that furry white trim.*

*And that's when I understood just how powerful and wonderful my father was.*

## Practise

While it is important to practise all speeches, it seems doubly so with the eulogy. This is because it takes courage and stamina to present your thoughts under such stress. Going over the speech until you can present it smoothly will ensure that you do a good job. Practising will also alert you to the parts that move you to tears. This allows you to get these out in the privacy of your home rather than in front of a group of people depending on you to capture the essence of the deceased.

However, do not be embarrassed if you do start to cry during your eulogy. Instead, be prepared by making sure you have a glass of water at your side and a tissue up your sleeve or in your pocket.

---

> ### THE EULOGY AT A GLANCE
>
> Here are some guidelines to help you prepare a eulogy.
>
> 1. Briefly explain your relationship with the person—how you knew him or her.
> 2. Describe the person's virtues, and recognize her or his humanity.
> 3. Explain how the person touched the lives of others.
> 4. Speak on behalf of those who knew the deceased and how they might be feeling.
> 5. Note the pain of the loss, and offer mourners comfort.
> 6. Keep focused on the deceased and not on how you personally feel.
> 7. Practise the speech and spend extra time on the parts that overwhelm you with emotion.
> 8. Bring a tissue with you in case you become teary eyed.

# PRESENTING AND ACCEPTING AWARDS

## Presentation Speeches

*Presentation speeches* are given before someone is presented with a gift or award. Hanna and Gibson (1995) write that such speeches should include the name of the award and the reason it exists, the criteria used in the selection process, and how the recipient met the criteria. Once that is done, the receiver is called forward to accept the award. Hanna and Gibson further note that any inscriptions on the award should be read to the audience. In all, the presenter's goal is to point out the significance and importance of the award and to explain the qualities, characteristics, or achievements of the recipient that made that person a suitable choice.

In situations where the award is physically large, be sure to help the recipient carry it, or provide a place to put it while she or he is making the acceptance speech. In situations where a wrapped gift is presented, it may not be proper for the recipient to open it in front of the audience. I once received a gift from students at Holy Angels High, an all-girls school, after making a presentation on gender and communication. The students waited eagerly while I unwrapped a beautiful journal. In that context, it was appropriate to open and acknowledge the gift. In other, more formal circumstances, it may not be.

# Acceptance Speeches

Depending on the type of award received, recipients may be expected to respond with an acceptance speech. The tone and language used should be in keeping with the award received. For instance, for more formal awards, such as a Nobel Prize or the Order of Canada, one expects acceptance speeches to be presented in a conventional and stately manner (tuxedo style). With other, more playful awards, such as the team member most likely to be late for practice, the acceptance speech would also be presented playfully (blue jean style). When giving an acceptance speech, two factors should concern you: content and demeanour.

## *Content*

One of the major challenges with the acceptance speech is keeping it short and at the same time, saying what people expect and want to hear. This may be disconcerting in situations when you are completely taken off guard by receiving the award. Nonetheless, never apologize for the speech you are about to make. Use the following guidelines to be a two-time success.

### *Acknowledge Individuals*

Begin by thanking the people who granted you the award and expressing your gratitude for the honour of receiving it. It is good form to acknowledge and say something positive about any competitors. You often see this done by Academy Award winners, especially those receiving the top acting or directing honours.

After that, move on to thank and acknowledge those who helped make the award possible. This is where it can get tricky. You want to avoid long lists that ultimately bore audience members. On the other hand, you want to ensure that everyone who helped is recognized. To deal with the dilemma, single out by name the most significant contributors, and then list the others in categories. For example, if you were accepting a Juno award for male vocalist of the year, you would thank your manager, producer, recording and mixing technicians, and musicians who worked on your CD. Thank family members and close friends, and then categorize the others, such as the hometown fans who supported you during the early years.

### *Acknowledge the Award*

After the "people" acknowledgments, turn to the values represented by the award. Explain what it means to you to receive such an honour, and how you will attempt to live up to it. While this last part may seem like it could take a long time, it can actually be taken care of with just a sentence or two. End the speech with a thank you, and step away.

### *Demeanour*

Equally important to the success of your speech is your demeanour, or approach. To accept an award in a dignified manner, one must be modest. Even though you may think you really deserved the award or it was about time that you were recognized, do not say this. While some humility may be conveyed through your content, much more about your attitude comes through your voice and nonverbal communication—so keep them in check, no gloating.

In situations where you know in advance that you will receive the award, it is expected that you will prepare an acceptance speech ahead of time. However, in those contexts where you are nominated with several others for an honour and you will not know the winner until it is announced at a public ceremony, you have a dilemma. If you plan and practise an acceptance speech, you may appear too confident and sure of yourself. In such cases, try to combine readiness with spontaneity. This can be accomplished by disclosing how you feel at the moment, and then moving on to express your planned sentiments.

On the other hand, some award nominees prepare absolutely nothing. Maybe they think that to do so will tempt fate. In any case, winners in that category can become so overwhelmed with excitement and emotion that they cannot speak coherently. They often later regret their missed opportunity to appear poised. Should you be the lucky recipient of some surprise award, breathe deeply to calm down, and then make the acceptance speech as if you are role-playing. Keeping the content outline in mind, say what you need to. Try to leave the emotional expressions for the celebration party.

---

**THE ACCEPTANCE SPEECH AT A GLANCE**

A good acceptance speech can be made by doing the following:

1. Acknowledge individuals who helped you attain the award or honours.
2. Acknowledge the value of the award and what it means to you.
3. Accept in a dignified, modest manner.
4. Be brief.

---

## ■ AFTER-DINNER SPEECHES

After a rich meal, most people just want to nod off for a bit. This is what you are up against when you present an after-dinner speech. As the name implies, an *after-dinner speech* follows a meal, although not necessarily just a dinner. You may find yourself making a presentation at a breakfast meeting.

However, because these epideictic speeches come after a meal, two major factors contribute to their success: (1) they must be entertaining, and (2) they must be short. In fact, Hanna and Gibson (1995) recommend that they last no longer than 10 minutes. While keeping after-dinner speeches short may suit you just fine, providing entertainment value may require considerably more thought.

## Content

To entertain an audience, the after-dinner speech should be light, yet inspirational in some way. Therefore, choosing a topic can be somewhat complicated. Topics that are too weighty, such as arguing a side of some controversial issue or trying to persuade an audience to invest in your new company, are not appropriate. In fact, the last thing you want to do is clutter your time with technical details, complex issues, or a list of statistics. Using a thorough set of visual aids is also out. On the other hand, you do not want the topic to be so light and airy that it completely lacks depth.

What should you do? First, get *audience-centred* by finding out as much as possible about the listeners. This will allow you to choose a topic that is within your expertise, but one in which the audience will also be able to relate. The next step is to adapt your subject to meet the specific needs of the listeners. For instance, if I were to present a quick speech on public speaking to the university business society, I could better meet their needs by providing ways to deal with nervousness rather than talking about gender differences in presentation styles.

Hanna and Gibson (1995) recommend the one-point speech for such occasions. You take some major, or central, theme and develop it by using anecdotes, stories, and interesting quotations, all of which should emphasize the main point you are making. An after-dinner presentation on nervousness would lend itself well to such a scheme.

After-dinner guests like to be entertained and they enjoy hearing funny material. You can add humorous stories to your speech, practising them until you have the timing and intonation right. Include funny narratives that appeal to a wide variety of people, not just the unique sense of humour shared by your family. Many communication specialists recommend that you make humour at your own expense—perhaps something directed toward your own foibles. This gives the audience insight into your personal approach to life, which in turn serves to establish a bond with the listeners. This tactic can be very appealing.

What do you do if you are not naturally inclined toward humour, and you cannot tell a joke well no matter how often you try? A speech about something light but interesting can work just as well—if it is short.

---

### ✍ EXPERT ADVICE

Remember what Polonius, said: "Brevity is the soul of wit." Practically everyone can relate a social occasion marred by a speech that was ill-conceived, poorly prepared, poorly delivered—perhaps all three—and, worse, too long for the occasion. Here are a few more tips Polonius might have offered to Laertes.

Prepare in advance, including rehearsing. "Winging" it is not acceptable if it's avoidable. Most of the time, we know in advance—make sure it shows.

Use the microphone. Not everyone can hear you. And, make sure it works.

Never use expletives. No matter what company you're in, coarse language is inappropriate for centre stage.

Easy on the punch. A drink can relax you—more can unhinge you.

*Mike Hunter, Department of Communication*
*Cape Breton University, Sydney, N.S.*

---

## Demeanour

When you will be giving an after-dinner speech, it is best either to eat before you attend or wait until after your speech. This will prevent indigestion, burping, or other potentially embarrassing bodily functions. Because most speakers are nervous, not eating presents little hardship. During the meal, just pick at your food. You might also sneak out to a quiet space—it may even have to be the bathroom—and take a quick look at your notes. Return well before it is time for you to speak.

# ▇ SPEAKING POLITICALLY

## Nominating a Candidate

For those of you who may be interested and involved in politics, you could easily find yourself in the position of having to offer a nomination speech. This generally occurs at political rallies or conventions, when you nominate a candidate to run for your party. Zarefsky and MacLennan (1997) suggest a three-step plan for such speeches.

First, begin the nomination with an overview of your "understanding of the importance of the office" (Zarefsky & MacLennan, 1997, p. 345). Discuss the responsibilities and issues the candidate would have to deal with, and couple this with the characteristics required to handle the job.

Second, signify why your candidate is right for the office. Do this by stating the candidate's position on relevant issues, and the role he or she has played in the past. You can also demonstrate how your nominee's qualities (talents, experiences, intelligence, and so forth) make her or him the ideal candidate. Zarefsky and MacLennan (1997) also discuss the notion of negative campaigning (making disparaging remarks about your opponents). Although this tactic has become more common in recent years, it should not be part of a nomination speech. The goal of such a meeting is to select the candidate who will best represent the party in the forthcoming election; everyone present supports the same party. Such attacks make the candidate look inadequate.

Third, formally place your candidate's name on the nomination roster. You may want to build up to a crescendo, but this must be rehearsed so it does not sound like barren hoopla.

## Accepting a Candidacy

If you have a keen interest in politics, you may be nominated to run for political office. If so, you will be required to make a series of speeches, the first of which is your acceptance speech. Zarefsky and MacLennan (1997) state that you should begin by accepting the nomination and pledging to do your best. As in an acceptance speech for an award, commend the losing candidates and solicit their support in the fight ahead. Then go on to note the magnitude of the task associated with the

Reprinted with special permission of King Features Syndicate.

position, and pledge to work hard. Overall, attempt to deliver the speech with the right blend of confidence and modesty. In addition, keep your message short and succinct. It is better to say a lot with a few words than to say little with a lot of words.

## MAKING INTERPERSONAL INTRODUCTIONS

Have you even been in a situation where you are talking to someone and a third person who knows your friend joins in? Good etiquette suggests that your friend should initiate the introduction process. However, this does not always occur, and you're left feeling awkward and even embarrassed.

Politeness is integral to success in the professional world. As Gaut and Perrigo (1998) note, "People simply won't do business with companies whose personnel are inattentive or rude" (p. 218). Introducing people is another form of social speaking, especially in business contexts. In addition, introductions, like ceremonial speeches, are guided by certain conventions. Gaut and Perrigo (1998) describe four rules that result in introductions that meet the highest etiquette standards. They are: (1) the biggest star always gets top billing; (2) the biggest star's name is always said first; (3) in professional/social situations, select the person who should be the biggest star; and (4) if you are unsure who the biggest star is, appoint the person you prefer to compliment (pp. 226–228).

Gaut and Perrigo (1998) also provide some instructions for determining who gets top billing. They suggest the superior in the workplace is the star over a subordinate, a client stars over anyone in the organization, visiting dignitaries from other countries over presidents of companies, top ranking politicians over company presidents, the woman in cases where a man and woman have equal status, and the elder of two people with equal status.

Once you have sorted out the star business, simply make introductions in the following manner:

"Dean Bujold, I would like you to meet our new accounts payable assistant, Sonya Poulette" or "Dean Bujold, allow me to introduce Sonya Poulette, our new accounts payable assistant.

# IMPROMPTU SPEECHES AND USING THE TELEPHONE

## The Impromptu Speech

An impromptu speech is one where you are given so little preparation time that it is almost spontaneous. For instance, a boss might ask you to provide a project update at a meeting, give your rationale for a new product line, or offer your thoughts on an issue. Although the idea of having to deliver an impromptu speech tends to make people apprehensive, you have really been speaking in an impromptu fashion your entire life—in classes when your instructor asks you a question or in small groups when you give your input. In fact, we spend much more of our life speaking spontaneously, or interpersonally, than we do in prepared forms. This is similar to giving an impromptu speech.

Nonetheless, here are four strategies that can help you develop a presentation fast: listen, adhere to a generic outline, keep it short, and practise.

### Listen

Part of doing a good impromptu presentation is listening to what others have said before you. In business contexts such as meetings or presentations, Lucas (2004) recommends that you, "Take notes of major points with which you agree or disagree" (p. 296). This will give you a basis for a presentation and enable you to link what others have said to what you are saying.

### Adhere to a Generic Outline

Impromptu speeches are similar to other types of presentations in that they have an introduction, a body, and a closing. Impromptu speeches are also short so you will probably only have time to make one, maybe two, main points. Therefore, an impromptu speech can be organized in five steps. The following generic outline can be used for a wide variety of topics.

1. Get the audience's attention—Think of something to garner the interest of the audience.
2. State the goal of your presentation—For an impromptu speech, it might simply be something like, "While others today have agreed with implementation of the new policy, I believe there is one major stumbling block that needs to be dealt with: how the men will respond."

3. Define the situation—In this segment, you provide your views or insight into the situation.

4. Support your stance—Use reasoning, examples, statistics, testimony, or anecdotes to support your stance or argument.

5. Close the presentation—A good way to do this is to repeat your point.

### Keep It Short

No one expects an impromptu speech to be long, and neither should you. Do not feel that you have to go on and on or ramble. Just say what you have to and end it. To try to expand too much can result in a muddled presentation.

### Practise

The final strategy to help you become an excellent impromptu speaker is to practise on your own whenever you have a chance. Select a topic that you are familiar with and use the five-step outline to prepare an impromptu presentation. Say it aloud as you drive along or wait in rush hour traffic lines.

Give yourself three minutes to organize an impromptu speech for the following events:

- giving a gift to an instructor
- raising a toast to someone who is heading out for a year-long trip around the world
- accepting an award for top speaker in your class
- introducing a new employee at a meeting

---

**FIVE STEPS TO IMPROMPTU SPEAKING**

1. Get the audience's attention.
2. State the goal.
3. Define the situation.
4. Support your stance.
5. Close the presentation.

---

# Voice Mail

Most people think that leaving a voice mail message is easy. To a degree, they are correct, but there is still substantial room for improvement. I was quite surprised to receive a message from another speech communication professor that I could hardly make out. He spoke very fast, and a strong accent blurred the unlisted number to which I was supposed to respond.

If you dislike leaving messages, decide in advance what you will say—even if the person might answer. That way you will not be put off when you hear the answering machine respond. It will also prevent you from leaving one of those rambling messages that do not get to the point, or those short sharp ones that do not contain enough information. All you need in the message is your name, a brief explanation of why you are calling, and a telephone number where you can be reached. To avoid playing telephone tag, indicate a time when you will be available. This should all be stated slowly and clearly.

Avoid leaving messages like "Hi, it's me!" even with your friends. It is presumptuous on your part to think that the receiver will recognize your voice, although these days call display helps. Also, make sure to leave your last name. Sometimes I get calls from students like "Hi, it's Jennifer. Can you call me about the assignment?" With over 100 students per semester, I do not always know which Jennifer is phoning. Further, without the courtesy of leaving a telephone number, I must track down all the Jennifers in each of my courses.

---

### A SAMPLE VOICE MAIL MESSAGE

Hello, this is Jennifer Riley from section 01 of your public speaking course. It is Wednesday, February 14, at 9:30 a.m. I am having some trouble with the speech outline assignment and hope you can help me out. You can contact me at 749-7731. I'll be at this number until 7:00 p.m. That's Jennifer Riley at 749-7731. Thank you.

---

Not only is the content of the message important, so too is how you say it. Messages need to be articulated slowly and clearly. Keep in mind too that if you are calling outside your geographical area, the message receiver may think you have an accent, which can cut down on the clarity of your message. Further, make a concerted effort to slow your voice down when you are leaving telephone numbers, addresses, names, or other unfamiliar information. In fact, it is not a bad idea to repeat such pertinent information.

# Telephone Etiquette

## *Answering the Telephone*

Often, the first impression that customers have of a business, or individuals have of someone they have not yet met, is created through the telephone. You can create a positive image by attending to a few simple details. First, say "Hello" rather than "Yeah," when you answer. If you are answering on behalf of a business or organization say "Good afternoon," followed by the appropriate name or department ("Good morning, Speech Communication Department").

If the call is for you, say something like, "Yes, this is Mary MacDonald," or "You're speaking with her." If the call is not for you but someone in your household, good manners would have you say, "One moment, please." After that, call the person, but make sure that you do not yell into the telephone. Remember that the caller can hear you, so keep that in mind when you are calling for someone else. Use polite, casual/dress code language, and keep your tone of voice pleasant.

If the call is not for you and the person being called is not in, say, "I'm sorry, Mary is not in just now. May I take a message?" Deliver this brief interaction in a pleasant tone of voice. It is commonly suggested that voices sound more pleasant when speakers smile when they speak.

## *Taking and Leaving Messages*

Be sure to have paper and a pen handy by the phone for message taking. Listen well, and ask the caller to spell names and repeat numbers or addresses. When the caller is finished, repeat the message to check for accuracy.

When you leave a message, make sure to leave your name, number, and a brief message. When you have finished, ask the person taking the call to repeat what you have said so you can verify that the message is accurate. This is your responsibility.

Sometimes people do not like to ask that their message be repeated. One way to get around this is to say something like "I'm not sure if I've told you everything. Could you please repeat the message?" In this way, you can correct any errors.

## *Making Calls*

When you call people, it is polite to ask for them as follows: "May I speak with Mary MacDonald?" This is much more professional than "Is Mary there?" or "Get me Mary."

## DEVELOPING A GOOD PHONE MANNER

To use the telephone in a professional manner, try to incorporate the suggestions provided by Dennis Becker and Paula Borkum Becker into your telephone-handling repertoire.

Beyond specific telephone skills such as taking and making calls, using the hold button, using a telemarketing script, and handling upset callers, there are also general skills you can apply to all your business phone calls. Keep in mind that telephone calls are an excellent opportunity to promote your company's image and develop a good relationship and reputation with your clients, customers, and colleagues.

We all know people who have a wonderful phone manner. They are the colleagues at work who never seem ruffled by even the most problematic callers, never get confused or thrown off balance by out-of-the-ordinary calls, and never view phone calls as interruptions, to be avoided at all costs. We've analyzed these people's skills to determine what elements make up a good telephone manner. By mastering the following skills, you'll gain telephone confidence and add to your business speaking skills.

1. Keep a positive attitude.
2. Live the golden rule: Do unto others as you would have them do unto you.
3. Never lose your temper.
4. Be a good listener. Everyone likes to be listened to.
5. Treat others with respect. *Everyone* gets special treatment.
6. Always speak politely and courteously.
7. Have patience and tolerance with the shortcomings of others.
8. Understand human behaviour, especially human needs.
9. Practice stress management regularly. Do whatever works for you, but do something.
10. Use the F-F-F technique frequently (see below).
11. Separate personal and professional attitudes and behaviours.
12. Sound appropriately concerned about people's needs.
13. Smile with your face and your voice.
14. Take messages well.
15. Use the hold button courteously.
16. Maintain a neat, professional appearance at all times. This helps maintain a positive attitude that can be heard over the phone.

17. Provide options when problem solving. Be open to the ideas of others.
18. Offer to help in any situation.
19. Develop alternate methods for ending a call. Remember—it's an opportunity, not an interruption.
20. Use people's last names with their titles frequently (Mrs. or Dr. Nikolof, not Ann). Be respectful, but not too chummy.

**THE F-F-F TECHNIQUE**

First F: "I understand how you *feel*." Be sure you don't say this until callers have said everything they want to say. Don't interrupt, even if you've heard the whole story before. If you do interrupt and upset the caller, what will the caller say?

"You don't understand; you won't even let me finish. You're not listening." So be patient.

Second F: "I have *felt* the same way." Here, use a 10-second personal anecdote to indicate that you can identify with the caller's feelings.

"I've felt the same way when I waited home all day for the telephone repair crew to show up. It wasted my whole day. I understand your feeling of frustration."

Don't take longer than 10 seconds. An upset caller doesn't want to hear a long story from you.

Third F: "I have *found* that what helps is. . ."

Then give a solution or plan for assistance.

# CHAPTER AT A GLANCE

- Social speeches are also called *epideictic* or *ceremonial speeches.*
- Social speeches are short speeches that typically take place on happy occasions and signify the reason for the gathering.
- A good introduction to a speaker prepares the audience to listen, provides background information on the speaker, and welcomes the speaker.
- Include a blend of prepared and spontaneous remarks when called upon to thank a speaker.
- When proposing a toast, give the reason for the toast, offer specific examples of accomplishments, and wish the individual well.
- Never make inside jokes or inappropriate remarks during a social speech.

- When giving a eulogy, explain your relationship with the deceased, expound on his or her virtues, describe how the person touched the lives of others, speak on behalf of the mourners, and offer comfort. Keep the focus on the deceased and practise beforehand.
- To present an award, include its name and the reason it exists, the criteria for the selection, and how the recipient met those criteria.
- When you accept an award, acknowledge people who helped you, state what receiving the award means to you, and be brief and modest.
- When you give an after-dinner speech, keep it short and entertaining.
- When you nominate a political candidate, Zarefsky and MacLennan (1997) suggest that you state the importance of the office, why your candidate is appropriate, and who your candidate is.
- When you do an impromptu speech, get the audience's attention, introduce your goal, define the context, offer examples, and close the presentation.
- Voice mail should be clear, concise, and contain all the necessary information.
- Always answer or make calls politely and with a pleasant tone of voice.

## APPLICATION AND DISCUSSION QUESTIONS

1. Answer the following questions in your communication journal:
   a. *Cognitive dimension:* From the various social speeches you have heard, what is one of the most common errors you've noticed speakers make? Explain.
   b. *Affective dimension:* Which characteristics of the epideictic speeches listed in the chapter (being brief, being funny, etc.) would make you the most nervous? What could you do to reduce your tension?
   c. *Behavioural dimension:* Describe your strengths and weaknesses as a social speaker. What will you do to improve your skills?
2. Select a letter of the alphabet, choose three words beginning with that letter, and then develop a three minute inspirational presentation on those words. Follow this with a list of at least five different situations where the speech could be presented. Include any adaptations that would be required for each context.
3. With a small group, share stories about good and bad epideictic speeches that you have heard. From those narratives, create lists of dos and don'ts that you could present as an after-dinner speech.
4. You have been hired as a speechwriter for the Juno Awards. Choose three of your favourite performers and outline an acceptance speech for each. Have your classmates select one of them, and then role-play the acceptance speech.

5. Write out a poor voice mail message. Exchange messages with a classmate, and rewrite the one you get to make it a good message. Have volunteers read the messages to the class.

6. Develop toasts you could propose
   a. at a friend's graduation
   b. at a friend's wedding
   c. at a friend's first child celebration
   d. at a friend's promotion celebration
   e. at a friend's memorial service

7. Go to the Pierre Elliot Trudeau Official Web site at *http://www.clevernet.net/ pierre_trudeau/justin_trudeau_eulogy.html* and read Justin Trudeau's eulogy for his father. Then complete a rhetorical analysis by answering the following questions: How do you think Justin felt about his father and what in the speech led you to think that? Describe how Justin explained his relationship with his father, described his father's virtues, explained how he touched the lives of others, spoke on behalf of those attending or watching the service, and offered them comfort. Did he focus on the deceased or on himself? In all, how would you rate the design and content of the eulogy? What language style did he use? Did he use inclusive language, language intensity, or abstract language? Did he incorporate the classical stylistic devices?

8. Have everyone in the class write a topic from the chapter (or course) on a small piece of paper and place it in a bag. Then have a volunteer student draw a topic, develop an outline in his or her head (in approximately one to two minutes), and deliver an impromptu speech. Perhaps the instructor could model this by going first.

## REFERENCES AND FURTHER READINGS

Barnard, S. (1996). *Speaking our minds: A guide to public speaking for Canadians* (2nd ed.). Scarborough, ON: Prentice Hall.

DeWine, S. (2001). *The consultant's craft: Improving organizational communication.* New York: St. Martin's Press.

Gaut, D.R., & Perrigo, E.M. (1998). *Business and professional communication for the 21st century.* Boston: Allyn and Bacon.

Golden, J.L., Berquist, G.F., & Coleman, W.E. (1983). *The rhetoric of Western thought* (3rd ed.). Dubuque, IA: Kendall/Hunt.

Hanna, M.S., & Gibson, J.W. (1995). *Public speaking for personal success* (4th ed.). Dubuque, IA: Brown & Benchmark.

Lucas, S.E. (2004). *The art of public speaking* (8th ed.). Boston: McGraw-Hill.

Osborn, M., & Osborn, S. (1994). *Public speaking* (3rd ed.). Boston: Houghton Mifflin.

Parr, C. (July 26, 2001). Personal communication.

Trudeau, J. (2000, September). Justin Trudeau's eulogy given for his father Pierre Elliot Trudeau. The Pierre Trudeau Home Page. Retrieved April 6, 2005, from http://www.clevernet.net/pierre_trudeau/justin_trudeau_eulogy.html.

Zarefsky, D., & MacLennan, J. (1997). *Public speaking: Strategies for success* (Canadian ed.). Scarborough, ON: Allyn and Bacon.

# Chapter 10
## Group Presentations

## CHAPTER GOALS

In this chapter, you will learn
- the different types of group presentations
- how to prepare group presentations
- how to deliver group presentations
- how to deal with group problems

# INTRODUCTION

At some point in your life, you will likely be called on to make a group presentation. Students in business courses, for example, often assemble in small groups for problem solving, discussion, and case development. In many instances, their results are presented to their class. Which do you think is easier, making a speech or doing a group presentation? If you are like many students, you might argue that a group presentation requires less effort because the workload is shared, speakers do not stand alone in front of the audience, and they do not do as much talking. Individuals can take a back-seat role. Many people believe this—until they actually have to work with a group to research and write a report, and then present the results to an audience. Then they declare that group work is much harder than a speech.

What makes group work so difficult? Although we tend to think that a group presentation is a one-shot deal, a single isolated event, it actually represents the group's final product. The work starts long before members set foot in front of an audience—it begins the minute they are assigned to or invited to join the group. The lead-up to the presentation has a great impact on the success of the event itself.

This chapter is designed to teach you how to do a polished group presentation. It begins by outlining various types of group presentations. Then it describes how to develop and deliver an engaging small group presentation. Because groups consist of individuals, a segment of the chapter is devoted to the "people part" of groups. In particular, it offers strategies to help you work well together and to deal with conflict when it arises. After reading this chapter, you should be better prepared for your next group presentation.

Through my work in different groups I have finally come to realize that there are definite peaks and valleys. Sometimes things go well, sometimes they don't. At least now I know that this is to be expected. This knowledge definitely helps when things get bad.

*Robin, Small Group Communication Student*

# ▍ TYPES OF GROUP PRESENTATIONS

## Panel Discussions

*Panel discussions* consist of three to six people and a moderator. The goal of the panel is to present an open discussion on some theme. It is the moderator's duty to direct the conversation and to ensure that all participants have an opportunity to express their opinions. Interestingly, you cannot always predict where the conversation will go.

Because individuals do not rehearse beforehand, the interaction can be lively and spontaneous, especially when the topic is a controversial one and panellists feel strongly about the issues. Although the discussion may become rather heated at times, participants speak in a formal language style. The tuxedo or casual/dress code approach is the norm in these settings.

You could arrange a panel discussion for your classroom. I am sure you can generate several contentious topics for discussion. For example, several students could discuss how the use of sex in music videos influences teens' perceptions of body image, or two men and two women could form a panel to discuss whether women and men have equal opportunities in the workplace.

## Symposiums

While panel discussions are spontaneous in nature, symposiums are more formal. Members gather with a specific theme in mind, and each person comes with prepared remarks on a specific aspect of the theme. Participants are given time limits in which to complete their remarks. Papers at the National Communication Association Conventions are presented in symposium format. I, like the others, have only about 11 minutes to describe my entire project.

You could organize a symposium on the topic of public speaking. For instance, one speaker would present information on organizing a speech, a second might focus on how to use your voice and body in the delivery, a third could deal with nervousness, a fourth could discuss visual aids, and a fifth could discuss the group presentation. I am sure you can think of many relevant, interesting topics that would make for a good symposium.

Symposiums also have moderators. Their job is not to direct the discussion but rather to introduce speakers and to keep time. After the presentations, the moderator might open up discussion with members in the audience. The moderator concludes the symposium by summarizing the presenters' remarks.

## Roundtables

In roundtables, as the name implies, participants sit in a circle. This enables everyone to have eye contact with one another. The feature that separates roundtables from other types of group presentations is that there is no audience. Participants gather to explore a particular issue. Koch (1995) writes that "This type of discussion is particularly suited to council and committee meetings, conferences, and classroom discussions" (p. 155).

Roundtables can accommodate a large number of participants. Perhaps you have inadvertently participated in a roundtable in some of your courses. Think back to times when professors have asked everyone to put their chairs in a circle, and then proceeded to conduct a group discussion. That would be classified as a roundtable.

The moderator's role is less obvious in roundtables than in other types of group presentations because he or she also takes part in the discussion. However, the moderator is still responsible for opening, closing, and timing the affair.

## Forums

In a forum, one speaker with a prepared speech makes a presentation to an audience. Upon its completion, the audience is invited to respond to the speaker's thoughts and ideas. The moderator opens the forum, introduces the speaker, facilitates the greater group discussion, and closes the event.

## Small Group Presentations

The small group presentation is the focus of this chapter. The major difference between this type of presentation and the others is that in small group presentations members work together before the event to formulate a response to an issue and then to format the delivery. For example, you may be asked to work with a group of interested students to solve a relevant campus problem—say, poor lighting in some areas. Afterward, you might present your recommendations as a group to the students' union and university administration. Small groups generally consist of five to seven members. Anything more than that is too large, and ultimately, members divide into subgroups. This might even occur with seven in the group. Having an odd number of participants is helpful should a vote be required because the group would not have to deal with a tie.

Small groups generally have a moderator, or leader, during their presentation. That person's role is basically to introduce the topic, introduce the participants, and maybe provide transitions from one topic to another. Participants may also use various

> Our team was definitely goal-oriented and committed to quality. I guess it started right at the initial "get to know you" stage. In fact, I think the very first topic we discussed was getting a high grade. From there we worked hard to develop a presentation that had good substantive content, but one that was also dynamic, and even entertaining. Well, we were successful. We learned a lot, we got an A, and we had great fun doing it. I loved working with that group and we became great friends.
>
> *Salena, Former Small Group Communication Student*

means to present their material: visual aids, role-playing, lecture/discussion, straight presentation of information and facts, and others.

Finally, small group presentations blend the panel discussion (where people may speak at will) with the symposium (where people have prepared remarks for the audience). Further, like an extemporaneous speech, the group knows the points it will make and how it will make them, but the presentation is not so structured that participants cannot react to or interact with the audience.

In many ways, small group presentations are more difficult than the other types because they require a lot of preparation and practice on the part of the participants. How this is done is described in the rest of the chapter.

## START WITH THREE KEY STEPS

Groups can take definite steps that will affect their later success. If members (1) deal with basic practicalities, (2) get to know one another, and (3) set some ground rules at the initial group meetings, they are more likely to work well together and to produce a better product.

## Basic Practicalities

### *Names*

Learn one another's names at the very first meeting. Write them down if you have to. It is embarrassing to ask someone who he or she is a couple of weeks into the project. Although it may seem silly, many people use rhymes (in their heads, of course) to help them recall names. For instance, *Mary* could be *Hairy Mary*, *Stacey* could be *Lacey Stacey*, *Joel* could be *Joel the Mole*, and so forth. They are only limited by their imaginations.

## Meeting Times

To promote efficiency, group members might also exchange addresses, telephone numbers (home and work), e-mail addresses, and even school/work schedules. Because group work requires so many meetings, it is imperative to be able to contact one another. In some instances, groups can actually work online. However, there still needs to be face-to-face interaction, and with busy lives and schedules, it can be difficult to isolate meeting times that are convenient for everyone.

Daniel Morrison, a student in my small group communication course, found it exceedingly difficult to schedule meetings that all his group members could attend. Exasperated, he designed a timetable sphere that he and the group completed. Group members were amazed to learn that the only times everyone could meet were on Thursday mornings from 9:00 a.m. until 11:00 a.m., and later that evening from 7:00 p.m. until 9:00 p.m. Time was open on Sunday evenings, but with group members living in different towns and each wanting family time, that option was quickly eliminated. See the accompanying box for the model Daniel developed for his group (Figure 10.1). You may want to use it to chart your group's availability. Then you can set up a schedule that will enable your group to get its work done within the prescribed time. Once you settle the dates and times for meetings, assign someone to book a quiet, convenient meeting space.

## Making the Most of Meetings

Efficient groups follow an agenda and include individuals who come well prepared to their group meetings. When I asked one particularly effective group their key to success, participants told me that they always had a goal for every meeting, meetings were guided by an agenda to help them achieve their goal, each member was assigned to research a particular topic, and everyone was expected to have results available at the next meeting.

The group also argued a lot and assigned a recorder at each meeting to log important decisions. Finally, this "super group" took 15 minutes at the end of every session to discuss how things were going. If anyone had a problem with the group interaction or how they were proceeding, it was brought up then. Rather than harbour bad feelings, this group got things out in the open.

**Figure 10.1—The Daniel Morrison Group Timetable Sphere**

## HOW TO COMPLETE THE TIMETABLE

1.  The numbers represent the meeting slots per day. The slots begin at 9:00 a.m. and end at 10:00 p.m.

2.  Each triangle segment represents a day of the week.

3.  Go through each hour of each day. If anyone in the group *cannot* meet at that time, then fill that hour in with a marker.

4.  Continue like this until every hour of the seven days has been assessed.

5.  Any spaces left open can then be used as meeting times.

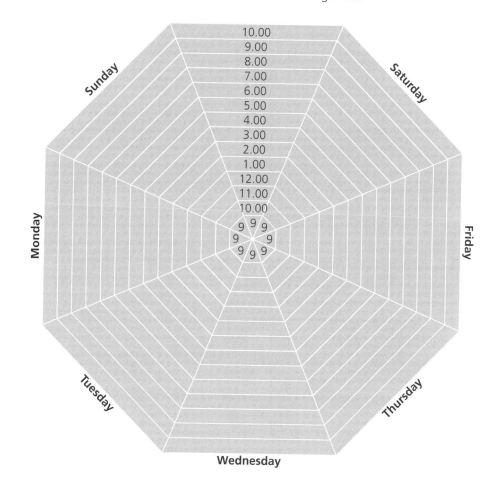

---

### ONE GROUP'S KEYS TO SUCCESS

- Have a specific goal for every meeting.
- Use an agenda at each meeting to help you meet your goal.
- Assign members homework, and expect them to report back at the next meeting.
- Have one person act as recorder at every meeting.
- Argue a lot.
- Leave time at the end of each session to discuss issues that are bothering you.

**Source:** Cory, Tassie, Tom, Phoebe, and Rodney.

---

## Get to Know One Another

A very influential factor in any group project is how well members interact with one another. This is often referred to as the group's *social dimension*. You can develop good relationships by getting to know one another. The more time you devote to this, the more insight you will have into why individuals behave and manage problems the way they do. Such insight goes a long way to strengthen the social dimension of your group. Then you are better prepared to handle the *task dimension*—what you wish to achieve as a group.

### Play the Commonalities Game

You can get better acquainted by determining what you have in common, what your goals are, what your likes and dislikes are, or what you do in your spare time. An icebreaker exercise I often use is to have group members find 15 weird things that they have in common with one another (also see Chapter 1). Commonalities must be truly weird, like they each have a dog with a white mark on its left hind leg. That they all attend the same university or are in the same class is not weird enough. With 20 minutes to find the commonalities, they quickly learn one another's similarities and differences. This exercise works— not only do groups uncover interesting things about themselves, but the exercise also helps to reduce the initial tension people may have felt about coming together.

### Develop a Positive Group Image

You might also wish to develop a group image. To help in this endeavour, group members can first discuss how they would like to operate as a group. Begin by answering the question "What would the ideal group experience be like?" Then the team members can develop an adage that will guide their group interactions so that they become such a group.

Lumsden and Lumsden (2000) explain, "The team image is a strong sense of its own identity that helps motivate and direct the members, just like a strong sense of personal identity may shape an individual's behavior" (p. 95). It is important to develop a positive image at the outset. In one of my classes, one group always felt like they did not fit; that they were the "leftover" group. They claimed that these feelings affected their productivity and their enjoyment of the group process.

# Ground Rules

Most group facilitators, or people who work regularly with groups, think that ground rules are a must. *Ground rules* refer to the expectations that members have of one another. These rules should also be created early in the group's life.

## Common Group Ground Rules

To help you develop your ground rules, have a discussion that focuses on the best and worst things that can occur in groups. Obviously, if you can prevent the worst behaviours by engaging in some specific, guided conduct, then that could become a *group rule*—a stated expectation. Essentially, ground rules can be thought of as group behaviour do's and don'ts. The box on page 314 lists group rules that are commonly used by students.

While it is one thing to create ground rules, it is quite another to enforce them. It is useful to form some policies to handle a situation when a group member violates one of the ground rules. This works best if the policies are developed at the initial meetings, when participants are fresh. While such an exercise may seem like a waste of time or one that stalls your progress toward the "real" work, small group scholars and theorists guarantee that such an effort pays off in the long run. Rather than grumble through conflict in the future, you will have a mechanism in place to handle it.

Once you have the basics under control, it is time to begin work on the task. This may involve selecting and researching a topic, and determining how the presentation will be formatted and conducted. These elements are discussed in the next section.

---

### COMMON GROUP GROUND RULES

This set of rules might provide some suggestions to help your group develop its ground rules.

1. All meetings will start on time.
2. Members who cannot make a meeting are expected to contact someone in advance. Anyone who misses more than five meetings will not have their name on the final project.
3. Members are expected to arrive at meetings with prepared materials.
4. Everyone is expected to contribute at each meeting.
5. Everyone should listen to others' ideas, particularly those of the more reticent members. People who find it easy to speak up might use their skills to encourage the quiet members to participate. Alternatively, everyone should make an attempt to join in the conversation. (Note: Quiet people are often surprised to learn that their silence actually makes other group participants uncomfortable because they have no idea what the shy members are thinking! This can be very disconcerting at times.)
6. Everyone will be treated with respect and dignity.
7. Members are encouraged to engage in constructive criticism of ideas but not to criticize people's personal characteristics.

---

# PREPARING THE GROUP PRESENTATION

## Choose and Research the Topic

Sometimes groups are assigned specific themes or problems to solve, but in most cases, their first step is to generate a suitable subject. One way to accomplish this task is to brainstorm a list of possibilities (see the accompanying box). From there the group can narrow it down to one. While this may appear to be a relatively simple procedure, finalizing a group's topic can take weeks, or even months if the time is available.

Once the topic is selected, divide it into subtopics and have group members research the areas that interest them most. To conduct the actual literature review, refer to Chapter 4, "Researching the Speech." The same techniques are employed for group searches. Keep in mind that the more information the group locates, the better informed their decisions will be. This in turn will affect their group presentation.

---

| **ONE WAY TO DO A GROUP BRAINSTORM** |
| --- |

1. Assign one or two people to record a list of all the topics that are suggested.
2. Use a flipchart, chalkboard, or whiteboard so all members can see the ideas.
3. When the recorders are ready, group members call out any topic that comes to mind.
4. The group abides by the following important rules:
   - No topic is too crazy.
   - No one criticizes or "disses" any of the topics or the person making the suggestion.
   - Topics are not discussed or analyzed during brainstorming.
   - Topics may be mixed and matched and adapted or grown from the others.
5. After everyone is exhausted and can think of no more topics, the group begins to make its decision.

# Develop the Topic

## *Select the Main Points*

Once the topic has been selected and researched, participants must decide how the information will be presented. Groups that make presentations are often required to submit a written document of some sort to an instructor, boss, organization, etc. Typically, they complete the writing and then assume that the bulk of the presentation is done—all they need to do is divide the paper for presentation.

However, as you may recall from Chapter 4, good speeches do not work that way. Written texts just do not translate well into the spoken word. Therefore, papers and reports must be adapted for oral presentation.

Note that it is not possible to put everything from the paper into the presentation—there will just not be enough time. Given that you will be able to cover only a certain number of major points in your presentation, your immediate task is to decide what those points will be. Therefore, select the highlights and provide lots of examples and illustrations to make the information come alive for the audience. Once the group decides what the specific content will be, the next step is to organize the points.

### *Organize the Main Points*

The presentation outline requires careful consideration. Think of it just as you would a speech outline with a beginning, middle, and ending. Your task at this stage is to finalize the material that will go into each section.

#### *Introductions to Group Members*

Regardless of how you decide to open your presentation, part of it should include introducing the group members. Think about how you will do this. Will one person act as chair and introduce everyone, or will individuals introduce themselves? Will they be named at the opening, or just before they give their part of the presentation? Will participants wear name tags?

The answers to these questions depend on how the presentation will be formatted. For instance, some groups open their presentation with a role-play, so they do not introduce themselves right away. You will better be able to consider the introductions once you have decided on how the presentation will be structured. Then you can choose an approach that fits smoothly into your overall design.

#### *Body and Conclusion*

Like a speech, the body of your presentation consists of the main points you wish to make. In the conclusion, you bring the presentation to a specific, definable closure. Again, check out Chapter 4 for possible ways to conclude your presentation.

## Format the Presentation

After you have considered the overall presentation, the next major step is to figure out how the material will be delivered. Unlike a speech, which has a prescriptive format, there are many possibilities for group presentations. For instance, you can use a lecture style, a lecture/discussion, or a role-play. You could incorporate a video, music, or even play a musical instrument. Consider, too, if and how visual aids will be used.

Developing a suitable format takes time and effort. You may, like many effective groups, decide to combine several options. Below are some alternatives to consider.

### *All in a Row*

Students with no training in group presentations generally present as singletons rather than as group associates. I am sure you have seen this: they sit or stand in a row, sometimes even leaning against the wall or a piece of furniture, and each person takes a turn presenting her or his information. In many instances, this "all in a row" format may be appropriate (as in a symposium), but in others, it can lack professionalism. If panel members lack good presentation skills, or read from prepared scripts, this approach can be downright boring.

### How to Make It Work

To make this style work, the group needs to present as a whole, not as individuals presenting their five-minute bits. If you choose this approach, have a moderator who will introduce the speakers and topics as you progress. They should also draw connections between the speakers. For instance, if the topic was *public speaking*, the moderator might say something like, "Tim has given us insight into how to deal with nervousness. Once we have that under control, we need to deliver the presentation in an effective manner. Our next speaker, Usah, will offer some suggestions."

Speakers using this style must also be attentive to one another, look alert throughout the entire presentation, and show some enthusiasm when they are speaking. In some cases, they might, as an aside, even interject their thoughts or offer something that one of the speakers forgot. Individual speakers could also refer to other group members or to the group as a whole. All this creates a good team effect. One final note: speakers *never* read from their notes. Instead, they talk to, or communicate with, the audience.

You may want to adapt an all in a row format that also includes role-plays, costumes, videos, and so on. When such formats are given careful consideration, they can be exciting and interesting for the audience.

I was really nervous about our presentation. I'm a business student and we present our cases very formally. However, my teammates were from other disciplines and they were used to more creative—far, oh, very far outside the box—types of presentations. Because I was outnumbered, I had to go along with them. Fortunately, I was able to keep the crazy (should I say stupid?) stuff out of it. But in the end, we reached a balance and had one of the best presentations. I'll probably try using some of the techniques in my business classes, especially in my marketing course.

*Roxanne, Business Student*

## *Lecture/Discussion*

In a lecture/discussion approach, speakers have a prepared text, but they deviate from it to pose questions to the audience. They might ask listeners to share examples or narratives of their experiences with the topic. Audience members generally like this approach because there is opportunity for involvement. Groups that use this interactive style must balance audience discussion with coverage of the intended material.

## *Role-Play*

To role-play, set up a situation and then act it out, making up the dialogue as you go. Barker, Wahlers, and Watson (1995) say, "During the role play, one or more participants are asked to assume a role based on how they think another person would act or feel" (p. 221). Each person responds spontaneously to one another and the results can be remarkably realistic. In addition, participants gain tremendous insight into the perspectives of others.

Role-playing can be great fun, and it is an excellent, entertaining way to illustrate a variety of concepts. Student groups in my gender and communication classes enjoy using role-plays to demonstrate male and female communication differences. When you insert role-plays into your presentation, you will also require debriefing segments. For example, sometimes presenters explain a topic and follow it with a role-play to illustrate its real-life application. This makes the concept clear for the audience. Other groups do the role-play first, which leaves the audience to make the connection between the theoretical and the applied. Because not everyone may see the association, it is critical to explain what has occurred. Some groups choose a person who dislikes role-playing to act as the commentator.

Do not hesitate to include several role-plays, but only if they complement the topic (not become the presentation) and if other dimensions are included in the presentation. Occasionally, a group will offer several hastily concocted role-plays and think it has met its group presentation requirements. It has not.

### *Practise, But Don't Overdo It*

Due to the spontaneous nature of role-playing, try not to practise the skits too much. Otherwise, you peak too soon, before there is an audience to see you. Further, the players tend to lose their enthusiasm and impulsiveness, two ingredients that make role-playing so successful. Certainly do not write out a script. To do so is to move from role-playing into the realm of scriptwriting and acting. When this happens, anxious students tend to focus on the written word.

## Costumes

Costumes also create an aesthetically pleasing impact. For example, students in a persuasion course worked in small groups to conduct and present an analysis of the persuasive strategies used in a television commercial. The first group selected the Scented Glad Bag commercial, and just as the actor in the commercial wore a white lab coat, so did the five group members. The class loved them. Their simple outfits clearly caught everyone's attention, raised their credibility, and showed a sense of group spirit and creativity. They also set high standards for the rest of the group presentations.

If your group plans to don unique attire or costumes, it is best to change into them just before the presentation. Otherwise, they will not have the impact you desire. However, you need not do your presentations in elaborate outfits. Even having identifiable group features (wearing similar-coloured shirts or sweaters, or specific pins) will establish a group bond and suggest that some thought has been put into the presentation.

## Creativity and Humour

Do not be afraid of creativity and humour. Often your instructor will set the tone in this area. If you are encouraged to use it, go for it. I always tell my students to take chances—and they do. One small group did its entire presentation as beatniks, sitting cross-legged on a large desk. As Andrea Curry strummed a guitar, her fellow group members kept the beat by rhythmically snapping their fingers. They each explained part of their topic in '50s-style beatnik poetry. That was innovative, interesting, and memorable. Another group gave a 15-minute presentation on the visual and vocal components of communication all in mime! Still, the messages were clear to everyone.

## Visual Aids

Visual aids can make a presentation more stimulating and understandable. If you include visual aids, consider when they will be used and who will control them. Using them will also require practice time. For example, while a dyad is performing a role-play, the visual aid person could ensure that the concept being played out is shown on a screen, or you could have a vaudeville poster person walk by holding up a sign with the concept printed in big, bold letters on it. This would get the audience's attention and help listeners comprehend and retain your message. While this particular approach would not be appropriate in a business meeting, it could work in other contexts—if it was well executed.

One group of interpersonal communication students chose the topic "How to Break Up with Your Partner" for their presentation. They used a variety of visual means to present their recommendations to the class. For starters, they had earlier videotaped real students telling their sad stories (one woman's husband broke up with her in an e-mail message that he forwarded to her at work!). After one group member (playing a commentator) showed a "sad story" video excerpt, a panel from within the group role-played experts who offered more effective interpersonal communication strategies. The expert panellists included a communication expert, a psychologist, and a love letter newspaper columnist—and each dressed the part.

In all, the visual aids were well coordinated in that the video excerpts were cued and ready to go, the volume was appropriate, and the moderator knew how to handle the equipment. The switches between the expert panel role-play and the video excerpts were also smooth—all orchestrated by the moderator. The group (Andrea, Kevin, Steven, Cherie, and Jeff) did a fine job.

## Music

Music can be used in a variety of ways. At the beginning of a presentation, it is particularly useful for setting the mood. If you have a creative, active small group presentation, music can be played to divide the segments. Just as listeners become familiar with television theme songs, they will quickly start to associate the music with one segment of the presentation ending and another beginning. Should you use music, make sure it is appropriate for the setting, is cued and ready to go, that you know when and how to use it, and so on—everything needs to be professionally done.

This section has offered a variety of techniques that can be integrated into a small group presentation. One caution though: don't overdo it. More is not always better. Whatever you choose should be tasteful, appropriate, and contribute to your presentation. For example, do not play music just for the sake of having music. The pieces you choose should enhance your overall theme. The same goes for any strategy you select.

## Decide Who Does What

Specific group members should be assigned to present certain parts of the presentation or have particular duties during the presentation. Such decisions are often made when planning the general format.

When planning who will do what, strive for balanced member participation. This means that everyone should speak or interact with the audience for approximately the same length of time. When one or two participants do all the talking, it suggests that they also did most of the work. For a group presentation, this does not look good.

A common problem among student groups is having one member who consistently misses meetings and rehearsal periods, but shows up for the final classroom

presentation. Groups generally scramble to include the deviates by having them introduce the team members. Should you have a truant in your group, consult with your
professor well in advance of the presentation, if possible. This is particularly important
in situations where the instructor has not made it clear how to handle this problem.
Many professors also allot a portion of the overall group mark to be awarded by group
participants. Each assigns a grade to everyone else and participants are not hesitant
about giving absentee members a failing grade.

---

At least we got through the presentation, barely. Marty, our "problem"
member, actually showed up. We figured he had to do something, so we
gave him some of the overheads and told him just to review them. Well, he
even screwed that up. He couldn't explain the graphs that he was supposed
to have made up for us! The whole thing really irked me. All the work we
put into the presentation and this guy ruins it for us.

*Jennifer, Former Communication Student*

---

## Create the Space

When you present a speech, you usually do so from a designated area, typically from a
podium. When groups make a presentation, they establish their own space. If your
group plans a variety of activities, such as role-playing, you will need plenty of space.
These issues should be considered before the presentation.

One way to accommodate a lot of activity is to place the podium to the audience's
right. In theatre, this is a strong stage position, and it works equally well in public
speaking settings. Suppose your group has six or more members. A little behind the
podium, but off to the side, place three chairs at an angle so that they half face the audience and half face the opposite side of the room, where three other chairs are set up in
a similar way (see Figure 10.2 on page 322). Have extra chairs if required for additional
manoeuvres. This set-up leaves a vacant space in the centre of the room to accommodate, say, role-play skits. Unless you are doing a panel presentation, this generic scheme
lends itself well to group activities.

You must also determine where to put any miscellaneous visual aids (CD players,
objects, etc.). They could be placed on a table at the back of your presentation area.
Also consider where flipcharts, overheads, and other devices will be housed. The setup

**Figure 10.2—A Possible Space Setup**

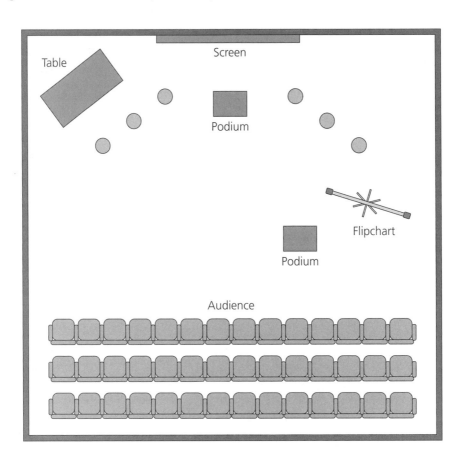

of the physical space should be finalized during your preparation and practice periods. Making on-the-spot decisions will reduce your group's credibility and makes for a second-rate, "make do" kind of presentation.

## Practice

The final consideration in preparing for the group presentation is practice. Audiences can distinguish between groups that have put in practice time and those that have not—the difference is usually very clear. As noted in Chapter 2, when students are asked what they would do differently if they could repeat their presentation, the most common response is that they would practise more. This is even more crucial in group presentations because the margin of error grows with each member added to the mix. You simply must know what the others are doing if you want to create a smooth, flawless flow. This will not happen if you start practising only 15 minutes before the presentation.

To give a presentation that will make you proud, assign time for a couple of run-throughs, and include any visual aids, costumes, and props. This way, you will be able to time the event, review who is going to be where, and when. Call it your dress rehearsal and work out the kinks until you have a polished performance that will earn both marks and prestige.

# MAKING THE GROUP PRESENTATION

So, you have survived weeks (maybe even months) of group work, you have organized and practised an innovative presentation, and finally it's showtime. Here are a few recommendations to help you with the actual presentation. They centre on being attentive to other group members, presenting as a team, using topnotch communication skills, and fielding questions.

## Be Attentive

There is nothing worse than watching group members who ignore one another and act as singletons. In the worst cases, they do not look at the person speaking, they whisper in loud voices to one another, and they shuffle through their notes. Some even check what is in their pockets, yawn, or gaze off into space or out a window. This is amateurish behaviour. Funny? Yes. Professional? No.

*Giving focus*, a theatrical term, has application for small group presentations. It means that if group members focus on the speaker, the audience will too. It is important to act like a group and provide visual support, or give focus to one another. When presenting, the speaker should stand while the other group members remain seated. In this way, the audience is not distracted by the others. Likewise, the moderator should sit or stand well off to the side during any role-play exercises.

## Present Like a Team

As a group, you must help one another. When teammates fumble or lose their place, rather than sit helplessly by and watch them fall apart, jump in and get them back on track. Do this in a natural, conversational manner and tone as if the pause was intended. Further, do not make faces or roll your eyes when someone deviates from your outline or something unplanned occurs. Instead, take it in stride and work together. In other words, be professional.

**EXPERT ADVICE**

## TIPS FOR GROUP PRESENTATIONS

### APPEARANCE
- Dress normally for the occasion—don't let your appearance distract or detract from your presentation.
- Occasionally your appearance (e.g., a costume) may be part of your presentation.
- Don't chew gum.
- Don't wear ball caps or outdoor clothing.

### THE ROOM
- Do a rehearsal in the room ahead of time.
- Make sure all members can be heard in all parts of the room.
- Make sure visuals can be seen in all parts of the room.
- Arrange furniture and equipment the way you want it *before* you start.
- Take charge of the space as you arrange chairs, screens, doors, lights, and the podium.

### EQUIPMENT
- Make arrangements to get whatever equipment you want well ahead of time (including extension cords).
- Practise with the equipment so you know that it works, how to work it, and who will be working it.
- The person who is speaking should not be running the equipment—the presentation should be coordinated so that when one person is speaking, another person knows when to turn a video on, what slide to put on the overhead, where to point, etc.

### VISUALS
- Make sure visuals can be seen/read from anywhere in the room.
- Word visuals should be headings or points—not a lot of text (don't put more words on a slide than you would on a T-shirt).
- Whatever you put on a screen, leave it long enough for people to read/look at the whole thing.
- Make sure visuals add to your presentation, not detract from it. They should never be the main part of your presentation.

- Make sure charts and graphs are clear and easy to understand. Better still, make sure *you* understand them!

## THE GROUP

- People not participating at the time should be comfortable, quiet, and at least appear to be paying attention to the speaker.
- Everyone should be introduced—either all at the beginning, or as each person gets up to speak, or both.
- There should be smooth transitions from one speaker to another—practise!
- Your rehearsals will allow you to ensure that the overall presentation is neither too short nor too long.

## THE INDIVIDUAL

- *Know your stuff!*—Go over material several times prior to the actual presentation. Stumbling over words or being puzzled about charts or graphs gives a very poor impression.
- Learn proper pronunciations (or find alternatives for words you have trouble pronouncing).
- The best presentations occur when a person "talks" from notes. If you are very nervous and feel you have to have your full text in front of you, at least try a couple of times to "talk" to the audience. The more often you try this, the better you will get at it.
- Look at the audience and don't focus on any one person, such as your instructor.
- Define any words or terms that some people may not understand. Don't use jargon unless you explain it.
- Try not to use the same word or phrase over and over—for example, "basically."
- Speak loudly and clearly enough to be heard in all parts of the room, and neither too fast nor too slowly.

*Professor Brian Seville, Retired Business Professor*
*Cape Breton University, Sydney, Nova Scotia*

I was wild during our presentation. Lynn, who was totally unprepared, left out a whole important section. I regret now not having addressed it during the presentation. If she didn't have the info, I know we all knew enough to pull it off or at least to say something on the subject. As a result, the presentation was way under time and the professor noted that this important issue had been overlooked.

*Cindy, Former Small Group Communication Student*

## Demonstrate Effective Communication Skills

Individually, everyone in the group must exercise top-notch communication skills. Remember to be enthusiastic, to use gestures and facial expressions, and to make eye contact with the audience. Refer occasionally to the other group members. Feel, look, and be confident, and avoid distracting repetitive adaptors such as adjusting your glasses or playing with a pen.

Speak loudly enough to be heard, and try not to race through the presentation. Try to enjoy it and to connect with the audience. After all, that is why you are there. Present your material extemporaneously and never read from notes. Be polite and professional with the other group members. Speak in a clear, articulate voice and use a suitable language style.

## Field Questions

It is common to have a question-and-answer period follow the group presentation. While many people feel apprehensive about fielding questions, my experience has been that the most shy presenters often communicate best when they respond spontaneously.

If a question is not directed toward any one specific person, then the team member with the most experience in that area should probably respond. If you are singled out and you know that someone else could better field the question, hand it over to him or her. Do not feel, however, that you cannot contribute at all. In fact, you may be able to offer further clarification or examples about the issue.

What happens if no one knows the answer to a question? Never give a fake response; this only lowers your credibility and it will embarrass you later. If no one can respond, just say that, and based on what you do know, offer an educated answer. Make it clear to your audience that you are doing this.

You can also turn the question over to the audience. It is perfectly legitimate to do this, and it can also enhance your bond with the audience. There is a good possibility that someone can offer insight, or at least steer the questioner in the right direction to get more information on the topic. Keep in mind too that people often pose questions so they can tell you what they think. Rather than offer a lengthy explanation, ask for their opinion. Question periods are meant to involve the audience, and this is another way to let them have their chance to interact with you. If someone in the audience keeps harping on one particular topic that has already been covered and that you do not wish to discuss further, simply and politely say so. However, invite the questioner to talk with you afterward. Do the same if someone poses a question that requires a long and complex response, or one that only a few audience members might be interested in.

## THE PEOPLE PART OF GROUPS

So far you have learned several ways to develop and conduct a group presentation. However, because groups do not always run smoothly, you can pretty well expect some not-so-pleasant things to occur. Conflict in groups is to be expected, and it is a natural phase in the stages leading up to a group presentation. However, being aware of potential problems enables you to deal with them. In your small group work, watch for the following: the midpoint crisis, social loafing, conflict of various types, group norms, conformity, and leadership struggles.

### The Midpoint Crisis

It is particularly useful to be aware that most teams and groups experience what is called a *midpoint crisis* (Gersick, 1988). Halfway through their allotted time for the project, groups are suddenly hit with the realization that time is running out. As a result, they make major adjustments in their topics, their approaches, and their relationships with one another. This occurs repeatedly in my classes. Further, periods of inertia, which are normal in group life, clear up after the midpoint crisis. This is also good to know.

While dealing with the midpoint crisis is not an enjoyable experience, it is a useful one. Keep this in mind as your group prepares for its presentation.

Our last meeting was a better experience, tenfold. It was successful in the sense that we accomplished the task at hand. We organized the presentation and arranged for rehearsal time. Dale brought in a copy/draft of the paper for the group to peruse and it was approved. Clearly, Gary was less stressed than at earlier meetings. I guess he realized there is more to being in a group than merely getting the task done. The big difference in the meeting was the degree to which we socialized in relation to the other times. I think Gary is learning how to work in groups, and we are all happier.

*Tom, Former Communication Student*

## Social Loafing

Social loafing (Szymanski & Harkins, 1993) occurs when members of a group do not make as great an effort as they would if they were working on their own. They depend on others to take the lead or carry the workload. Students like hearing about this concept and quickly pinpoint the loafers in their groups. However, social loafing is not only confined to student groups. It occurs in industry and government, on boards of directors (Atkinson & Salterio, 2002), in employee profit-sharing businesses (Long, 2000), and even in cheerleading groups (Schwarz, 1988).

There are a couple of things groups can do reduce social loafing. Szymanski and Harkins (1993) recommend building a self-evaluation program into your group. Lumsden and Lumsden (2001) report that several communication studies on social loafers have found that evaluation is an effective motivator. Other ways to reduce social loafing is to build team spirit. Finally, Lumsden and Lumsden (2001) note that social loafing is often related to a general lack of interest. Therefore, social loafers might be motivated by doing something relevant. One way to find out what that is, is to ask loafers what they would like to do to contribute to the group.

## Conflict

Definitely expect to encounter conflict during your group interactions. You may be surprised to learn that disputes and clashes are actually good for a group. Groups that disagree and argue over ideas make superior decisions and create better presentations than groups that do not. This is because the argumentative process allows them to critically evaluate their work, and as a result, lame and underdeveloped ideas are not accepted. It is a rare group that does not experience conflict, and those groups that do fall into such a category end up with projects and presentations that are mediocre at best.

## Substantive Conflict

Good groups engage in what is called *substantive conflict*—that is, arguments over procedures (how to get the project done) or the substance of the work (what information should be included in the project). These areas of disagreement, when resolved, add greatly to the quality of the work. Clearly, substantive conflict is positive.

## Affective Conflict

Conflict is not productive when it is directed at individuals. Labelled *affective conflict*, these disagreements move away from the issues and focus on the person. The arguments become personal and people refer to these as personality conflicts. For example, Carl and James disagree with one another on some issue. After a series of longstanding disagreements, Carl begins to take James's arguments as personal attacks, rather than as an attack on the matter at hand. Carl is unable to separate the person from the argument and stops communicating with James. This type of affective (as in emotional) conflict is extremely detrimental to a group's progress. It can also destroy once good interpersonal relationships and bring a lot of stress to the group.

Groups need not endure such strife and dissension. To deal with affective conflict, make members aware of it. Then develop group norms and rules so that it will not be

I once worked with a horrible man who was very much into control and he made everyone feel uncomfortable, inferior, and even nervous. When I get nervous, I lose my verbal skills; it's like I just can't talk, can't seem to spit out the right words. Because of that, I never confronted him. I didn't want to look stupid. However, I realized I could sound stupid but be smart by dealing with him, or I could sound smart but really be stupid for letting him walk all over me. I eventually got up the courage to confront him, and you know what—after that he quit speaking to me, which I perceived as a gift rather than a punishment.

*Julie, Former Communication Student*

tolerated. Ask individuals who are engaging in affective conflict to focus on the ideas, not the person. Sometimes groups are afraid to confront such members because they can also be bullies. However, the longer groups put it off, the more they will be subjected to such negative behaviours. This does not make for a pleasant group experience, nor does it contribute to the calibre of the final group presentation.

## Other Types of Conflict

There is a tendency to think of all conflict as substantive or affective. However, if you look a little closer, you may uncover some specific differences that can also account for some struggles: a structured versus an unstructured approach to life, a task orientation versus a social orientation, or a keep-ahead-of-the-deadline versus a do-it-at-the-last-minute approach to time. None of these approaches is any better than the others—they are all just different strategies that can drive teammates crazy.

For instance, some people are very structured in their approach to life while others are not. You know these people: the former always comes to class prepared, has an extra pen just in case the first one runs out of ink, and takes careful notes; the latter never seems to have a pen or a piece of paper. The structured person considers the unstructured person scattered, while the unstructured person considers the structured person anal and uptight. It is very difficult for either person to work with the other. Being aware of these differences and discussing them when they become obvious can add to group harmony. Here is where some humour can also help.

How people approach a task is another potential source of conflict. Some are very task-oriented: they have no time for idle chitchat and prefer to get to the work at hand. These people are sometimes considered unfriendly or are labelled task masters. Others prefer to shoot the breeze before getting down to work. They might be labelled slackers by the task-oriented people. You can see how these differences could affect group interaction.

## Group Norms

The notion of setting group rules was discussed earlier in the chapter. A related topic is *group norms*, which are unstated expectations that are placed on group members. For instance, if a group sits by and allows a bully to pick on others, the bullying becomes a group norm. Group norms might include eating candy throughout your meetings, starting meetings late (or on time), teasing certain members about their favourite sports team, sitting in certain places, using a particular type of humour, using a lot of profanity, and so forth. It is group norms that give groups their synergy, or group personality.

Watch the types of norms that develop in your groups because they may affect your group's progress in a negative way. For instance, bullying causes emotional pain for its victims, and they will not work to their best ability—they may even start to dread group meetings. Consistently starting meetings later than scheduled might affect the quality or the completion date of your project. A "putdown" type of humour might be taken seriously by a team member, who may subsequently refuse to cooperate with the rest of the group.

## Conformity

Two types of conformity are relevant to small group interactions: conformity of thought and conformity to group norms. Conformity of thought is bad news. It is the variety of unique responses that allows groups to make solid, innovative decisions. When everyone in the group thinks the same way and agrees with everyone else, two things can happen: (1) the group produces an inferior final product because members do not critically evaluate their ideas, strategies, and conclusions, and (2) groupthink occurs.

*Groupthink*, although rare, occurs when members become so wrapped up and entrenched in their own ideas and convictions that they refuse not only to look critically at their work, but also to listen to advice from external experts that may differ from or contradict the group's beliefs. The group becomes so cohesive and insular that they end up making grave errors. For instance, many believe that those at NASA responsible for the space shuttle *Challenger*'s 1986 explosion suffered from groupthink—several people knew there was a problem with the shuttle, but no one spoke up (or at least not loudly enough).

Conformity to group norms is good. *Deviates*, or individuals who do not adapt to prevailing norms and rules, cause problems for groups. When everyone else arrives on time, for example, the deviate is late. When everyone shows up with useful, relevant information for the group, the deviate has some excuse for having nothing. While everyone likes to meet for three-hour sessions, the deviate prefers short, quick meetings.

Bormann (1975) does a good job of describing how groups handle deviates. At first, such individuals are treated politely and encouraged by the other group members to conform. Group members then start to taunt and tease the nonconformists. If the deviates still fail to adhere to the group's expectations, they may be told outright to shape up. After this stage, if deviates still do not conform, the group ignores them. The group carries on as if the renegade members do not belong, and those members are ultimately ostracized by the group.

## EXPERT ADVICE

Knowing how to work in groups is a valuabie asset for students as it allows them to become confident in expressing their ideas and opinions. They need to avoid groupthink. I always think back to one of my bosses informing me to be open in expressing my ideas and opinions, even if they were different than his. He said, "Dale, if we are always thinking the same, one of us is not needed."

*Dale Caume, Department of Communication*
*Cape Breton University, Sydney, N.S.*

## Leadership Struggles

Conflict can occur when more than one person vies for leadership of the group. While communication theorists once thought that only one person emerged as leader, we now know that groups often share leadership. In fact, *superteams*—teams that are deliberately composed of people with diverse talents and personalities—generally share leadership. That is, each "expert" takes leadership for that particular aspect of the group.

Conflict also occurs when group members dislike the leader's style. Three leadership styles are *autocratic* (my way or the highway), *democratic* (tell me what you think and we'll make a decision that works for the majority), or *laissez-faire* (do it as you like—just get the work done by the deadline).

Businesses and organizations are now encouraging the development of *transformational leaders.* Their goal is to share leadership with other group members by empowering and motivating them to self-actualize, or work to their full potential. Transformational leaders do this by helping others through difficult times, by helping them to recognize and develop their individual skills and abilities, and by encouraging them to take ownership of their projects. I think this leadership style lends itself well to productive and satisfying student groups.

# CHAPTER AT A GLANCE

- Group presentations can be panel discussions, symposiums, roundtables, forums, and small group presentations.
- Spend time taking care of the practicalities (such as setting meeting times), getting to know your group members, and setting some ground rules.

- Group presentations are organized like speeches in that they have a beginning, middle, and ending.
- Group presentations can include an all in a row approach, a lecture/discussion, role-playing, costumes, creativity and humour, visual aids, and music.
- Designate who will do what, and practise your presentation, including setting up the space.
- During the presentation, present like a team, demonstrate effective communication skills, be attentive to one another, and be prepared to field questions.
- Conform to group norms, but also be prepared to disagree with, and argue over, ideas.
- The midpoint crisis, social loafing, conflict and leadership struggles are all to be expected. It is how you deal with these challenges that makes the difference between a good and a bad group presentation.
- Styles of leadership include shared, autocratic, democratic, laissez-faire, and transformational.

## APPLICATION AND DISCUSSION QUESTIONS

1. Answer the following questions in your communication journal:
   a. *Cognitive dimension:* Of the topics discussed in this chapter, which ones have most increased your knowledge of working with groups? Explain.
   b. *Affective dimension:* What types of conflict have you or others you know experienced in groups? Explain how you were affected by it.
   c. *Behavioural dimension:* As a result of reading this chapter, what will you do differently the next time you have to make a group presentation?
2. Discuss or think about times when you were in an effective group and when you were in an ineffective one. What behaviours helped or hindered the group's progress? How did the group presentation work out? Try to look at what you did as well as what the other group members did.
3. Take a few moments to write down the reasons you would make a good group leader.
4. Ask your instructor to have students conduct a panel discussion, symposium, roundtable, forum, or small group presentation. Does one type of presentation appeal to you most? If so, why?
5. Develop an outline of a group presentation and then decide on its format. What techniques would you use: lecture/discussion, role-playing, costumes, etc.?

6. After you have completed your group project, discuss with your group the following:
   a. the group rules and norms that were established and how each helped or hindered the group's progress
   b. who vied for leadership and who emerged as leader, or whether there was shared leadership
   c. what the group would do differently if it could do the project over again
   d. what each group member learned about group theory and practice
7. For groups that are going to work on a project together, you might consider the following opening exercise. Take some time to share with one another what the ideal group experience might be like. From there, ask yourselves if your group experience could be an ideal one. What reasons prevent the group process from achieving such a standard and how might the group make up for these? From there, develop a group motto (that everyone buys into) and use it to guide group members' behaviours.
8. For students who have worked in online discussions groups, compare and contrast your virtual group experiences with your physical group experiences. Describe the pros and cons of working in each type of group.

## REFERENCES AND FURTHER READINGS

Atkinson, A., & Salterio, S. (2002). Function vs. form. *CMA Management, 76*(6), 23–27.

Barker, L.L., Wahlers, K.J., & Watson, K.W. (1995). *Groups in process: An introduction to small group communication* (5th ed.). Boston: Allyn and Bacon.

Bormann, E.G. (1975). *Discussion and group methods: Theory and practice.* New York: Harper & Row.

Ellis, D.G., & Fisher, B.A. (1994). *Small group decision making: Communication and the group process.* New York: McGraw-Hill.

Gersick, C.G.C. (1988). Time and transition in work teams: Toward a new model of group development. *Academy of Management Journal, 31*(1), 9–41.

Koch, A. (1995). *Speaking with a purpose.* Boston: Allyn and Bacon.

Long, R. J. (2000). Employee profit sharing: Consequenced and moderators. *Relations Industrielles, 55*(3), 477–505.

Lumsden, G., & Lumsden, D. (2000). *Communicating in groups and teams: Sharing leadership* (2nd ed.). Belmont, CA: Wadsworth.

Rolls, J.A. (1995, June). *Women and leadership: Communication strategies that enhance leader emergence in mixed-sex small groups.* Paper presented at the Twelfth Annual Institute of the Canadian Psychological Association's Section on Women and Psychology (SWAP). Charlottetown, PEI.

Schwarz, J. (1988, March). Loafing in groups. *Omni, 10*(6), 31.

Szymanski, K., & Harkins, S.G. (1993). The effect of experimenter evaluation on self evaluation within the social loafing paradigm. *Journal of Experimental Social Psychology, 29*(3), 268–286.

# Chapter 11
## Employment Interviews

## CHAPTER GOALS

In this chapter, you will learn
- what it takes to do an artful and skilled interview
- what is involved in organizing and structuring an employment interview
- how to pose questions that elicit revealing responses
- how to conduct a behavioural interview
- how to be a good interviewee

The interview techniques we learned in the communication course actually helped me get a job last summer. Because I knew what an interviewer was supposed to do, I wasn't nervous at all. That really surprised me. In fact, there were probably a couple of things that the interviewer could have improved. Like, his organization was weak and he didn't ask any follow-up or probing questions.

*Devon, Former Communication Student*

# INTRODUCTION

## Why Study Interviewing?

Most of the interview training that students and other job-seekers receive focuses on their role as the interviewee rather than as the interviewer. While this may be helpful, there are three strong arguments for learning to conduct an employment interview as well as participate as an interviewee. First, you will be able to compensate for poor interviewers who do not enable you to demonstrate the strengths you will bring to the position; second, you will become a more confident interviewee; and third, you will gain a surprisingly valuable skill. Communication research shows that one of the best ways to learn to be a good interviewee is to learn how to be an effective interviewer. This chapter attempts to offer enough information so that you will know the ins and outs of how to conduct an interview. It also provides the interviewee perspective. This approach should help students prepare for both roles.

### *Compensate for Poor Interviewers*

Research suggests that less than 60 percent of campus interviewers have had some sort of interview training (Posner, 1981). This means that you can be put at a disadvantage when you are interviewed by an inexperienced individual because the interviewer may not allow you to demonstrate how your training, experience, and personality make you a fitting candidate for the position. Even though you may have the qualifications and skills to do the job, you may not be hired because your unique qualities and abilities are not discussed during the interview

However, if you know how an interview should be conducted, you can compensate somewhat for poor interviewer skills. Do this by offering additional information about your previous work experience and by providing specific examples of your skills.

### Gain Confidence

Knowing what to expect when you are being interviewed helps to demystify the entire process. This in turn can reduce your apprehension and thus allow you to present yourself in an assured, qualified manner. Then you are more likely to land the position you want. Students repeatedly report they got a job because they understood the interview process. Knowing how to be a competent interviewer resulted in them being adept interviewees as well.

### Learn a Valuable Skill

The third reason to become a proficient interviewer is simply because you will use this skill surprisingly often in both your professional and personal life. Whether you are hiring contractors to work on your home or selecting an administrative assistant, knowing how to structure and conduct an interview could be of great benefit to you.

## THE ART OF INTERVIEWING

Regardless of the type of interview you are conducting (employment, media, profile, health, research), they all share certain properties: there are two or more parties, there is a specific goal, the parties influence each other, and there is an exchange of questions and answers (Barone & Switzer, 1995).

Further, the interviewer's attitude greatly influences the outcome of the interview. This suggests that how interviewers conduct themselves interpersonally (the art of interviewing) is just as important as their knowledge of how to structure the interview. That is, your approach is as critical as your organization. By approach, I mean the attitude or philosophy that you bring—how you treat interviewees and react to their responses. The same holds true for interviewees. Their overall approach influences whether or not they will be selected for the postion.

It takes four important qualities to make an interviewer artful: responsibility, rapport, open-mindedness, and good listening skills. Each of these is discussed below.

## Artful Interviewers Are Responsible

Artful interviewers recognize that the success or failure of the interview lies with them, not with the interviewee, as many believe. Therefore, it is up to the interviewer to elicit the type and depth of information required to properly evaluate the candidate. In many instances, this presents little challenge. For example, it requires no effort to draw out lively and outgoing individuals. However, not all interviewees are outgoing. People who are nervous or lack interview skills may feel awkward, and this in turn prevents them from expressing themselves effectively. In such cases, it is the interviewer's responsibility to ensure that the degree of information uncovered about such interviewees equals that of the more outgoing candidates.

For example, a communication student, Jean, felt that her graded in-class employment interview went poorly because her interviewee, Yu-Kyung, spoke in a low, unenthusiastic voice and was not open and forthright in her responses. Although Yu-Kyung provided only short, nondescriptive answers, a review of the videotaped interview showed that Jean (the interviewer) posed mostly closed, yes/no–type questions. While these may have worked with talkative interviewees, they did not work with Yu-Kyung. Had Jean been an artful interviewer, she would have worked harder to develop a rapport and to pose questions that encouraged longer, more descriptive replies. When Yu-Kyung seemed to seize up, Jean should have provided encouraging feedback. Therefore, the failure of the interview rested with Jean. You too have to be prepared to interview a wide variety of people, some of whom will be less easy to draw out than others.

### What About the Interviewees?

The interviewee must also take some responsibility for the process. Even though you may feel nervous, shy, or intimidated, try to communicate in a professional manner. Prepare for the interview by anticipating some of the questions and consider how you might respond. Speak in a voice that can be heard, and expand on your responses.

## Artful Interviewers Build and Maintain Rapport with Interviewees

Paramount to the success of any interview is making interviewees feel comfortable and relaxed from the beginning and keeping them that way throughout the duration. The more relaxed interviewees are, and the more comfortable they feel with

Interrogative interviews were always set up in an adversarial manner. But now police officers recognize the importance of putting the interviewee at ease and developing a rapport. When they do this they find suspects more willing to cooperate, and the interrogation goes more smoothly for everyone.

*Pat, Police Sergeant and Former Communication Major*

the interviewer, the more likely they are to provide good breadth and depth of information. You do not want to lose good employees merely because they feel uncomfortable in interviews.

## Building and Maintaining Rapport

To build rapport, take time at the beginning of the interview for a bit of informal small talk. If interviewees are still apprehensive after this opening conversation, you may have to candidly address their anxiety. Encourage them to relax and tell them it is normal to feel nervous.

Throughout the interview, give interviewees your undivided attention and appropriate verbal and nonverbal feedback. If about 65 percent of face-to-face communication comes from nonverbal cues (Birdwhistell, 1970; Burgoon, 1994), then it is important to be sensitive to the nonverbal messages you are sending. For example, make plenty of eye contact, nod your head, and use suitable facial expressions. Get involved in the interview, and occasionally, go beyond the questions to add support material or other relevant comments. Sit leaning forward a little, keep an open posture (don't fold your arms), and smile to further reveal your curiosity and concern. Laugh when something is funny, and do not be afraid to let your personality come through.

---

### S-O-F-T-E-N

Some people use the word **SOFTEN** to help them remember to be more open to communication with others, and hence to be perceived as more approachable:

    **S** — Smile
    **O** — Open posture
    **F** — Forward lean
    **T** — Touch (but not too much—handshaking is appropriate)
    **E** — Eye contact
    **N** — Nod

---

## What About the Interviewees?

This is your time to put to use some of the things you have learned. Dress the part, make eye contact, avoid using adaptors (drumming your fingers, jiggling jewellery, playing with a pen), sit up straight, and demonstrate a forward lean. Provide as much information and examples from your previous work experiences as you can. If you are straying too much, the interviewer will let you know.

Always follow the lead of the interviewers. If they communicate in a formal manner, you respond in kind. If they demonstrate humour, enjoy it, although you do not want to get carried away telling your favourite jokes. And, just as interviewers are trying to read your verbal and nonverbal communication, you too need to be reading their messages.

With a lack of vitality or enthusiasm in his voice, Chad had the habit of responding to all his interviewee's comments with "That's interesting," while he simultaneously looked down at his notes for the next question. Clearly, Chad's interviewee was not receiving the kind of attention to keep him feeling comfortable and involved in the process. Chad seemed more interested in getting through the interview than listening to the answers. Such behaviour does not make for a productive transaction between the two parties, and does nothing to add to the rapport.

*Stan, Former Communication Student*

## Artful Interviewers Are Open-Minded

While most people believe they are open-minded, they cannot help but perceive and process the world through their individual biases and attitudes. However, successful interviewers recognize and minimize stereotypes associated with culture, race, gender, ethnicity, language style, and so on. Stereotypes are generalizations, based on a few characteristics, which people make about various groups. They are often hard to destroy because people are not always aware of the assumptions on which stereotypes are based.

We live in a pluralist, multicultural, open society where the *Canadian Human Rights Act* entitles all individuals to equal employment opportunities. Therefore, to curtail discrimination, it is illegal in Canada to ask interviewees questions that are related to marital status, national origin or race, age, criminal background, disabilities, sex or gender, sexual orientation, religion, size, or health (Canadian Human Rights Commission, 2001).

### *What About the Interviewees?*

What can you do if an interviewer asks you an inappropriate question? Sharon Graham, from the Graham Manage Group based in Milton, Ontario, suggests that you have four options. You can answer the question if you think that the intent of the question is

"Any references other than your parole officer?"

FARCUS® is reprinted with permission from LaughingStock Licensing Inc., Ottawa, Canada. All rights reserved.

related to or relevant to the job. However, if you answer the question, you are still providing inappropriate information that may well hurt your chances for getting the position. Another option is just to refuse to answer the question, but Graham suggests that it is a good idea to explain why. You can ignore the question and move on to something else. Finally, you can terminate the interview and leave the room if you think the question represents blatant discrimination. In such cases, you will be better off finding a job in a non-discriminating workplace.

## Implicit Personality Theory

*Implicit personality theory* is another notion related to a lack of open-mindedness (Trenholm & Jensen, 1995) and it can be another form of prejudice. The notion holds that individuals have a tendency to group personality characteristics together and this results in creating both positive and negative impressions about an individual. Take the following scenario, for example. A young, blond woman with her hair tied on top of her head and wearing big hoop earrings is running her two Yorkshire Terriers in the park. She plays catch with them and talks baby talk. She digs for treats in her pocket and as she pulls them out, so too comes a variety of makeup—lipsticks, powders, tubes, eye shadow, eyeliner, and mascara. What occupation do you think this woman has? Now, imagine another scenario and a young, blond woman is walking through the park with her two Yorkshire Terriers. Her hair is tied back in a clip, she is wearing a dark suit, and she has a brisk air about her. She does not play with her dogs, but has a businesslike approach. What do you suppose her occupation is?

According to implicit personality theory, most individuals would attribute a professional occupation to the woman in the suit and a more casual, maybe artsy job for the playful woman. Based on this theory, interviewers need to be very careful about the impressions they have of interviewees until they learn more facts about them.

 ## PUBLIC SPEAKING IN THE 21ST CENTURY

### INAPPROPRIATE INTERVIEW QUESTIONS

You can learn more about this issue by going to Sharon Graham's article titled "Handling Inappropriate Interview Questions" at *http://www.albertajobs.com/ document.cfm?task=view&documentid=207.*

The site offers many examples of illegal questions that are related to topics such as sex, religion, marital status, and so forth. It also contains more information on how interviewees can deal with inappropriate, illegal questions.

### WATCH THOSE FIRST IMPRESSIONS

Interviewers are greatly influenced by the presentation and appearance of the candidate's application (Dipboye, 1982; Dougherty et al., 1994; Rasmussen, 1984). Further, Stewart and Cash (2001, p. 238) note that "interviewers tend to make their decisions within the first four minutes in unstructured interviews." This works to create a self-fulfilling prophecy on the interviewer's part.

Once the decision to hire someone is consciously or unconsciously made, the interviewee's responses are evaluated accordingly. For example, two candidates, Jacques and Janette, have both held a series of jobs in the past two years. The interviewer has decided from a first impression (perhaps based on Jacques' appearance and demeanour, how he carries himself, the feel of his handshake, or maybe just his wild and crazy tie) that Jacques should be hired.

Jacques' employment history is interpreted as indicating that he is trying to get ahead, willing to make changes, and wanting to better himself.

Janette makes a less favourable first impression (she seems nervous and has a limp handshake). The interviewer interprets Janette's similar work history as showing a lack of personal responsibility, and her behaviour as suggesting that she cannot hold down a job. While this is an untested theory, you can see how interviewees might not be treated fairly.

### What About the Interviewees?

Interviewees need to be aware of the kind of impressions they are making during the interview. This is why it is important to dress appropriately, speak clearly, and use good grammar. In other words, you want to play the role of an adept interviewee and a potential employee. Given that 65 percent of face-to-face communication comes in the form of nonverbal communication, interviewees need to be aware of the nonverbal messages they are sending.

## Artful Interviewers Are Good Listeners

Finally, artful interviewers listen well and give genuine, positive feedback to interviewee responses. This helps to maintain rapport and to encourage interviewees to give even more information. Interviewers who "nod off" and engage in pseudolistening greatly limit the details they can learn and recall about the applicants. This, of course, can later hamper the selection process.

### What About the Interviewees?

It is equally important for interviewees to listen so they have a clear understanding of the questions they need to answer. If you cannot hear the interviewer or understand what is being asked, do not hesitate to ask. It is also important to listen to any information about the position and follow up after the interview.

## CONDUCTING THE EMPLOYMENT INTERVIEW

If you are conducting an interview, it is imperative that you know and work through the proper channels within your organization. Many businesses, institutions, and government agencies have advertising, interviewing, and human resource policies in place to guide the interview process. Having said that, the selection interview is typically divided into five steps: (1) prepare for the interview, (2) open the interview, (3) conduct the body of the interview, (4) close the interview, and (5) do the follow-up.

# Step 1: Prepare for the Interview

## *Review Applications*

To prepare for the interview, determine which candidates will be interviewed. This is based on certain criteria: their education, past work experience, and any special skills they may possess. You match candidates' assets with the qualifications required to satisfy the job description. Therefore, you must have a thorough knowledge of the position you want to fill.

As you read candidates' résumés, note areas for further probing. Many interviewers write questions on the résumés and take them to the interview. For example, during the interview, you will want to verify candidates' credentials and experience, and get detailed descriptions of their past on-the-job behaviours (Barone & Switzer, 1995).

Although résumés may list degrees and diplomas, different university and college programs emphasize different dimensions and have diverse assessment standards. These are the kinds of things to note in your interview guide (explained below) and to check out during the interview.

## *What About the Interviewees?*

Just as implicit personality theory suggests that people attribute further personality characteristics inferred from a series of initial qualities or characteristics, so too do employers make judgements about candidates based merely on the set up of their resumes. Therefore, take care to ensure your spelling is accurate, that the overall format adheres to accepted standards, that the information is current, and that the application is clean and printed on good quality paper. Attention to the details in your resume will make a difference in how you are perceived before you even step into the interview.

## *Prepare an Interview Guide*

You will also want to create an *interview guide*, an overview of the interview process to help you. This is similar to a speech outline (see the accompanying box for an example). It provides a review of the specific steps to follow during the interview to help you through the process. In addition, the interview guide sets out the types of questions to ask. Essentially, it presents an overview of the interview.

## *What About the Interviewees?*

Interviewees can also prepare by developing an overview of the questions they think will be posed regarding their educational background, their previous work experiences, and how these have made them qualified for the position. Review the interview guide box to help you in the interviewee role. Check out some of the many Web sites that help individuals prepare for an interview by offering sample questions and how they might be answered.

---

### AN INTERVIEW GUIDE

#### INTERVIEW OPENING

*Goal:* To set the tone and develop a rapport

1. Greet the interviewee.
2. Introduce yourself (shake hands).
3. Verify the interviewee's name.
4. Engage in some chitchat (about the weather, parking, the new building, something topical) to reduce tension and set the tone of the interview. Take your time with this.

#### INTERVIEW BODY

*Goal:* To determine candidates' suitability for the position

1. State the position being applied for.
2. Ask questions about the interviewee's educational background (programs, relevant courses, extracurricular activities, degrees, diplomas, certificates). Listen, probe, and ask for examples.
3. Ask questions about the interviewee's previous job experiences (duties, degree of responsibility, projects initiated, aspects that relate to the specific position being applied for).
4. Ask behavioural questions to learn whether the candidate possesses the special qualities required for the position or to fit in with the organizational culture (questions related to leadership qualities, ability to get along with others, ability to deal with pressure, ability to deal with conflict, a sense of humour, professionalism, and so on).
5. Describe the position, including the salary range, benefits, and other relevant information.

---

**INTERVIEW CLOSING**

1. Ask interviewees if they have any questions or anything they would like to add.
2. Review any specifics, make arrangements for any further documents that either you or the interviewee will provide, give the interviewee an idea of when to expect to hear the outcome of the interview.
3. Ask again whether there are questions.
4. Thank the interviewee and show her or him out.

## Contact Interviewees

While larger companies have personnel and human resources departments to set up interviews, smaller organizations may not. If you are setting up interviews, begin by booking an appropriate space. Then contact the candidates and give them plenty of lead time.

# Step 2: Open the Interview

## Develop Rapport

In the interview opening, you try to develop rapport and put interviewees at ease. Welcome candidates, introduce yourself, shake hands, and state your position in the company. Introduce, by name and position, any other interviewers or observers who may be present. Offer interviewees a seat.

Then take time for some informal chitchat to help relax interviewees. Do not rush this important step.

## What About the Interviewees?

Interviewees should also shake hands in a firm, but not clenching, grip. Make eye contact with the interviewer or team and respond to the introduction with something like, "It's nice to meet you."

## State the Position Being Applied For

After everyone has loosened up, introduce and briefly describe the position for which the candidates are being interviewed. Do not spend a lot of time describing the job as it is more important to learn about the interviewees. Note that novice interviewers tend to talk too much. Anderson and Killenberg (1999) write that, "Most experts suggest interviewees should probably talk, on average, two to three times as much as interviewers" (p. 169).

Another reason to state the position being applied for is because there can be the occasional mix-up. Finding that you are interviewing, or being interviewed, for the wrong position halfway through the interview is embarrassing to both parties.

### *What About the Interviewees?*

At this point, engage in the opening chitchat and maybe even say something like, "I am very excited about this position." Be polite.

## Step 3: Conduct the Body of the Interview

Once you dispense with the preliminaries, get into the body of the interview. Ask questions about three areas: educational background, work experiences, and specific qualities and skills required for the position. You also ask for clarification regarding any details on the résumé or application form. Try to use a variety of questions, and avoid hypothetical ones—use behavioural questions instead. These are discussed later in the chapter (also see the box on page 352).

Some interviewees are so strong that they can have an intimidating effect on interviewers, actually causing them to doubt themselves. Interviewers who have experienced this phenomenon start to think that they are the only ones who feel that way. However, like forms of abuse, this is actually a common occurrence, but one that is not often discussed.

*Janine, Accountant*

### *Pose Questions*

Do not be afraid to ask hard questions. If you have reservations about something the candidate says or something in the résumé, do not hesitate to probe further until your doubts are confirmed or dispelled. Continue to ask questions until you have probed all applicable areas and feel that you know enough about the person to make an informed decision about his or her suitability for the position. Take notes as you go, briefly listing both positive and negative qualities. These will help you to make and justify your hiring decision.

Because there are so many different kinds of questions to ask, and ways in which to ask them, an entire section of the chapter, following this one, is devoted to this topic.

## What About the Interviewees?

Interviewees should also familiarize themselves with the types of questions that will be posed. This contrasts with the content of the question. The type, which you will read about in an upcoming section, will alert you to how you should structure your response.

Interviewees should feel positive and confident as they answer questions. If you are asked tough questions, respond honestly to them. For example, if you did not get along well with the boss in the last position, it is appropriate to indicate that. However, how you convey that information is important. Rather than say things like, "Oh, he was a jerk. Nobody liked him," it would be better to say something like, "We had different ideas about where the department should go," or "We had different work styles." Such statements could be followed with examples, but be sure not to speak negatively about the former boss. Be professional.

## Listen and Observe

Throughout the interview, listen carefully and watch the interviewee's nonverbal responses. One international company has observers sit in on interviews, not to ask questions but rather to get an overall feel for the person. Rolls and Strenkowski (1994) note that for most technical jobs, employers think that candidates possess the requisite specialized skills. What employers look for are individuals who also possess the soft skills—interpersonal competence, or the ability to work well with others.

## What About the Interviewees?

Interviewees should also have their nonverbal radar turned on. Notice the reactions you are getting from the interviewer and modify your behaviour and verbal responses accordingly. If, for instance, you received a look that suggests that you might provide more information, do so. If the interviewer's facial expression indicated a lack of understanding of some sort, then further explain what you are attempting to convey.

## Provide Relevant Information

In the final part of the interview body, describe in more detail what the position entails. Include a general description, the work hours, any benefits (such as a pension plan, insurance plan, vacation time, etc.), the salary range, and other important details.

## What About the Interviewees?

This is the interviewees' opportunity to learn more about the position and employee benefits. Students always ask if they should inquire about salary. If they have done their homework, and researched the company and the position, they should have a good idea of the salary range. If the interviewer does not provide such information, ask. However, note that how you ask is as important as what you ask. Asking about salary range is different than saying something like, "How much will I be making?" or "How much vacation time do I get?"

## Step 4: Close the Interview

To close the interview, ask interviewees whether they have questions or would like to add anything. Then, provide some information about the interview process itself. For instance, you might disclose the number of people being interviewed, verify any further interactions or materials that either party will provide (for example, the interviewee's references, a second interview with someone else in your organization), and disclose time frames. It is good form, for example, to let candidates know if and when they will be contacted about the interview outcome. Finally, ask again whether there are any questions, thank interviewees, and show them out.

### What About the Interviewees?

Interviewees should thank the interviewer and indicate when they will get any follow-up documents to the potential employer. If they are going to be away in the next while, they might also leave an alternative telephone number or e-mail address where they can be contacted.

## Step 5: Do the Follow-Up

### Check References

*Always* check references, even if you have a good feeling about the candidate. People behave and communicate differently in different contexts, and your experience with an interviewee is very limited. Further, referees are more likely to be candid in conversations than they are in recommendation letters. And, do not hesitate to ask hard questions—although you must be diplomatic when you do so.

Do a thorough job with your assessment because, in many cases, you will have to work with the people you hire. Make sure the person can actually do the job and will be an industrious, honest, and fair employee. Remember too that individuals who interview well do not always make the best employees. Interviewers should also be watching candidates for clues as to whether they'll fit into the corporate culture.

## What About the Interviewees?

Always seek permission to use someone's name as a reference. Make sure their contact information is current and correct. It can also be helpful to supply the person with a copy of your resume. He or she will be able to speak more highly of you if updated information is at hand.

## Consider Others' Opinions

In today's interview settings, more and more you will find yourself on an interview team. Always consider the opinions of others because they could possess insight into candidates that you may be missing; perhaps they are sensitive to some nonverbal communication you are overlooking, for example. And, although it is difficult to articulate a "gut feeling," that does not negate its accuracy.

In situations where half the team feels strongly in favour of one candidate and the other half favours another candidate, it might not be wise to hire neither on a full-time basis. It is better for *everyone* to feel good about the candidate, when all team members can "live with" a particular individual.

---

### COMMON CATEGORIES OF QUESTIONS

*Open questions:* Allow interviewees to answer in a variety of ways.
*Closed questions:* Elicit either a specific or a yes/no response.

*Primary questions:* Introduce a topic.
*Secondary questions:* Probe responses to primary or open questions.

*Multiple choice questions:* Provide answers from which interviewees choose a response.
*Challenge questions:* Probe previously stated positions or opinions.

*Hypothetical questions:* Ask what interviewees would do in hypothetical future situations.
*Behavioural questions:* Ask what interviewees did in past situations.

---

## Offer the Position

Once the decision is made, follow the proper organizational channels for hiring. Inform the successful candidate. Only after he or she has accepted the position should you contact the unlucky interviewees. Never discuss the details of the decision process with anyone outside the hiring circle, not even with the individual who is selected. Do not, under any circumstances, disclose qualities of the unsuccessful candidates with the new employee.

# ASKING QUESTIONS

The goal of the employment interview is to find the best candidate for the position. Interviewers use one major tool to achieve this end—questions. While the types of questions were discussed in Chapter 4 in relation to research interviews, they are described here in terms of the employment interview.

## Open/Closed Questions

*Open questions* allow interviewees to respond in a number of ways. For example, questions that begin with "How do you feel about," "Tell me about," "Give me some examples of," or "Explain what accounts for," are open questions. Open questions generate a wide variety of information, encourage interviewees to provide descriptive and candid answers, and provide insight into people's values and attitudes. They also encourage interviewees to open up and get involved in the interview.

    *Closed questions*, in contrast, require short, specific answers, often just a yes or no. For example, "Do you have CPR training?" "How long did you work in that department?" and "Was a communication course part of your training?" are closed questions.

    Inexperienced interviewers typically pose far too many closed questions. This results in the interview ending very quickly and uncovering little information about the candidate. Novice interviewers think they are asking open questions when in fact they are not. See the accompanying box for examples of questions that only *sound* open.

    Closed questions are not bad—they just have to be used at the proper time in the interview. Use closed questions when you want to get specific information fast, when you need quantified answers ("How many years did you work there?"), or when you want to get back control of the interview from an interviewee who rambles. They also make excellent probing questions. Good interviewers use a variety of closed and open questions throughout the interview.

## What About the Interviewees?

If you have an interviewer who asks all closed questions, make sure you provide lots of information and examples.

## CLOSED QUESTIONS THAT SOUND OPEN

The following questions demonstrate how the same questions can be posed as closed or open. Notice how much more information is garnered from the open questions.

**Sounds Open:** Did you like working in the human resources department? *(Yes.)*
**Is Really Open:** Tell me about working in the human resources department. *(Well, five interns worked there—three doing data entry and two setting up pre-interview schedules. I was with data entry and worked in three different positions over the course of my time there. I liked that because you get to know a lot and I worked with some really great people.)*

**Sounds Open:** Would you say that your IT training program was a good one? *(Yes, it was.)*
**Is Really Open:** Describe your IT training program for me. *(It was a year-long course and we took classes in programming, systems analysis, software design . . .)*

**Sounds Open:** Did you do the same job all the time you worked at Thomson Nelson? *(No, I also worked in sales.)*
**Is Really Open:** Tell me about the different jobs you had at Thomson Nelson. *(When I first started, I worked in sales and did that for three years. I liked it, but I was becoming more and more interested in acquisitions. From working in the field, I was getting a good sense of the types of textbooks that were needed, especially in the public speaking area.)*

## Primary/Secondary Questions

*Primary questions* introduce a topic. They can be open or closed, and can be prepared in advance. *Secondary*, or *probing*, *questions* are used to follow up on primary ones. For example, if you want to know whether a candidate had communication training, you might introduce the topic with the primary question "Did you take any communication courses in your program?" To learn more about the course, you would pose secondary questions such as "Tell me about the topics that were covered." This probes the interviewee to provide further information.

Probing questions ask for more details on answers that lack particulars or ones that spark a provocative line of thought. They allow interviewers to get more complete information or a more thorough knowledge about the candidate. Interviewees who do not use probing questions miss opportunities to gain better insight into candidates.

## Multiple Choice/Challenge Questions

Most of you are familiar with *multiple choice questions*—they frequently appear on tests and exams. The ones used in interviews are the same, but not as tricky. For example, "Do you prefer to work mornings, afternoons, evenings, or backshift?

Do not confuse multiple choice questions with multiple questions. In multiple choice questions, you provide several possible options from which the interviewee selects one. In multiple questions, you unintentionally pose several questions all at once. Usually only the last one gets answered.

*Pegah, Employment Counsellor*

---

### DEALING WITH PROBLEM INTERVIEWEE RESPONSES

*Short responses, rambling responses*, and even a *lack of response* are common in interviews. Here are some tips to help you get the information you need from the interviewee:

- *Short responses:* Ask lots of probing questions, and try to turn your closed questions into open ones that call for plenty of description. If you are still not getting what you need from an interviewee, try something like, "I'm not getting a clear picture of the responsibilities of your last job. Can you tell me more?"
- *Rambling responses:* Interrupt the interviewee with something like, "In the interest of time, I need to move on to another topic." You can also interrupt with a series of closed questions.
- *Lack of response:* Rephrase the question and allow the interviewee more time to develop a reply. You might even say, "It's OK if you don't understand my question. Can I clarify something for you?" You may also supply an example of what you are looking for.

*Challenge questions* confront a previously stated opinion or position. For example, "You said earlier that you did your undergraduate studies at the University of Toronto. How did you come to take courses at Ryerson?"

# Hypothetical/Behavioural Questions

Hypothetical questions typically look to the future and ask what a person would do, think, or say in a particular situation. They are often used in selection interviews, but I would take interviewee responses with a grain of salt. Hypothetical questions lead to hypothetical answers—that is, people can make up the answer they think interviewers want to hear. Most intelligent, resourceful people applying for jobs will concoct the best solution they can, but there is no guarantee they will behave that way in real-life situations. However, hypothetical questions can work well for creative or artsy types of positions.

A far better type of question to ask is a behavioural one. While hypothetical questions focus on the future, *behavioural questions* probe the past. Instead of asking people how they *would handle* a conflict situation in the workplace (a typical hypothetical question), a behavioural question elicits more realistic information because it explores how they *have already handled* conflict in their previous work environments. "Tell me about a time when there was a conflict at work. Describe it to me," is an example. By using follow-up questions, you can find out much more about individuals. This approach is discussed in more detail in the next section.

## *What About the Interviewees?*

If you are asked a hypothetical question, answer it very briefly and supplement it with examples from past educational, work, and other similar experiences.

---

### COMMON PITFALL QUESTIONS

There are several types of questions to avoid. These are what Stewart and Cash (2001) call *pitfall questions*. They lack clarity, confuse the interviewee, and detract from the overall effectiveness of the interview. Being aware of these troublesome questions is your first step to eliminating them.

*Double-barrelled or multiple questions:* These are several questions asked at once. They confuse interviewees, who typically answer only the last question.

*Questions that are too long:* These muddle the issue and confuse interviewees. Instead of formulating thoughtful answers, interviewees are trying to figure out

---

what you are actually asking. As with double-barrelled or multiple questions, interviewees will probably answer only the final part of the question.

*Questions that are too short:* These questions are often incomplete and short, and do not provide enough information to tell the interviewee how to answer the question.

*Jargon and acronym-filled questions:* Avoid technical language or terms specific to your organization. Communication is curtailed when interviewees do not know what you are talking about.

*Leading questions:* Try to avoid questions that include the anticipated response. For example, "Of course, you would be willing to work overtime if required?" or "So travel wouldn't be a problem?" Interviewees will likely tell you what you want to hear, whether it is true or not.

## ◼ CONDUCTING THE BEHAVIOURAL INTERVIEW

### Basics

The behavioural interview is based on the notion that people's past behaviours are the best predictors of future behaviours in similar contexts or situations (Janz, Hellervik, & Gillmore, 1986; Janz, 1989). The focus is shifted from candidates' credentials and opinions to their actual prior work experiences. By probing the candidates, interviewers are often surprised at the amount and type of knowledge they uncover, all of which helps them to make wise hiring decisions. Anderson and Killenberg (1999) note that the employment interview process has changed substantially in recent years in that employers are engaging in far more behaviour-based interviewing.

### Benefits

To warrant an interview, candidates must possess the requisite education and skills for the job. However, as Stewart and Cash (2001) write, "Fit and match with the organization is a growing emphasis because organizations are discovering that a well-qualified applicant who does not match the organization's ethos and culture is likely to result in poor performance and high turnover rate" (p. 238).

The behavioural interview is well suited to weeding out those potential employees who are not a good fit. Behavioural questions elicit information that provides insight into candidates' communication styles, attitudes, and values (Rolls & Strenkowski, 1994).

## Setting Up the Behavioural Interview

The major difference between a conventional employment interview and a behavioural one is in the types of questions that are asked. The steps in the interview process are similar—preparation, opening, body, closing, follow-up. You still verify credentials and past work experience, but then you shift to actual incidents.

To prepare your behavioural questions, think about the interpersonal or specific communication or behavioural qualities that candidates require for the position. Also, get a sense of the personal traits that are required to work well within the organizational climate. If the organization is sales-driven, then employees might be expected to demonstrate traits such as drive, independence, creativity, or gregariousness. List these. Then, develop behavioural questions that allow you to determine whether interviewees possess these or other special qualities.

### *Example*

If applicants were screened for a position that required them to work under a lot of pressure, behavioural questions would give you more of a sense of their actual performance. If you ask interviewees a hypothetical question (*Would you be able to handle the pressure that's associated with this position?*), candidates would most likely respond that they could handle the pressure, whether or not that was true. However, if a behavioural question is posed (*Tell me about some of the worst types of pressure you have had to work under in the last couple of years?*), the interviewer can get a better idea of what candidates perceive as pressure. This, in turn, provides greater insight into interviewees' ability to do the job.

Behavioural questions like the following ones uncover more realistic information about candidates. It is up to the interviewer to probe each response.

- Describe a time in your work when you handled a particularly difficult customer. What did that person demand, and how did you react?
- Give me an example of a time when you disagreed with a decision your boss made. How did you deal with this?
- What kinds of people do you like to work with most? Why? What kinds of people do you like to work with least? Why?

Behavioural questions start with words like "describe," "explain," "tell me about," "recount," or "portray." Ask for lots of descriptions and examples, and keep asking until you get a better understanding of the candidate. Check out the accompanying box for a list of stock behavioural questions that get at characteristics such as leadership abilities, professionalism, interpersonal skills, and so on.

## STOCK BEHAVIOURAL INTERVIEW QUESTIONS

### PRESSURE
- Give me an example of when you handled pressure well. Tell me about a time when you did not. How would you change your behaviour if you were to have a similar experience again?
- Describe a time in your life when you were juggling several responsibilities at once and someone asked you to take on yet another task.
- Describe a person you know who works well under pressure. Explain that pressure and compare it with your perception of how you deal with pressure.
- Describe one of the busiest times you ever had at work. How did you handle it?

### CONFLICT
- Recount a time when a person at work made you angry. Tell me about it.
- Describe the most common kinds of conflict you have had at work.
- Tell me about a time when your boss asked you to do something that you did not want to do.

### LEADERSHIP
- Tell me about a time when you were in a position of authority or power. How did you deal with those under you?
- Recount an event when you had to criticize a co-worker's or subordinate's behaviour, work, or attitude.
- Tell me about a time when you were criticized.
- Did you ever have to make a "touchy" decision? How did you do it?
- In your professional or personal life, are you the type of person who organizes everything? Why or why not?
- In your opinion and based on your experience in positions of authority, what characteristics should subordinates possess?

### INTERPERSONAL SKILLS

- Did you ever have to resolve a personality conflict between employees? If there was no personality conflict, what other types of conflict have you resolved?
- Tell us about a time in your work experience when you found yourself in an awkward position. How did you resolve it?
- Concerning your relationship with others with whom you have worked, what is your greatest asset? Explain. What is your greatest weakness? Explain.

### HUMOUR

- Share a time in your previous work experience where you felt embarrassed or unsettled about something and now, upon reflection, you see the humour in the situation.
- Tell me about a time when you were able to laugh at yourself.
- Tell me something funny that happened to another person at work.

### PROFESSIONALISM

- In your previous work experience, explain how you demonstrated professionalism.
- What types of deadlines have you had to meet in your previous positions? How did it go? What strategies did you use to meet them?

**Source:** Some of these questions come from Rolls and Strenkowski (1994).

## Behavioural Interviewer Skills

It takes three skills to be an effective behaviour-based interviewer. While they seem easy and straightforward, they require patience and practice to incorporate them into your interviewing style.

### *Get Relaxed with the Process*

First, you have to become relaxed with the process. This means that you listen well and give respondents plenty of time to reply. If they have had no previous experience with this line of questioning, interviewees may feel a little overwhelmed. So might you. Get comfortable with silence, and encourage interviewees to take as long as they need to think.

### What About the Interviewees?

Interviewees also need to become familiar with this style of interviewing. To help you become more relaxed with the process, look at the stock behavioural interview questions contained in the accompanying box and think about how you would answer them.

### Recognize Descriptive Responses

You also need to learn to recognize when interviewees have actually provided a descriptive—or as one student referred to it, a behavioural—response. A behavioural response is one where the candidate provides a story, example, or description that you then probe further.

Interviewees have a tendency to fall into the "what they would do" mode. Do not accept these types of responses because you will not have gleaned enough, or possibly anything, revealing. Instead, politely but firmly ask interviewees to elaborate on specific instances from their previous work experiences.

### What About the Interviewees?

The best way to answer behavioural questions is to provide plenty of description. Talk about the work experiences you have encountered in the past and explain how you dealt with them.

### Listen and Probe

Finally, you need to become comfortable asking lots of follow-up questions. When candidates provide only basic, short replies, query them further for specifics. So that you do not sound like you are trying to interrogate interviewees, frame your questions like you're just interested in the topic. Remember too that you are looking for past behaviours in *similar* situations. So, if interviewees have no experience with conflict in the workplace, probe other contexts, such as volunteer work, school experiences, committee activities, or sports involvement. If they still cannot isolate any examples, ask for a description of the interpersonal strategies they use that enable them to avoid friction with others.

## ▨ THE INTERVIEWEE

Now that you know what to expect from a good interviewer, you should be more relaxed in the interviewee position. A few things may further increase your chances of being a successful applicant. Keep in mind that interviewers make decisions based on the information you supply. During the interview, you have two vehicles through which to provide this information: your nonverbal communication and your verbal communication. Therefore, it is up to you send the right kinds of nonverbal messages. Recall too that how you use your voice is also included with nonverbal communication so attend to tone and pronunciation. It is up to you to provide as much information about your education and experience as you can. Do not skimp on this. The more details you provide, the better the interviewer is able to get insight into your skills and abilities.

## Characteristics of Successful Candidates

Anderson and Killenberg (1999) reviewed the research on the differences between successful and unsuccessful interviewees and found the following:

- Successful interviewees generally had clearer career goals, and these were consistent with the position applied for.
- They preferred a career rather than a job, and understood how the job description being applied for related to them.
- During the interview, they used more evidence and statistics, and elaborated on their stories and qualifications—in other words, they gave examples.
- They used more active language, more positive descriptions, more technical jargon, and had good articulation and fewer grammatical errors.
- They were animated, showed fewer nervous habits, and used more positive nonverbal cues, such as smiling and affirmative nodding. They also had better eye contact.

In all, successful interviewees were thought to be more dynamic, enthusiastic, professional, and assertive (Anderson & Killenberg, 1999, p. 197). The next time you go for an interview, keep these professional and communication behaviours in mind.

## Preparing to Be Interviewed

You may be subjected to pre-interview written tests. This is common for government competitions. For the interview itself, always prepare by learning about the company, organization, or agency and the position you are applying for. Because many employers are still asking questions like, "Why should we hire you?" and "What qualities do you bring to this position?", give these types of questions some thought before the interview. See the accompanying box for Web sites that feature commonly asked interview questions and how best to respond to them.

"I always wear my lucky hat for job interviews."

## WEB SITES FEATURING COMMON INTERVIEW QUESTIONS

Quintessential Careers: *http://www.quintcareers.com/interview_questions.html*

Job-interview.net: *http://www.job-interview.net/Bank/QuestionBank InDepth.htm*

Monster Career Center: *http://content.monster.com/jobinfo/interview/questions*

Job-interview-questions.com: *http://www.job-interview-questions.com*

Today's interviews are also longer than they were a decade ago. Be prepared for a committee or team interview, and for some positions, expect to go through a series of interviews before the final decision is made. Be ready to engage in a behavioural interview, because they are rapidly growing in popularity.

Finally, remember that as you are being interviewed for the position, you are also assessing whether the position or company is a good match for your skills and talents. Give some thought to the questions you want to ask too.

## ✍️ EXPERT ADVICE

### WHEN DO I SELF-DISCLOSE A DISABILITY?

Because it is illegal for an employer to discriminate against a person based on a disability, it is up to the person with the disability to choose the most appropriate time to identify their special needs. Self-advocacy refers to the ability to articulate your needs, abilities, strengths, and limitations. By understanding your disability, you can communicate your needs to an interviewer. But, when is the most appropriate time to self-disclose: in the job application, in the cover letter, during the interview, or on the job?

For persons with invisible disabilities, such as learning disabilities, you may choose not to disclose until you require specialized computer software to complete your duties. For persons with visible disabilities such as hearing loss or loss of vision, you may choose to discuss the appropriate accommodations required in the employment interview.

It is a matter of personal choice to decide when, where, and to whom you disclose. Employment equity legislation prohibits discrimination based on a disability. Employers have a responsibility to provide reasonable accommodations for persons with disabilities to the point of undue hardship and as long as bona fide occupational requirements (i.e., safety) are not compromised. Many employers refer to employment equity hiring practices in their job advertisements and encourage people to disclose their special needs.

Remember, it is very important to identify your disability in terms of what you can do. Focus on your strengths, not your shortcomings. You could introduce your disability in the cover letter by writing, "Although I have a permanent disability, a few adjustments and/or accommodations will allow me to perform the duties associated with this position." For further information on this topic, see "Duty to Accommodate" at the following site: *http://www.tbs-sct.gc.ca/pubs_pol/hrpubs/tb_8521/ppaed1_e.asp*.

*Deanne Williams, Disability Resource Facilitator*
*Department of Education, Nova Scotia*

# PREPARING TO INTERVIEW

If you combine the information contained in this chapter with some extemporaneous interviews, you should find yourself well outfitted to conduct interviews. An *extemporaneous interview* is one in which you prepare a question guide and even practise with a friend. But when you conduct the actual interview, you do so with a person with whom you have not interacted. This gives the exercise a more realistic flavour for both the novice interviewer and interviewee. It more closely approximates what might happen in a genuine interview. It also gives you a chance to assess your interview strengths and weaknesses. For example, you may be good at dealing with problem responses but find that you need more practice with probing. As an interviewee, for example, you may find that you use too many adaptors or provide short, abrupt responses.

In many communication classes, students practise an interview with a classmate and then perform it for the entire class. While one or two of these might serve as interview models, they do little to actually help you perfect the art of interviewing. That only comes by engaging in extemporaneous interviews, where you do not know in advance how the interviewee will respond to your questions. This type of practice makes interviewers good at what they do. Interviewees who role-play and give spontaneous fictitious responses also learn from the experience.

# CHAPTER AT A GLANCE

- The success or failure of the interview rests with the interviewer.
- Paramount to the success of the interview is making the interviewee feel comfortable and relaxed.
- Even though you have an outline or plan for the interview, you need to listen carefully and read and respond to the interviewee's nonverbal cues.
- Be open-minded—do not let accents or cultural, racial, gender, or other characteristics shape your perceptions.
- Ask a variety of question types, and avoid pitfall questions.
- If interviewees talk too much, ask closed questions. If they do not talk enough, ask open questions. If they look dazed and confused, rephrase your question.
- Opt for behavioural rather than hypothetical questions.
- The best way to become a good interviewer (and a good interviewee) is to practise.

- Interviewees can prepare for an interview by learning about the organization to which they are applying, learning how interviews are organized, thinking about potential questions and how they might respond, learning to provide plenty of information during the interview, being sensitive to the nonverbal messages they are both sending and receiving, and by engaging in practise role-play interviews as both the interviewer and the interviewee.

# APPLICATION AND DISCUSSION QUESTIONS

1.  Answer the following questions in your communication journal:
    a.  *Cognitive dimension:* Describe, in your own words, the difference between hypothetical questions and behavioural questions. Give examples, and then explain the benefits of using behavioural questions.
    b.  *Affective dimension:* Describe the feelings you typically experience when you are being interviewed. How could you change your feelings to become a more effective interviewee?
    c.  *Behavioural dimension:* What are your strengths and weaknesses as an interviewer? As an interviewee? Develop a plan to help you improve.
2.  List some of the common stereotypes that are associated with gender, race, religion, and culture. Come up with ways in which people can be helped to see beyond the stereotypes.
3.  If questions can be divided into open and closed questions, into which category would the following be placed: hypothetical questions, behavioural questions, probing questions, multiple choice questions, challenge questions, and leading questions?
4.  With a partner, make up a script that includes both questions and answers for a behavioural interview, and perform the interview for your class.
5.  Make up an interview guide and conduct an unrehearsed interview. Have a person role-play the interviewee. Then discuss how this interview differs from the scripted one.
6.  Think about the next time you will be interviewed. Develop a series of questions you could be asked, and then plan how you would respond.
7.  Read Stan's student narrative on page 342 where he describes the poor interview skills of another student. If you were being interviewed by such a person, what could you do as an interviewee to make the interviewer give you more attention?

# REFERENCES AND FURTHER READINGS

Anderson, R., & Killenberg, G. (1999). *Interviewing: Speaking, listening, and learning for professional life.* Mountain View, CA: Mayfield.

Barone, J.T., & Switzer, J.Y. (1995). *Interviewing: Art and skill.* Boston: Allyn and Bacon.

Birdwhistell, R. (1970). *Kinesics and context.* Philadelphia: University of Pennsylvania Press.

Burgoon, J.K. (1994). Nonverbal signals. In M.L. Knapp and G.R. Miller (Eds.), *Handbook of interpersonal communication* (2nd ed., pp. 229–285). Thousand Oaks, CA: Sage.

Canadian Human Rights Commission. (2001, February). *A guide to screening and selection in employment.* Retrieved April 19, 2002, from http://www.chrc-ccdp.ca/publications/index.asp.

Dipboye, R.L. (1982). Self-fulfilling prophecies in the selection–recruitment interview. *The Academy of Management Review, 7*(4), 579–586.

Dougherty, T.W., Turban, D.B., & Callander, J.C. (1994). Confirming first impressions in the employment interview: A field study of interviewer behavior. *Journal of Applied Psychology, 79*(5), 659–665.

Janz, T. (1989). The patterned behavior description interview: The best prophet of the future is the past. In R.W. Eder & G.R. Ferris (Eds.), *The employment interview: Theory, research, and practice* (pp. 158–168). Newbury Park, CA: Sage.

Janz, T., Hellervik, L., & Gilmore, D. (1986). *Behavior description interviewing: New, accurate, cost effective.* Boston: Allyn and Bacon.

Posner, B.Z. (1981). Comparing recruiter, student and faculty perceptions of important applicant and job characteristics. *Personnel Psychology, 34*(2), 329–339.

Rasmussen, K.G. (1984). Nonverbal behavior, verbal behavior, resume credentials, and selection interview outcomes. *Journal of Applied Psychology, 69*(4), 551–556.

Rolls, J.A., & Strenkowski, M. (1994). Rationale and description of the video resume model. *The Journal of Cooperative Education, 29*, 77–83.

Stewart, C.J., & Cash, W.B. (2001). *Interviewing principles and practices* (9th ed.). Boston: McGraw-Hill Higher Education.

Trenholm, S., & Jensen, A. (1995). Social cognition: How we perceive individuals, relationships, and social events. In J. Stewart (Ed.), *Bridges not walls: A book about interpersonal communication* (pp. 158–169). New York: McGraw-Hill.

# Copyright Acknowledgments

# Index